# Global Resource Scarcity

A common perception of global resource scarcity holds that it is inevitably a catalyst for conflict among nations; yet, paradoxically, incidents of such scarcity underlie some of the most important examples of international cooperation. This volume examines the wider potential for the experience of scarcity to promote cooperation in international relations and diplomacy beyond the traditional bounds of the interests of competitive nation states.

The interdisciplinary background of the book's contributors shifts the focus of the analysis beyond narrow theoretical treatments of international relations and resource diplomacy to broader examinations of the practicalities of cooperation in the context of competition and scarcity. Combining the insights of a range of social scientists with those of experts in the natural and bio-sciences—many of whom work as 'resource practitioners' outside the context of universities—the book works through the tensions between 'thinking/theory' and 'doing/practice', which so often plague the process of social change. These encounters with scarcity draw attention away from the myopic focus on market forces and allocation, and encourage us to recognise more fully the social nature of the tensions and opportunities that are associated with our shared dependence on resources that are not readily accessible to all.

The book brings together experts on theorising scarcity and those on the scarcity of specific resources. It begins with a theoretical reframing of both the contested concept of scarcity and the underlying dynamics of resource diplomacy. The authors then outline the current tensions around resource scarcity or degradation and examine existing progress towards cooperative international management of resources. These include food and water scarcity, mineral exploration and exploitation of the oceans. Overall, the contributors propose a more hopeful and positive engagement among the world's nations as they pursue the economic and social benefits derived from natural resources, while maintaining the ecological processes on which they depend.

**Marcelle C. Dawson** is a Senior Lecturer in the Department of Sociology, Gender and Social Work, University of Otago, New Zealand, and a Senior Research Associate at the Centre for Social Change, University of Johannesburg, South Africa.

**Christopher Rosin** is a Senior Lecturer in the Department of Tourism, Sport and Society at Lincoln University, New Zealand.

**Navé Wald** is a researcher at the Higher Education Development Centre, University of Otago, New Zealand.

# Earthscan Studies in Natural Resource Management

**Global Resource Scarcity**
Catalyst for conflict or cooperation?
*Edited by Marcelle C. Dawson, Christopher Rosin and Navé Wald*

**Food, Energy and Water Sustainability**
Governance strategies for public and private sectors
*Edited by Laura M. Pereira, Catlin McElroy, Alexandra Littaye and Alexandra M. Girard*

**Environmental Justice and Land Use Conflict**
The governance of mineral and gas resource development
*Amanda Kennedy*

**Soil and Soil Fertility Management Research in Sub-Saharan Africa**
Fifty years of shifting visions and chequered achievements
*Henk Mutsaers, Danny Coyne, Stefan Hauser, Jeroen Huising, Alpha Kamara, Generose Nziguheba, Pieter Pypers, Godfrey Taulya, Piet van Asten and Bernard Vanlauwe*

**Transformational Change in Environmental and Natural Resource Management**
Guidelines for policy excellence
*Edited by Michael D. Young and Christine Esau*

**Community Innovations in Sustainable Land Management**
Lessons from the field in Africa
*Edited by Maxwell Mudhara, Saa Dittoh, Mohamed Sessay, William Critchley and Sabina Di Prima*

For more information on books in the Earthscan Studies in Natural Resource Management series, please visit the series page on the Routledge website: http://www.routledge.com/books/series/ECNRM/

# Global Resource Scarcity
Catalyst for Conflict or Cooperation?

Edited by Marcelle C. Dawson,
Christopher Rosin and Navé Wald

First published 2018
by Routledge
2 Park Square, Milton Park, Abingdon, Oxon OX14 4RN

and by Routledge
52 Vanderbilt Avenue, New York, NY 10017

*Routledge is an imprint of the Taylor & Francis Group, an informa business*

First issued in paperback 2019

© 2018 selection and editorial matter, Marcelle C. Dawson,
Christopher Rosin and Navé Wald; individual chapters, the
contributors

The right of Marcelle C. Dawson, Christopher Rosin and Navé
Wald to be identified as the authors of the editorial material, and
of the authors for their individual chapters, has been asserted in
accordance with sections 77 and 78 of the Copyright, Designs and
Patents Act 1988.

The Open Access version of this book, available at www.taylorfrancis.com,
has been made available under a Creative Commons Attribution-Non
Commercial-No Derivatives 4.0 license.

*British Library Cataloguing-in-Publication Data*
A catalogue record for this book is available from the British
Library

*Library of Congress Cataloging-in-Publication Data*
A catalog record for this book has been requested

ISBN: 978-1-138-24102-2 (hbk)
ISBN: 978-0-367-37692-5 (pbk)

Typeset in Bembo
by Swales & Willis Ltd, Exeter, Devon, UK

# Contents

| | |
|---|---|
| *List of figures and tables* | vii |
| *Acknowledgements* | viii |
| *Notes on contributors* | ix |

1  Introduction: resource scarcity between conflict and
   cooperation                                                        1
   MARCELLE C. DAWSON, CHRISTOPHER ROSIN AND NAVÉ WALD

## PART I
## Reframing scarcity and resource diplomacy                          19

2  Taking the scare out of scarcity: the case of water                21
   LYLA MEHTA

3  Cooperation in the power sector to advance regionalisation
   processes and sustainable energy flows                             39
   ANDREAS LINDSTRÖM, KEVIN ROSNER AND JAKOB GRANIT

## PART II
## Resource scarcity and tensions in international relations          57

4  Phosphorus security: future pathways to reduce food system
   vulnerability to a new global challenge                            59
   STUART WHITE AND DANA CORDELL

5  Peasant mineral resource extractivism and the idea of scarcity     73
   KUNTALA LAHIRI-DUTT

vi *Contents*

6 Whose scarcity, whose security? Multi-scalar contestation
of water in the Indus Basin 89
DOUGLAS HILL

7 Protecting our global ocean heritage: unprecedented threats
will require bold interventions 107
TODD L. CAPSON

**PART III**
**Building resilience through resource cooperation** 129

8 Food sovereignty and the politics of food scarcity 131
ALANA MANN

9 Rare earth diplomacy: mitigating conflict over
technology minerals 146
ELLIOT BRENNAN

10 Going with the flow: can river health be a focus for
foreign policy? 164
DAVID TICKNER

11 Don't forget the fish! Transnational collaboration in
governing tuna fisheries in the Pacific 184
VICTORIA JOLLANDS AND KAREN FISHER

12 A world without scarcity? 203
MARCELLE C. DAWSON, CHRISTOPHER ROSIN AND NAVÉ WALD

*Index* 207

# Figures and tables

## Figures

| | | |
|---|---|---:|
| 4.1 | The growth in production of phosphorus fertilisers by source | 61 |
| 4.2 | Outcomes of a vulnerability assessment for phosphorus in Australia | 64 |
| 4.3 | Illustration of methods by which rock phosphate consumption could be reduced using a combination of supply side and demand side measures | 66 |
| 4.4 | Examples of policy tools | 69 |
| 7.1 | Increases in global catches | 109 |
| 7.2 | Oceanic whitetip shark in the Eastern Pacific Ocean (IATTC) | 115 |
| 9.1 | Criticality matrix for green technology substrates | 150 |
| 10.1 | Examples of freshwater ecosystem services and links to elements of river health | 169 |
| 10.2 | Focusing 'six streams' of foreign policy interventions through the lens of flow regime to help attain outcomes for river health and for improved cooperation and reduced conflict | 175 |
| 11.1 | WCPO tuna fishery governance arrangements | 193 |
| 11.2 | WCPO tuna fishery actors | 194 |

## Tables

| | | |
|---|---|---:|
| 1.1 | Forms of environmentalist response | 10 |
| 2.1 | Diverse ways to view scarcity | 31 |
| 9.1 | Selected applications for REEs | 149 |
| 9.2 | Global production and known reserves | 150 |
| 10.1 | Selected examples of links between changes in the health of rivers and dimensions of conflict/cooperation | 170 |
| 10.2 | Indicative suggestions for foreign policy interventions to support improved cooperation for river health | 176 |

# Acknowledgements

We would like to thank the committee members of the University of Otago Foreign Policy School for their efforts in hosting the 49th meeting of the School, out of which this book has emerged. The financial support of the university's Vice Chancellor and Humanities Division helped to bring together a vibrant group of scholars and practitioners from around the world, whose contributions to the School shaped the direction and outcome of this book. The efforts of some of the speakers are reflected in these pages and we would like to thank them for their enduring commitment to this project. It has been a long journey with many personal ups and downs, both for the contributors and the editors, and we are grateful to each and every author for seeing this project through.

Given that some of the original conference participants were unable in the end to contribute to the book, we tapped on a few shoulders of people whom we knew were working on topics that would allow us to round out the book. We recognise that it is challenging to join a process mid-stream, when one has not had the benefit of a direct exchange with peers, and we are thankful to those authors who came on board in the months following the Foreign Policy School.

We are sincerely grateful to the team at Routledge who have guided us along the way, and we owe a special thanks to Tim Hardwick and Amy Johnston for their patience.

Finally, the editors would like to thank their families and loved ones who provided much-needed support along the way.

# Notes on contributors

**Elliot Brennan** is a non-resident research fellow at the Institute for Security and Development Policy (Sweden) and a non-resident WSD Handa fellow at the Center for Strategic and International Studies' Pacific Forum (USA). Most recently he worked as conflict analysis and early warning specialist with the Joint Ceasefire Monitoring Committee in Myanmar. His research interests include resource security, crisis management and strategic foresight.

**Todd L. Capson** has more than 21 years of experience in the US and developing world as a consultant with the Department of State and the Smithsonian Tropical Research Institute. His work focuses on building programmes to address ocean acidification, the strengthening of protected areas, and drug discovery in tropical ecosystems. He received his PhD in Medicinal Chemistry from the University of Utah. As a post-doctoral fellow of the National Institutes of Health at Pennsylvania State University, he studied the kinetics of DNA synthesis and the structure of enzyme-DNA complexes. He was an Executive Branch Fellow of the American Association for the Advancement of Science (AAAS) in the Office of Marine Conservation at the State Department.

**Dana Cordell** is Research Director at the Institute for Sustainable Futures at the University of Technology Sydney. Dana co-founded the Global Phosphorus Research Initiative in 2008 with colleagues in Sweden and Australia. She has led research and provided policy advice globally and in Australia on phosphorus scarcity and management. She is the recipient of Banksia Award, an Australian Museum Eureka Prize and was named as one of Australia's 100 Women of Influence.

**Marcelle C. Dawson** is Senior Lecturer in Sociology at the University of Otago (New Zealand) and Senior Research Associate at the Centre for Social Change (University of Johannesburg). She is mainly interested in the study of social movements and popular protest, and much of her work addresses grassroots resistance to neoliberalism. Together with Chris Rosin, Marcelle co-directed the 49th Annual University of Otago Foreign Policy School, from which this book has emerged.

x  *Notes on contributors*

**Karen Fisher** is a Human Geographer in society-environment interactions. Karen is a Senior Lecturer at the University of Auckland in the School of Environment. Her current research investigates how knowledge is produced and subsequently used to inform environmental governance and management in New Zealand. Her research interests fall broadly under the following areas: sustainable development, political ecology, environmental governance and development, and science, knowledge and policy.

**Jakob Granit** is Director General of the Swedish Water and Marine Management Agency (SwAM) and former Center Director at Stockholm Environment Institute. Jakob Granit holds a PhD in geography and has over 20 years of experience working on the development and management of transboundary water resources and interlinked development opportunities. Jakob has held many senior positions at national and international level. His research focus is on how to achieve collective action on shared water systems, regional integration and the water and energy nexus.

**Douglas Hill** is Senior Lecturer at the Department of Geography, University of Otago (New Zealand), where he teaches Development Studies. He has published widely on issues related to transboundary water management in South Asia.

**Victoria Jollands** is an environmental, marine and fisheries science and policy specialist with eight years' experience in policy, research and project management of complex issues in New Zealand and in the Pacific. Victoria is the Managing Director of the Auckland based consultancy firm, Ocean Research Consulting and Advisory Limited. Victoria is also undertaking a PhD in marine policy at The University of Auckland. Her research investigates economy-environment relationships to develop a fisheries governance framework appropriately embedded in Pacific socio-ecosystems at different scales.

**Kuntala Lahiri-Dutt** is a Senior Fellow (Associate Professor) at the Resource, Environment and Development (RE&D) Program at the Crawford School of Public Policy, College of Asia and the Pacific, The Australian National University. Kuntala's research has deepened scholarly understanding of precarious and gendered livelihoods in environmental resource dependent communities in both the transient chars (river islands) or in the mines and quarries of mineral-rich tracts. Her research has primarily focused on India but has later expanded to Indonesia, Lao PDR and Mongolia. Kuntala's books include *The Coal Nation: Histories, Politics and Ecologies of Coal in India* (edited, Ashgate, 2014); *Dancing with the River: People and Lives on the Chars in South Asia* (co-authored, Yale University Press, 2013); *Gendering the Field: Towards Sustainable Livelihoods for Mining Communities* (edited, ANU Press, 2011); and *Women Miners in Developing Countries: Pit Women and Others* (co-edited, Ashgate, 2006). Besides these primary areas of research, Kuntala pursues an interest on marginal communities; her book, *In Search of a Homeland: Anglo-Indians and McCluskiegunge* has been used as the basis for a BBC documentary.

**Andreas Lindström** is a Research Fellow at the Stockholm Environment Institute (SEI). He holds an MEng in Civil and Environmental Engineering and has several years of experience of issues related to the water and energy nexus in different regions of the world, including the EU and the Nordic countries. In the field of water and energy, Andreas has co-authored and provided research to a number of reports and projects. He has developed research on environmental implications of various kinds of energy generation as well as providing recommendations on best practice. Andreas is a civil engineer educated at the Royal Institute of Technology (KTH) in Stockholm.

**Alana Mann** is Chair of the Department of Media and Communications within the Faculty of Arts and Social Sciences at the University of Sydney, Australia. Her research focuses on the engagement of citizens and non-state actors in activism and policy debates to inform the creation of just and sustainable food systems. Her book on food sovereignty campaigns in Latin America and Europe, *Global Activism in Food Politics: Power Shift* was published in 2014 by Palgrave Macmillan.

**Lyla Mehta** is a Professorial Fellow at the Institute of Development Studies (University of Sussex, United Kingdom), and a Visiting Professor at Noragric, Norwegian University of Life Sciences. Her work focuses on the politics of rights and access to water and sanitation and the politics of scarcity and uncertainty. She has extensive research and field experience in India and southern Africa. She has published about 90 scientific publications including the books, *The Politics and Poetics of Water* and *The Limits to Scarcity*.

**Christopher Rosin** is a Senior Lecturer in the Department of Tourism, Sport and Society at Lincoln University (New Zealand). He has research interests in the interactions of humans and the environment especially in relation to issues of sustainability and climate change response and mitigation in agriculture and food systems.

**Kevin Rosner** is an Associate with the Stockholm Environment Institute and Senior Fellow with the Institute for the Analysis for Global Security in Washington. He holds a PhD in Political Science and serves as the Director of Research for the Institute for Natural Resources and Sustainable Development at the University of Ottawa. Over the past decade he has helped pioneer the water-energy-security nexus with SEI and other organisations including the Swedish Defense Research Agency, the African Center for Security Studies at the National Defense University in Washington, the US Army Corps of Engineers, and most recently as Senior Fellow with the Robert S. Strauss Center for International Security and Law at the University of Texas.

xii *Notes on contributors*

**David Tickner** is Chief Freshwater Adviser at WWF, based in the UK. He provides oversight of river conservation programmes across the globe, leads research and innovation on strategic water management, and guides WWF's engagement on water issues with governments, the private sector and academia. He is currently also an Associate Editor of the journal *Frontiers in Environmental Science*. Dave began his career as a civil servant in the UK's environment ministry. More recently he has led WWF's programme for the Danube River, served as a Visiting Research Fellow at the University of East Anglia, been a non-executive director of Water and Sanitation for the Urban Poor (WSUP, a not-for-profit company) and acted as a sustainability adviser to Standard Chartered. Dave holds a PhD in freshwater ecology and has published a wide range of technical and popular articles on water and environment issues. You can follow him on Twitter (@david_tickner).

**Navé Wald** is a development geographer whose previous work focused on issues of rural development, food politics, radical politics and civil society. His doctoral research focused on the rural geographies of grassroots peasant-indigenous organisations in northwest Argentina. Navé is currently a researcher at the Higher Education Development Centre in the University of Otago, where his work involves a variety of pedagogical as well as political aspects of higher education.

**Stuart White** is the Director of the Institute for Sustainable Futures at the University of Technology Sydney and leads a team of researchers across a range of aspects of 'creating change towards sustainable futures'. His own research has focused on the future of resources use, including technical, economic and policy means to reduce the inefficiency of resource use. Stuart has had a lifelong interest in the use of phosphorus in agriculture, starting with his early years growing up on a sheep and cropping farm in Western Australia.

# 1 Introduction

## Resource scarcity between conflict and cooperation

*Marcelle C. Dawson, Christopher Rosin and Navé Wald*

### Why scarcity and cooperation?

As indicated by its title, this is a book about the relationship between what are perceived to be scarce natural resources and the tendency for access to them to lead to international conflict or cooperation. It is apparent from our reading of existing literature and from the contributions to this book that experts are often situated in positions that find little opportunity to engage or interact outside of academic disciplines or geographically and resource-specific practice. This diversity of forms and levels of engagement with resource scarcity and its implications for international relations poses particular problems when one attempts to provide a summary, but insightful, overview to those with more general interests in scarcity or politics. This book—in its structure and content—is the result of just this sort of exercise, having roots in the organisation of the 2014 University of Otago Foreign Policy School, an annual conference directed at early career staff from the New Zealand Ministry of Foreign Affairs and Trade. It was soon apparent that the invited speakers (many of whom are contributors to the following chapters) did not always share a similar epistemology or ontology in their treatment of scarcity, as its use ranged from that of a physical reality to an element of discourse. Whereas the implied lack of cohesion might have laid the framework for a failed conference, participants emerged with a strong sense of the common theme regarding the potential to engage or move towards cooperative relations in response to scarcity, irrespective of how it was conceived. It is on this premise that we organised the book as a collation of outwardly disparate manifestations and interrogations of 'scarcity' with the intention of directing our readers' attention to the potential for international collaboration.

On one hand, the scarcity of resources and the likelihood of such scarcity leading to international conflict (economic, political or military) is a common feature of public discourse and speculation. On the other, the potential for scarcity (or perceptions thereof) to initiate forms of international collaboration or cooperation is a much less common element of how we understand the world. This seems to us to be an unfortunate situation. Existing examples of international cooperation around such resources as fresh water, biodiversity conservation and ocean fisheries suggest that a common concern for the viability of a resource that extends beyond political boundaries can provide the basis for peaceful interactions among otherwise competing countries. It is just such positive examples that provide hope for a world that is defined less by bellicose confrontation over essential resources and more by a shared interest in the ability for greater equality in access to those resources and their societal benefits to facilitate cooperation—and potentially even peace.

In the remainder of the introduction, we will provide an explanation of the pathway we have navigated in assembling this collection. It will begin with a brief engagement with some of the literature on resource scarcity and its part in international relations. This review necessarily begins with—and is dominated by—the vast literature on the threats of scarcity to humanity more generally and its potential to initiate conflict between and within countries. It concludes with more recent literature on successful experiments with collaboration and coordination of resource access and use where the location and benefits of the resource extend beyond political boundaries. We suggest that our navigation of this literature helps us to get to grips with the diverse perspectives of scarcity (some more overtly stated than others) found in the chapters from our contributors. It also provides the rationale for the division of the book into three parts. This includes providing roughly parallel chapters, which present the potential tensions related to a situation of scarcity and specific examples of cooperation. We will conclude with an invitation to read the book as a whole in order to develop a broader understanding of scarcity and its relevance to international relations.

## Scarcity and conflict

The predominance of the linkage between instances of resource scarcity and potential conflict is by no means surprising. In a global context framed by increasing attention to environmental issues and concerns with readily appreciated international implications and the heightened economic and political competition among nations, scarcity portends an unavoidable escalation in tensions among already hostile or would be hostile actors. Examples from the Middle East and Central Asia provide vivid examples of the potential for access to oil and natural gas to lead to armed conflict and to create situations in which regional and global powers insert themselves with the likelihood of for wider scale conflict. Conflict over resources is not limited to military confrontation, with indications that the dominance of supply and processing chains can be used to impose economic pressure and constraints on competing economies (see the chapters on rare earth minerals and phosphorus in this volume). In yet other contexts, the perception of potential scarcity can lead to continued or renewed exertion of colonial forms of exploitation in the Global South as demonstrated in the 'land grabbing' investments that divert the productive capacity of large tracts in Africa, South America and elsewhere to meet consumption demands in the Global North. These are all well documented and publicised instances of conflict that grab public attention—especially to the extent that they elicit spectres of global war, hidden economic agendas and exacerbated inequalities between global haves and have nots. This association between scarcity and conflict is deeply embedded on our social consciousness.

By comparison, the achievements in cooperative efforts to manage and regulate resources receive less attention. This is probably most notable in the case of fresh water where the resource crosses the borders of countries that, often, already experience tensions due to cultural, religious or ideological differences. Whereas conflicts over resources are presented as potentially escalating to even higher levels, the efforts at cooperation are commonly seen as tenuous at best given the underlying tensions involved. In this context, there is little expectation that cooperation is a viable and sustainable response to scarcity.

The relative emphasis on the association between resource scarcity and conflict is also a feature of the academic literature. In this case, the argument revolves around the assumption that social relations are strongly influenced by competition and any form of scarcity will exacerbate existing tensions between countries or among class, cultural or ethnic divisions within countries. This position is commonly based on theorised impacts of projected scarcity or on more vivid case studies of conflict in which resource scarcity is identified as a contributing factor. A less recognised literature on the potential for scarcity to galvanise pursuit of peaceful relations has been constructed within peace and conflict studies, which focus on the need for common goals and benefits as the basis for facilitating cooperation.

## Scarcity (and environmental degradation) as a threat to security

The association between resource scarcity and social conflict and strife has an ancient history. It is common for such treatments of scarcity to reflect political economic perspectives with the assumption of competitive relations between political rulers and nation states (at an international scale) or social groups such as class, race or religion (at a regional scale). Implicit to this perspective is the expectation that increasing demand for resources (attributable to population growth, changing consumer preferences, etc.) will outpace supply and generate tensions around access to and availability of resources that can only be addressed from the perspective of a zero-sum game. The assumption that any gains by one group of resource users necessarily involve a loss among others creates the circumstances in which conflict becomes an inevitable feature.

In more recent and current debates, this conception of scarcity has become more tightly focused, most notably through the framing introduced by the British clergyman and economist Thomas Malthus and his warning that, if left unchecked, population growth would outstrip food production and lead to catastrophe and societal collapse. In 1798, Malthus anonymously published his prophetic thesis under the title, *An Essay on the Principles of Population*, in which

4 *M.C. Dawson, C. Rosin and N. Wald*

he identified three principles of population. The first two principles stipulate that the population cannot grow without the necessary means of subsistence, and that growth will take place when such means become available. Malthus saw these principles as established ideas, which he attributed to Adam Smith, David Hume and others. His main contribution in the *Essay* was the third principle, where he argued that population growth stays in check vis-à-vis the means of subsistence 'by the periodical or constant action of misery or vice' (Malthus, 1798: 144). For Malthus, this is inevitable because population, which grows exponentially, will always outpace increases in food production, which can only grow linearly. Checks will thus come into play and these can be either 'positive', such as higher mortality rates, or preventative, in the form of birth control. Both, nevertheless, necessitate misery or vice (Winch, 2013).

The resultant view of scarcity as a natural law is also known as the 'scarcity postulate' and is rooted in classical liberalism and classical economics, with which Malthus was affiliated. The scarcity postulate positions scarcity as a nearly ubiquitous condition affecting human society. It recognises the social dimension of human needs and desires, but sees their pursuit as rational and socially desirable. This view of scarcity, which underpins the field of economics, is essentially a modern conceptualisation. Periods during which vital resources were scarce are common historical events; but, prior to modernity, these were often anticipated and provision could be made to mitigate their effect by diverse means, including cooperation and conflict. These scarcities were furthermore perceived as spatially and temporally confined, in comparison to modern representations of scarcity as an omnipresent condition that encompasses all aspects of human life and wellbeing (Xenos, 1987). Thus, modern scarcity, where need and desire are inseparable and where the spread of desire is pivotal for sustaining society, is manifested in a paradoxical relationship between abundance and scarcity. An ever-accumulating society has more and more, but cannot fulfil its ever-increasing desires, which in turn propel even greater accumulation. This paradox of modernity, Xenos (1987; 2010) argues, results in a society living with perpetual scarcity.

In spite of the shared philosophical roots of the Malthusian principles and classical economics, over the latter decades of the twentieth century a notable division developed between neo-Malthusian and neoclassical economic theories and their proponents. At that time, nearly 200 years had passed since Malthus's gloomy prophesy in which substantial population growth did eventuate but without outpacing food production. For neoclassicists this was evidence of the ability of the free market—and its signalling mechanism of price related to supply and demand—to efficiently allocate resources and incentivise innovation so that Malthusian misery is largely avoided. For neo-Malthusians, in contrast, Malthus's prediction still looms large as a Cassandra syndrome; that is, Malthus may have got the timing wrong but the essence of his prediction stands. Neo-Malthusians, therefore, maintain that overpopulation will lead to resource scarcity and environmental degradation, and subsequently to competition and conflict. The market, they posit, has not been able to avoid the environmental damage caused by the accelerating production needed to meet humanity's growing needs and desires. Their conclusion is that there are limits to growth. In spite of the notable differences between these perspectives, both apply similar philosophical underpinnings regarding the inevitability of scarcity in their policy recommendations (Matthaei, 1984).

Thomas Homer-Dixon (1999), a notable proponent of the resource scarcity–conflict nexus, identified three main positions in the ongoing debate around the outcomes of environmental scarcity. Neo-Malthusians, as noted above, still propagate the idea that having finite natural resources means there is a limited capacity for sustaining human society, which, if exceeded, will result in poverty and social unrest. Economic optimists are a second group that includes neoclassical economists and others who believe in the capacity of efficient markets and functioning institutions to effectively 'guide' conservation, substitution and investment so that capacity limits are not exceeded. Homer-Dixon calls the third group in the debate the 'distributionists.' This group believes that the real issue involves unequal and inadequate distribution of resources and wealth, and thus poverty and inequality should be seen as causes of population growth and resource depletion, and not their result. This view, which was relatively influential in the Global South during the 1970s and 1980s and particularly popular among Marxists, has had less purchase since then. Homer-Dixon recognised that this typology, while useful, carries the risk of oversimplification. Nonetheless, these positions became so entrenched that the debate became sterile.

Frerks, Dietz and van der Zang (2014) contend that the binary between the pessimism of the neo-Malthusians and the optimism of neoclassical economics no longer dominates debates around resource scarcity as they have in the past. Rather, these authors suggest that it has become widely accepted that environmental degradation and resource scarcity may be contributing factors to conflicts, but that such conflicts are rarely solely resource-driven. This position essentially combines elements of the otherwise distinctive perspectives of the neo-Malthusians, economic optimists and the distributionists. For example, such an approach accepts that, in a particular case, degradation could be a result of conflict, and not the other way around, while also recognising the importance of strong institutions for environmental management and peacebuilding. But, even if such a convergence between the different positions has indeed taken place, it does not automatically render the previous typology redundant. Having a more nuanced approach towards instances of scarcity and conflict is important, but it is often still possible to identify a commentator's worldview or ideological inclination. The debate may thus have become less sterile, and we share the sentiment that '[i]nstead of overarching theories, there is presently a need for contextualised knowledge, and complexity needs to be explicitly acknowledged' (Frerks, Dietz and van der Zang, 2014: 14), but as the chapters in this volume suggest, Homer-Dixon's (1999) typology still provides a useful analytical tool for assessing dominant views within the debate.

Notwithstanding the argument in the literature that the debate around environmental or resource scarcity has become more nuanced and context specific, it is the association of scarcity with conflict, violence and insecurity that has for a long time been the more visible facet of the debate. The relationship between resource scarcity and conflict has been well recognised and has received extensive attention, especially in the fields of international relations, environmental studies and security studies (Dinar, 2011). That the combination of scarce resources and growing population is a threat to national security and human wellbeing is largely taken for granted; it is merely common sense. One notable example is Homer-Dixon's (1999) *Environment, Scarcity, and Violence*, which analyses links between environmental scarcity and violent conflict and predicts that violent conflict is likely to become more common as access to renewable resources becomes increasingly scarce. Michael Klare's (2001) *Resource Wars* is a similar example, in which he argues that increased demand for resources, coupled with shortages and contestation over ownership, is likely to create new pressures leading to conflict. Neighbouring countries who share resources are at a higher risk of such tensions escalating into conflict. More recently, Klare (2012) extended his analysis of resource competition in *The Race for What's Left*. Whereas the race for resources often involves commercial corporations, '[f]or nation-states', Klare (2012: 214–215) argues, 'the fight for resources has equally high stakes: those that retain access to adequate supplies of critical materials will flourish, while those unable to do so will experience hardship and decline.' Another notable author linking natural resources with violence is Philippe Le Billon (2004; 2005). Unlike Homer-Dixon (1999), Le Billon does not dedicate much attention to the concept of scarcity, but his focus on the role of natural resources as an underlying factor in war and violent conflict is similar.

## Scarcity as an impetus for peacebuilding

In contrast to arguments that associate scarcity with conflict, another set of authors suggests that scarcity (especially around shared resources) can be a catalyst for peace (Brock, 1991; Carius, 2012). This literature approaches scarce resources from the perspective of peacebuilding, that is, with the examination of projects and policies promoting peaceful relations among international or domestic actors who are otherwise in conflict. It is also largely populated by applied, as opposed to theoretical, analysis with the objective of providing recommendations for more successful promotion of peace in the context of scarcity. The underlying argument is that a shared interest in the current and future benefits of access to resources—or ecosystem services deriving from them—provides a basis for engagement within which cooperation is a more viable and advantageous response than conflict. Currently, the most common areas for such peacebuilding involve transboundary management of water, nature conservation parks and international or global governance agreements.

Whereas observers such as Homer-Dixon, Klare and Le Billon interpret the access to surface and groundwater in water scarce regions as a likely point of contention that can (or inevitably will) trigger conflict, there is emerging evidence of collaboration in such situations. Perhaps the most notable examples involve progress in efforts to develop cooperative governance and management arrangements between otherwise belligerent groups in the Middle East. Kramer (2008) reports on the progress and achievements of the Regional Water Data Banks and Good Water Neighbors projects involving participants from Israel, Jordan and the Palestinian community. She identifies significant areas of cooperation around the allocation of water in the region. In addition to these projects, in his review of mechanisms and practices leading to successful peacebuilding efforts, Carius (2012) lists similar efforts in the Nile and Okavango River Basins in Africa and there is a growing literature on collaborative governance of the Mekong Basin in Southeast Asia (Jacobs, 2002). While these reviews of the achievements associated with transboundary water management emphasise the potential for appreciable positive outcomes and benefits to both regional societies and environment, Zeitoun et al. (2014) caution that the narrow focus on cooperation may overlook the ability for some participants to exploit their relative power to negotiate agreements that favour their position in comparison to weaker neighbours.

A further area of emphasis for peacebuilding is nature conservation, highlighted by the development of peace parks located in areas of contested resource access or transboundary regions (often in the context of challenges to national sovereignty). In making a claim for the relationship between nature conservation and debates about scarcity, Ali (2007a) states that scarcity should be viewed as being measurable in terms of quality—that is, a degraded resource is also a source of scarcity—as well as quantity. In that context, Matthew et al. (2002) review a series of case studies in which conservation efforts have been used to mitigate tensions around poverty and resource access in areas of highly biodiverse tropical rainforest. From the case studies, contributors to the book offer insight to policies and practices with the potential to reduce tensions caused by restraints on land and resource use imposed through conservation, while also identifying income potential for local communities through managed exploitation and ecotourism. Similar connections between biodiversity conservation and shared benefits for locally impacted communities are identified in parks that traverse international boundaries (Ali, 2007b). In his introduction to a collection of peacebuilding case studies, Ali (2007a) argues that the potential for conservation to facilitate peaceful relations is often sidelined by the more dominant theoretical arguments linking environmental issues to conflict. While not in evidence in the literature, the cautions identified by Zeitoun et al. (2014) are likely as much in play in the development of international peace parks.

A further arena for international cooperation around resources lies in the growing number of international treaties and agreements related to the governance of resources, including such diverse agreements as the Montreal Protocol (to mitigate the scarcity of ozone), the Convention of Biological Diversity, Regional Fisheries Management Organisations (see Jollands and Fisher, this volume) and

## 8 *M.C. Dawson, C. Rosin and N. Wald*

the Intergovernmental Panel on Climate Change (IPCC) negotiated climate change mitigation agreements. Such agreements demonstrate the power of scarcity (whether understood as actual or created) to impel more collaborative actions among international participants. That said, the extent to which the negotiation of international agreements is frequently reliant on the willingness of a small number of more powerful states (including the US, China, and large European powers), and often pivots around the recognition of 'special conditions' in weaker countries of the Global South, points to similar issues of power inequalities as noted above.

### Alternative approaches to understanding scarcity

Beyond perspectives that emphasise the peacebuilding potential of actual or perceived scarcity, there are numerous other approaches that seek to challenge the dominant view of an inevitable relationship between resource scarcity and conflict. In contrast to the fear-inducing Malthusian approach, growing numbers of commentators are promoting the idea of scarcity as a socially constructed concept, exposing the ability of powerful groups (e.g. government and industry) to craft certain resources as scarce, while simultaneously promoting their own interests by offering political or commercial solutions to the 'scarcity problem' (see, for instance, Lyla Mehta's chapter in this volume).

Notably, from a political ecology perspective, scholars such as Theisen (2008) and Bretthauer (2015), suggest that evidence in favour of Malthusian-inspired claims about a causal relationship between resource scarcity and conflict is inconsequential. In their work, they have identified other factors such as poor governance, corruption, institutional instability and other location-specific and structural conditions as confounding variables in the spurious relationship between resource scarcity and conflict. For instance, Peluso and Watts (2001: 5) argued that 'violence [is] a site-specific phenomenon rooted in local histories and social relations yet connected to larger processes of material transformation and power relations.' Deepening these findings, Bretthauer's (2015) research— a comparison of 31 resource-scarce countries, in which 15 displayed high levels of armed conflict and 16 were conflict free—shed light on some of the specific social, economic and political conditions under which violence or conflict are likely to occur. She concluded that the absence of education—or what she called 'low levels of ingenuity'—is the most significant necessary condition for conflict, followed by high levels of dependence on agriculture and excessive poverty (Bretthauer, 2015: 604–605). Moreover, challenging the view of the economic optimists, Bretthauer (2015) noted that a low or no conflict outcome was more strongly associated with lower reliance on agriculture than with economic development.

There has been much criticism of market solutions to 'the scarcity problem' that have been proposed in the form of resource substitution, technological innovation, increased investment, labour intensification and all manner of 'efficiencies' packaged as 'development' or 'progress'. As discussed earlier, rampant resource exploitation in the name of growth or prosperity, coupled with an exponential increase in the world's population, led to a momentary revival of Malthusian-esque trepidation in the 1970s. However, unlike the earlier phase of panic about running out of resources, new anxieties were articulated around the long-term consequences of soaring levels of pollution and environmental degradation. Meadows et al. (1972), authors of the widely-publicised *Limits to Growth* (LtG) thesis, referred to these outcomes as 'negative feedback loops' in the global system. According to them, unchecked population growth and resource depletion could lead to 'a sudden and uncontrollable collapse' of the global system, which would ultimately scupper the positive feedback loops of capital expansion and population growth (Meadows et al., 1972: 158).

Critics of the LtG thesis censured its seemingly woeful conclusions, arguing that it was possible to introduce measures to 'weaken the loops or to disguise the pressures they generate so that growth can continue' (Meadows et al., 1972: 157). However, Meadows et al. were firm in their view that '[s]uch means may have some short-term effect in relieving pressures caused by growth, but in the long run they do nothing to prevent the overshoot and subsequent collapse of the system' (p. 157). Unlike the pessimistic and over-deterministic overtones of Malthusian claims, the LtG thesis contained a message of hope; a call to action that could potentially avert disaster. Meadows et al. (1972: 24) argued that

> [i]t is possible to alter these growth trends and to establish a condition of ecological and economic stability that is sustainable far into the future. The state of global equilibrium could be designed so that the basic material needs of each person on earth are satisfied and each person has an equal opportunity to realize his or her individual human potential.

The term, 'equilibrium' alludes to the possibility of encouraging economic development without overshooting the earth's limited carrying capacity (see Randers, 2000). However, this concept failed to impress policymakers and captains of industry in the western world, who equated it with stagnation. Nevertheless, in 1986, when the Brundtland Commission (renamed the World Commission on Environment and Development in 1987) repackaged this idea as 'sustainable development', it soon became ubiquitous. The commission defined the term as 'development that meets the needs of the present without compromising the ability of future generations to meet their own needs' (WCED, 1987: 43). The resemblance to the term 'equilibrium' is clearly discernible, but in the early 1990s it was 'sustainable development' that became the 'watchword for international aid agencies, the jargon of development planners, the theme of conferences and learned papers, and the slogan of developmental and environmental activists' (Lélé, 1991: 607).

Despite extensive uptake of the word, conceptual fuzziness and myriad interpretations continue to hamper efforts to achieve the stated objectives

## 10  *M.C. Dawson, C. Rosin and N. Wald*

of sustainable development. In the minority are those who regard sustainable development as a contradiction in terms; an impossible objective, as well as those who have tended to (mis)interpret 'sustainable' as 'sustained'. For example, Nigerian academic Francis Idachaba (1987: 18) claimed in an address to the World Bank's seventh symposium on the agriculture sector, that '[s]ustainability in agricultural development . . . refers to the ability of agricultural systems to keep production and distribution going continuously without falling. It refers to how agricultural growth and development can be sustained into the future.' When challenged by an audience member about his lack of consideration for the environment, Idachaba responded with a suggestion that environmental concerns—while understandably a preoccupation of the developed world—were 'second generation problems that tend to give way to more immediate concerns' in the developing world (Hopcraft, 1987: 54).

Notwithstanding these outliers, Robinson (2004) has grouped the majority of the perspectives of environmentalist responses to resource scarcity into two camps (see Table 1.1). The first regards sustainable development as compatible with growth, while the second bases its views on the critical assumption that development is not synonymous with growth. It follows, then, that the first camp endorses technical fixes as part of the solution to scarcity, while the second promotes value change as the way forward. Robinson (2004: 372) also noted the first group's preference for the term 'sustainable development', while the second camp tended to use 'sustainability', entirely dropping the notion of 'development' because of its conflation with growth. Robinson (2004: 371) admitted that his typology was 'suggestive, not definitive', but even so, contrasting the views in this way highlights the vexed and contested nature of sustainable development as an approach to dealing with resource scarcity.

Several commentators have condemned the hijacking of the term 'sustainable development' by government officials and industry representatives, who seem intent on ramping up growth efforts under the guise of sustainable development. Critics have labelled their efforts variously as 'market environmentalism' (Anderson and Leal, 1991; Bailey, 2007), 'cosmetic environmentalism' or 'fake greenery' (Robinson, 2004: 374), 'green neoliberalism' (Bakker, 2010) or 'green capitalism' (Heartfield, 2008; Tienhaara, 2014), which Prudham (2009: 1595) defines as 'a set of responses to environmental change and environmentalism that relies on harnessing capital investment, individual choice, and entrepreneurial innovation to the green cause.' Such a view, promoted by the 'technical fixers', is distinctly at odds with the 'value changers', who

*Table 1.1* Forms of environmentalist response

|  | *Technical fix* | *Value change* |
| --- | --- | --- |
| Natural area management | Conservation (utilitarian) | Preservation (romantic) |
| Pollution and resources | Technology (collective policies) | Lifestyles (individual values) |
| Preferred language | Sustainable development | Sustainability |

Source: Robinson (2004: 372)

distinguish between development and growth. For example, as Daly (1990: 1) explained, 'growth is quantitative increase in physical scale, while development is qualitative improvement or unfolding of potentialities. An economy can grow without developing, or develop without growing, or do both or neither.'

While the *sustainable development* approach implies some degree of growth, *sustainability* sits more comfortably with the idea of what Meadows et al. (1972) referred to as a non-growth equilibrium state. This notion—also known by the term 'steady-state economy'—has some purchase among environmentalists in the US today. However, it has been dismissed in certain European circles, where a strategy of 'degrowth' is being promoted (Martínez-Alier et al., 2010). Pioneered in 1971 by French economist and statistician Nicholas Georgescu-Roegen, 'degrowth' has recently been resurrected by European scholars and activists. Despite ostensible parallels with the LtG thesis—particularly with regard to the shared disdain for the solutions proposed by the economic optimists—Georgescu-Roegen's disagreement with the notion of a steady-state economy became increasingly apparent (Levallois, 2010). For him, the only viable response to resource scarcity lay in 'retracting consumption levels in countries such as the US which he understood was already consuming excessively' (Martínez-Alier et al., 2010: 1743). It is clear that proponents are not proposing degrowth as a *global* strategy to address resource scarcity and environmental degradation, but instead are suggesting that 'Southern countries or societies, where ecological impacts are low relative to their biocapacity, [be allowed] to increase their material consumption and thus their ecological footprint' (ibid.). The mutually influential relationship between the burgeoning scholarly literature on degrowth and the increasingly energetic degrowth movement, signals a new, and potentially quite exciting, direction with regard to resource scarcity. Although not pursued in this book, it is a line of thinking and action that centres global inequality in the scarcity debate and questions what the world might look like if there were 'prosperity without growth' (Jackson, 2017) in advanced economies.

## Overview of chapters

As noted above, the contributions to the book have been purposefully organised in order to reflect the tensions and the hopefulness attributed to resource scarcity both in the academic literature and policy orientations. We look to achieve this by arranging the contributions into three parts based on their treatments of scarcity. Part I specifically challenges readers to rethink their conceptions of scarcity in a manner that eliminates the sense of inevitable conflict. Parts II and III are intended to offer paired accounts of scarcity in particular resource categories—agriculture, mining, fresh water and marine—framed in terms of the tensions that develop or the examples of cooperation achieved. The contributions to these parts are neither wholly alarmist nor uncritically optimistic; but each pair allows readers to gaze over the edge of the abyss, while also glimpsing the safe (if perhaps indistinct) footholds and pathways for navigating the crossing. As a whole, the contributors propose a more hopeful engagement among the world's nations as they pursue the economic and social benefits derived from natural resources while maintaining the ecological processes on which they depend.

The presentations of scarcity within the contributions vary significantly, highlighting the diverse professional backgrounds of our contributors—from academics to policy analysts, consultants and activists. As a result, the book does not offer a coherent theoretical treatise on the relevance of specific elements or aspects of scarcity. We suggest, however, that the diverse voices, styles of argument and focuses of analysis more accurately represent the breadth of engagements with scarcity in our global society—and the collection has value precisely because it forces each of us to confront scarcity in its multiplicity of meanings, implications and applications.

Contributors to Part I use the examples of water (Mehta, Chapter 2) and regional energy pools (Lindström, Granit and Rosner, Chapter 3) to re-evaluate the concept and boundaries of 'scarcity'. Both chapters challenge the scarcity postulate, where scarcity is regarded as a universal and permanent condition that underlies human existence. These two chapters are quite different in their approach to scarcity, which is telling of the epistemological and ontological diversity that can be found in this volume. The explicit conceptual analysis of scarcity that is presented in Chapter 2 reflects a critical approach prevalent in the social sciences, while the more implicit understanding of scarcity in Chapter 3 is more typical of a practice-oriented public policy approach. Lyla Mehta's chapter in this collection is a continuation of her critique of scarcity as a seemingly meta-level value-neutral reasoning for actions that, in effect, are laden with ideological dispositions. Mehta focuses on fresh water as an example of a renewable resource that is often being portrayed as dangerously scarce. This dominant discourse on water scarcity tends to emphasise economic problems and (market-led) solutions that are of importance to powerful groups over social, cultural and political concerns. Mehta promotes a critical lens that incorporates elements from both post-structural deconstruction and structuralist Marxist analysis.

The chapter by Andreas Lindström, Jakob Granit and Kevin Rosner examines regional energy cooperation as a strategy for achieving sustainable economic development and peace through the formation of stronger ties among neighbouring countries. The increasing demand for a stable supply of electricity has prompted transboundary cooperation in areas where energy resources are unevenly distributed. The authors note the potential for 'regionalism' and regional collaboration to generate political, economic and social benefits. They also emphasise deregulation and the mechanisms of the market as being instrumental for achieving a transboundary energy pool. Scarcity appears in this chapter, not as a theoretical concept, but in the form of constraints on electricity production imposed by costs of infrastructure and demands for alternative energy sources.

The chapters in Part II address some of the key tensions resulting from scarcity and the potential for response. As they demonstrate, scarcity of a natural resource may be influenced by various physical as well as socio-political factors, of which limited supply and growing demand are only two. In Chapter 4, Stuart White and Dana Cordell examine tensions surrounding the increasing global demand for phosphorus (phosphate rock), a non-renewable natural resource with a relatively low profile in popular debates about resource scarcity. This is in spite of phosphorus being an essential element for plant growth and thus for agriculture production and global food supply. In this chapter, the authors outline the key issues concerning this resource, including its sensitive geopolitical context and the absence of an international governance framework. The authors maintain that phosphorus is not scarce solely because there is a fixed amount of it in the earth's crust, but rather because of a number of factors affecting supply and demand that combine to limit its availability. The authors argue that because phosphorus security is directly linked to food security, and because there are many stakeholders involved, there is a dire need to establish an international body to coordinate collaborative solutions.

In Chapter 5, Kuntala Lahiri-Dutt focuses on the logic and practice of extractivism (as opposed to a particular natural resource), which refers to the accelerated exploitation of resources for fast economic growth. Under neo-liberalism, extractivism is often framed and legitimised through discourses of crisis and scarcity. These concepts are perceived as politically shaped and as reflecting a materialist worldview where natural resources and human needs are closely related. The chapter draws attention to the effects of this economic logic and strategy on peasants, who, in many countries in the Global South, have become artisanal, small-scale miners. Through their mining activities, they have—to varying degrees—contributed to the degradation of the environment on which they depend for subsistence. The peasant-miners operate at the margins of the mining industry, often as part of the informal economy, and tend to be ignored.

Doug Hill adopts a multi-scalar lens in Chapter 6 to examine how issues of water security in South Asia have been understood and constructed by different stakeholders. The discursive rationale for the use and management of water in this region commonly preferences a particular notion of scarcity and security that privileges a supply-side approach in the form of a volumetric understanding of water, and ignores other possible understandings. The particular geopolitics of the Indus Basin adds another layer of complexity, where water security is deemed to be of national importance to both India and Pakistan, who share the basin. Hill also mentions the secrecy around water data, which shuts down debate and obstructs possible alternative actions that may entail greater cooperation between stakeholders. He acknowledges the region's history of international and intra-national disputes over water, but calls for alternative understandings of water that do not solely serve the interests of powerful groups in the name of national security.

14   *M.C. Dawson, C. Rosin and N. Wald*

Chapter 7, by Todd Capson, examines the scarcities associated with the degradation of marine environments, including fisheries, as an important source of protein for many people. As with fresh water, marine resources may not be confined within a single political territory and are thus of interest to a broader range of stakeholders. Capson argues that the sustainability of this resource in the face of growing demand and environmental pressures necessitates transboundary cooperation and bold action, such as the formation of marine protected areas. Scarcity enters the discussion in its most conventional economic form as the result of demand exceeding a limited supply. Capson does not, however, regard it as a universal or permanent situation and posits sustainable management as the opposite of scarcity. However, high and growing demand will result in higher prices, with increasing numbers of consumers being unable to enjoy this resource. Scarcity, therefore, may refer to the quantity of fish stock available in the ocean or to the availability of these stocks for human consumption. The two are closely interrelated but not identical.

In Part III, our contributors shift to a more explicit focus on the potential for scarcity to act as the impetus for collaboration and a de-escalation of the tensions identified in Part II. The chapters reflect some of the existing work on peacebuilding noted above in relation to transboundary water management, but also extend the scope to a broader set of resources, including food, rare earth minerals and marine fisheries. In addition, they draw attention to the diverse forms and scales of coordination that use scarcity as a means to organise collaborative action across political, cultural and social boundaries. As a whole, they offer hopeful perspectives on resource use and access, which—while tempered by real world challenges—help to belie the inevitably of conflict.

Alana Mann addresses the concept of food scarcity as a threat to food security at both local and global scales in Chapter 8. She argues that the efforts of La Via Campesina to champion the capacities and rights of small-scale agricultural producers internationally is rooted in a vision of promoting increased self-sufficiency for societies and cultures. These efforts are encapsulated in the concept of food sovereignty, which promotes the right for self-determination in food production and consumption. Food sovereignty also involves the implicit rejection of a focus on scarcity and hunger in international food policy, with a concerted emphasis on the productive capacity of small farmers. The potential of La Via Campesina's efforts is apparent in its ability to draw together diverse peoples (from Latin America, to Africa, Asia, Europe and North America) and interests (across social strata, gender positions and other subjectivities).

Whereas the consumption of food is a shared experience that can lead to mutual interest in promoting socially and culturally appropriate means of production, Chapter 9 exposes the tendency for consumption of high-tech electronic goods to lead to the concentration of access. In this chapter Elliot Brennan shows that the potential for collaboration is more tenuous, emerging from realisation that control over the supply chain for rare earth minerals—which are, in fact, not physically scarce—has severe consequences for mineral dependent economies. In this case, scarcity has had implications for conflict, but it has also provided the impetus for the development of alternative sources (through recycling and new mining areas), resources (through substitution) and demand. Because of the dispersed nature in which rare earth minerals are distributed globally, these solutions offer the potential for collaboration, especially among those countries less endowed with their own reserves.

In Chapter 10, David Tickner focuses more squarely on the role of international relations and diplomats in promoting transboundary management of water resources. He argues that the foreign policy community can raise awareness of the need for collaboration by focusing on the ecosystem health of rivers and the associated benefits to human and environmental wellbeing. He suggests further that greater collaboration is an achievable goal, which can be facilitated through a set of 'six streams' of interventions. The implication of the model for improved collaboration around water management is that scarcity is not alleviated through conflict, but can certainly be mitigated through shared governance focused on the ecological role of rivers beyond the quantity of water they contain.

The emphasis on the potential for international diplomacy to enable cooperative governance of scarce resources is also apparent in Chapter 11 by Victoria Jollands and Karen Fisher. In their case, the scarcity of the resource (tuna species) is the result of its furtive nature (many tuna species traverse large expanses of ocean) and the accelerating demand in the marketplace. As the pressures of exploitation have impacted on the availability and size of the tuna fisheries, there is growing awareness of the need to regulate the activities of the fishing boats. Rather than a source of conflict among large and wealthy consuming nations, Jollands and Fisher demonstrate how these characteristics have facilitated the empowerment of the small South Pacific island states that have banded together to enable collaborative governance of fisheries. The experiences of these efforts points to both the potential and the challenges of cooperation related to resource scarcity.

## The value and significance of diverse views on scarcity

As a whole, the contributions to this book offer a distinctive insight into the role of scarcity in the relations among social actors who share an interest in and a desire to exploit a natural resource. Whereas, individually, the chapters may orient attention to specific resources, they do not provide an encyclopaedic introduction to the scarce resources of the world. Similarly, none of the contributors offers an all-encompassing explanation of or solution to conflicts related to contested resource access. They do, however, introduce a variety of engagements with and uses of scarcity as a localised reality, a dispersed or geographically uneven constraint on unfettered demand, a strategically created bottleneck on supply, or a more universal manipulation of access and regulated exploitation. These encounters with scarcity shift attention away from the myopic focus on market forces and allocation, and encourage us to

## 16  *M.C. Dawson, C. Rosin and N.Wald*

recognise more fully the social nature of the tensions and opportunities that are associated with our shared dependence on resources that are not readily accessible to all. We are confident that, read as a collection, this book will persuade readers to pursue cooperation—across the boundaries of disciplines, professions and institutional positions as well as those of nation states and social divisions—as a mechanism for more equitable and sustainable exploitation of resources that simultaneously mitigates tensions.

## References

Ali, S.H. (2007a) 'Introduction: a natural connection between ecology and peace?', in S.H. Ali (ed.) *Peace Parks: Conservation and Conflict Resolution*. Cambridge, MA: MIT Press, pp. 1–22.

Ali, S.H. (ed.) (2007b) *Peace Parks: Conservation and Conflict Resolution*. Cambridge, MA: MIT Press.

Anderson, T.L. and Leal, D.R. (1991) *Free-Market Environmentalism*. London: Palgrave Macmillan.

Bailey, I. (2007) 'Market environmentalism, new environmental policy instruments, and climate policy in the United Kingdom and Germany', *Annals of the Association of American Geographers*, 97(3), pp. 530–550.

Bakker, K. (2010) 'The limits of "neoliberal natures": debating green neoliberalism', *Progress in Human Geography*, 34(1), pp. 5–20.

Bretthauer, J.M. (2015) 'Conditions for peace and conflict: applying a fuzzy-set qualitative comparative analysis to cases of resource scarcity', *Journal of Conflict Resolution*, 59(4), pp. 593–616.

Brock, L. (1991) 'Peace through parks: the environment on the peace research agenda', *Journal of Peace Research,* 28(4), pp. 407–423.

Carius, A. (2012) 'Environmental peacebuilding: conditions for success', *ECSP Report*, Issue 12. Washington, D.C.: Wilson Center.

Daly, H.E. (1990) 'Toward some operational principles of sustainable development', *Ecological Economics*, 2(1), pp. 1–6.

Dinar, S. (2011) 'Resource scarcity and environmental degradation: analyzing international conflict and cooperation', in S. Dinar (ed.) *Beyond Resource Wars: Scarcity, Environmental Degradation, and International Cooperation*. Cambridge, MA: MIT Press, pp. 3–22.

Frerks, G., Dietz, T. and van der Zang, P. (2014) 'Conflict and cooperation on natural resources: Justifying the CoCooN programme', in M. Bavinck, L. Pellegrini and E. Mostert (eds) *Conflicts over Natural Resources in the Global South—Conceptual Approaches*. Leiden, The Netherlands: CRC Press, pp. 13–34.

Georgescu-Roegen, N. (1971) *The Entropy Law and the Economic Process*. Cambridge, MA: Harvard University Press.

Heartfield, J. (2008) *Green Capitalism: Manufacturing Scarcity in an Age of Abundance*. London: Mute Publishing Ltd.

Homer-Dixon, T.F. (1999) *Environment, Scarcity, and Violence*. New Jersey: Princeton University Press.

Hopcraft, P. (1987) 'Policy issues for sustainability—Rapporteur's comments', in T.J. Davis and I.A. Schirmer (eds) *Sustainability Issues in Agricultural Development*. Washington, DC: World Bank, pp. 54.

## Resource scarcity between conflict and cooperation 17

Idachaba, F.S. (1987) 'Sustainability issues in agriculture development', in T.J. Davis and I.A. Schirmer (eds) *Sustainability Issues in Agricultural Development*. Washington, DC: World Bank, pp. 18–53.

Jackson, T. (2017) *Prosperity Without Growth: Economics for a Finite Planet* (second edition). London: Routledge.

Jacobs, J.W. (2002) 'The Mekong River Commission: transboundary water resources planning and regional security', *The Geographical Journal*, 168(4), pp. 354–364.

Klare, M.T. (2001) *Resource Wars: The New Landscape of Global Conflict*. New York: Henry Holt.

Klare, M.T. (2012) The Race for What's Left: The Global Scramble for the World's Last Resources. New York: Metropolitan Books.

Kramer, A. (2008) *Regional Water Cooperation and Peacebuilding in the Middle East*. Brussels, Belgium: Initiative for Peace/Adelphi Research.

Le Billon, P. (ed.) (2004) *The Geopolitics of Resource Wars: Resource Dependence, Governance and Violence*. London: Frank Cass.

Le Billon, P. (2005) *Fuelling War: Natural Resources and Armed Conflict*. London: Routledge.

Lélé, S.M. (1991) 'Sustainable development: A critical review', *World Development*, 19(6), pp. 607–621.

Levallois, C. (2010) 'Can de-growth be considered a policy option? A historical note on Nicholas Georgescu-Roegen and the Club of Rome', *Ecological Economics*, 69(11), pp. 2271–2278.

Malthus, T. (1798) *An Essay on the Principle of Population as it affects the Future Improvement of Society*. London: John Johnson.

Martínez-Alier, J., Pascual, U., Vivien, F.D. and Zaccai, E. (2010) 'Sustainable de-growth: mapping the context, criticisms and future prospects of an emergent paradigm', *Ecological Economics*, 69(9), pp.1741–1747.

Matthaei, J. (1984) 'Rethinking scarcity: Neoclassicism, neoMalthusianism, and neo-Marxism', *Review of Radical Political Economics*, 16(2/3), pp. 81–94.

Matthew, R., Halle, M. and Switzer, J. (eds.) (2002) *Conserving the Peace: Resources, Livelihoods and Security*. Winnipeg, Canada: International Institute for Sustainable Development and IUCN – The World Conservation Union.

Meadows, D.H., Meadows, D.H., Randers, J. and Behrens III, W.W. (1972) *The Limits to Growth: A Report to the Club of Rome*. New York: Universe Books.

Peluso, N.L. and Watts, M. (eds). (2001) *Violent Environments*. Ithaca, NY: Cornell University Press.

Prudham, S. (2009) 'Pimping climate change: Richard Branson, global warming, and the performance of green capitalism', *Environment and Planning A*, 41, pp. 1594–1613.

Randers, J. (2000) 'From limits to growth to sustainable development or SD (sustainable development) in a SD (system dynamics) perspective', *System Dynamics Review*, 16(3), pp. 213–224.

Robinson, J. (2004) 'Squaring the circle? Some thoughts on the idea of sustainable development', *Ecological Economics*, 48(4), pp. 369–384.

Theisen, O.M. (2008) 'Blood and soil? Resource scarcity and internal armed conflict revisited', *Journal of Peace Research*, 45(6), pp.801–818.

Tienhaara, K. (2014) 'Varieties of green capitalism: economy and environment in the wake of the global financial crisis', *Environmental Politics*, 23(2), pp. 187–204.

WCED (1987) 'Our common future, Chapter 2: Towards sustainable development', available: http://www.un-documents.net/ocf-02.htm [accessed 11 May 2017].

Winch, D. (2013) *Malthus: A Very Short Introduction*. Oxford: Oxford University Press.

Xenos, N. (1987) 'Liberalism and the postulate of scarcity', *Political Theory*, 15(2), pp. 225–243.

Xenos, N. (2010) 'Everybody's got the fever: scarcity and US national energy policy', in L. Mehta (ed.) *The Limits to Scarcity: Contesting the Politics of Allocation*. New York: Earthscan, pp. 31–48.

Zeitoun, M., Warner, J., Mirumachi, N., Matthews, N., McLaughlin, K., Woodhouse, M., Cascão, A. and Allan, T.(J.A.) (2014) 'Transboundary water justice: a combined reading of literature on critical transboundary water interaction and "justice", for analysis and diplomacy', *Water Policy*, 16, pp. 174–193.

# Part I

# Reframing scarcity and resource diplomacy

# 2 Taking the scare out of scarcity

## The case of water[1]

*Lyla Mehta*

## Introduction

Ideas about resource scarcity and their implications for human wellbeing, economic growth and human security lie at the heart of global policy debates. Yet scarcity remains a contested concept, meaning different things to different groups. In this chapter, I demonstrate that spreading fear about the planet's diminishing resources serves the status quo and can result in keeping poor people poor (see Rayner, 2010). I argue that the assumption that needs and wants are unlimited and the means to satisfy them are scarce has led to scarcity emerging as a totalising discourse in both the North and South (see Hildyard, 2010). The 'scare' of scarcity has led to scarcity emerging as a political strategy for powerful groups. But scarcity is not a natural condition: the problem lies in how we see scarcity and the ways in which it is socially generated (see Mehta, 2010). Thus, we need to focus on the fundamental issues of resource allocation, access, entitlements and social justice, rather than drawing on simplistic, neo-Malthusian and universalising notions of scarcity. These issues are developed in this chapter through the case of water in the context of global debates and experiences from the Global South.

Since the mid-1990s, I have been working on the politics and social construction of water scarcity and questioning how it has been naturalised in policy debates as well as programmes. This work began in western India in Kutch, Gujarat, where I looked at how large dams were made out to be the panacea of water scarcity (see Mehta, 2005). A few years later I was concerned with examining the intellectual history of scarcity and its application to current policy and practice (see Mehta, 2010). I will draw on both of these as well as more recent work. The discussion begins by providing a background of recent scarcity narratives. It then turns to mainstream debates of scarcity within economics, namely the scarcity postulate and alternative perspectives. It unpacks these issues within the water domain before ending with thoughts on ways forward.

## The scare of scarcity

Of late, there has been a flurry of scarcity reports and concerns. In the late 2000s, the global financial crises, as well as dramatic increases in world food and fuel prices, were accompanied by growing concerns over climate change, population growth and increasing global inequalities in wealth and access to crucial resources. Dramatic increases in world food prices, causing much social unrest in both the South and North, coupled with processes of large scale land acquisitions—so called land and water grabs—have led to massive changes in local lives, livelihoods and reallocation of limited and life-sustaining resources (see Borras et al., 2012; Mehta et al., 2012). Since the 2008 World Economic Forum, key global players, including members of the corporate sector, have highlighted growing water, food, climate and energy security and scarcity threats and the need to resolve them through the so called 'nexus' approach (see Allouche et al., 2014; Hoff, 2011; SABMiller and WWF, 2014; World Economic Forum, 2014).

The past few years have also witnessed growing concerns about water scarcity and its threat to human wellbeing and livelihoods, economic and agricultural production, as well as the threat of 'water wars' having both national and international dimensions. Does all this suggest a déjà vu perhaps of the 1970s, where resource scarcity was a prominent political concern due to the oil shocks and accompanying financial crises? The 1970s raised critical questions regarding the existence of scarcity among plenty and abundance, about the need to set 'limits' to growth (cf. Meadows et al., 1972) and about the imperative for all humankind to coexist on 'spaceship earth', our one planet, which was increasingly being viewed as fragile and vulnerable. More than 40 years on, and in the midst of another global financial crisis, climate change poses new challenges to both human existence and resource availability. 'Water wars' and food shortages still appear as news stories. Resource scarcity continues to be linked with population growth and growing environmental conflicts, and science and technology or innovation are usually evoked as the appropriate 'solutions'. Scarcity remains an all-pervasive fact of our lives.

Take water scarcity, for instance. Water resources are under pressure from a number of competing uses, which cause different resource stress dynamics in different regions. These competing uses include domestic consumption, use in food production processes, urban demand, and use in industrial processes. According to the European Commission (2012), pressures on water availability will continue to grow, not only through the need to feed and hydrate a growing global population, but also as a result of changing patterns of consumption. Chatham House (2012) predicts that by 2030 global water demand could outstrip supply by 40 per cent. The Earth Security Group (2015) predicts that India will reach severe water stress by 2025, and that by 2030 both India and China will face severe water deficits. The OECD (2012) estimates that by 2050 there will be a 55 per cent increase in global water demand. Broken down by sector, that means a 400 per cent increase in demand for manufacturing, a 140 per cent increase for electricity generation and a 130 per cent increase for domestic use. All these reports call for innovative technologies, policy changes, regulation or water pricing as solutions to facilitate the market access of innovative water technologies. But with the endless call for solutions, we also need to step back and ask how the problem of scarcity is being framed in the first place. I now turn to the intellectual history of scarcity before moving on to scarcity debates in the water domain.

## The legacy of the scarcity postulate: from scarcities to scarcity

> ...the whole human existence, at least up to now, has been a bitter struggle against scarcity.[2]
>
> (Jean-Paul Sartre)

Jean-Paul Sartre sums up nicely what is taken to be a given in dominant academic and policy thinking: scarcity is an all-pervasive fact of our lives and much of human existence has been caught up in struggles against scarcity.

According to popular opinion, scarcity is the creation of economists. In part, this has to do with Lionel Robbins' famous definition: 'Economics is the science which studies human behaviour as a relationship between given ends and scarce means which have alternative uses' (Robbins, 1932: 16). But his conception was highly misleading for the 1930s when resources were not scarce but unavailable.

The scarcity postulate (i.e. that human wants are unlimited and the means to achieve these are scarce and limited) underpins modern economics, which, in turn, has helped promote a universalised notion of scarcity. Nicholas Xenos in *Scarcity and Modernity* (1989) systematically shows how certain attributes of modernity have given rise to the universal notion of scarcity. The etymological roots of the word 'scarcity' go back to the Old Northern French word *escarcté*, which meant insufficiency of supply. Until the late nineteenth century, scarcity connoted *a* temporally bounded period of scarcity or a dearth. Scarcity was experienced cyclically, dependent usually on poor yields. After the industrial revolution—which led to cataclysmic changes creating new needs, desires and the frustration of desires—the concept acquired a new meaning, which culminated in its 'invention' in neoclassical economic thought of the eighteenth century (Xenos, 1989: 7). From *scarcities*, which were temporally bound and spatially differentiated, came the scourge of *scarcity*, 'a kind of open-ended myth' (ibid: 35) from which deliverance was sought. Scarcity, not *a* scarcity or *scarcities*, was essentialised and its simplistic universalisation led to the obscuring of ambiguities and regional variations. In modernity, the elusive twin of scarcity is abundance, making scarcity 'the antagonist in the human story, a story with a happy ending; vanquishing of the antagonist and a life of happiness ever after and abundance for all' (ibid: 35).

Universal notions of scarcity legitimise the need to allocate and manage property either through the means of the market or through formalising rights regimes (formalisation of water rights, for example, has gained much currency in contemporary donor discourses, not least due to 'scarce' water resources).

It is thus economic goods, that is, goods that are scarce, that are made the objects of systematic human action. Of course, it is highly contested whether all 'resources' or goods can be viewed unproblematically as 'economic' goods. The declaration of water as an 'economic good' in 1992 at the Dublin conference on water and the environment (ICWE, 1992) is still deeply controversial in the water domain since many still feel that this legitimises the commodification of a life-giving resource and justifies its privatisation. This is because access may depend on one's ability to pay (see Dawson, 2010 and Nicol et al., 2011 for a further discussion of these debates).

Dominant definitions tend to privilege certain material aspects of resources over other cultural and public good aspects. Moreover, aggregate and technical assessments of resources rarely capture their multifaceted nature and embeddedness in culture, history and politics. All of this has a bearing on how resources are valued and thus rendered scarce or not. For example, water is simultaneously a natural element or $H_2O$, essential for the ecological cycle, a spiritual resource for millions who worship at holy river banks and oceans, a commodity which can be tapped, bottled, sold and traded, and a life-giving element without which human survival is not possible. These multiple purposes of water are rarely captured in global water assessments or dominant water scarcity and 'water wars' debates (which I will turn to shortly).

In the environmental security discourse, analysts such as Homer-Dixon (2001) and Baechler (1999) have made powerful links between resource scarcity, population growth and conflict. Often resource scarcity is seen as a constant variable in the context of environmental change and the cause for social and political conflicts. However, as argued by Dalby (2014) and Peluso and Watts (2001) the real problem may lie in distributional issues and ethnic rivalries as well as socio-political factors. Also, as the development literature suggests, violence often arises from resource abundance rather than scarcity. This is particularly true in regions where apart from resource extraction there are few other economic and livelihood options (see Le Billon, 2001).

## Challenges to the scarcity postulate

These powerful framings of scarcity have been challenged by diverse thinkers and disciplines that I now briefly explore. I demonstrate that there are different ways to view scarcity from economic, institutional, socio-political and human development perspectives.

Karl Polanyi (1944; 1957) stands out as one of the few economists who argued that economic theory and several of its core tenets (such as scarcity) are not universally applicable. Instead, Polanyi underscores the principles of the distinction between 'real' and 'fictitious' commodities, the latter being linked to human existence and not produced for sale (e.g. land, labour, water). Thus, market mechanisms cannot be the sole regulators of these 'fictitious commodities'. Crucial is the distinction between the formal and substantive meaning of 'economic'. Substantive economics is concerned with 'man's dependence for his living upon nature and his fellows. It refers to the ways in which people interact with each other and nature to satisfy their basic material wants. By contrast, the formal meaning of economics draws on the choice between the alternative uses of insufficient means' (Polanyi, 1957: 243). According to Polanyi, the two are quite distinct. While the formal meaning implies choice between alternate uses of scarce means, the substantive meaning need neither contain choice nor insufficiency of means. He then goes on to caution that the current concept of economic fuses the 'subsistence' and the 'scarcity' meanings of economic without a sufficient awareness of the dangers to clear thinking inherent in that merger (ibid: 244). These debates are very relevant for the water domain where the multiple characteristics of water (e.g. social, cultural, symbolic resource) are often negated in favour of promoting water as an economic good.

From anthropology, Marshall Sahlins (1972) has offered a series of critiques of the use of the universalist scarcity postulate. In his *Stone Age Economics*, Sahlins questions the assumption that material wants are limitless and can never be satisfied. He begins with the postulate that human wants can be limited and few. People, he claims, can enjoy material abundance and plenty with a low standard of living and are thus free from market obsessions with scarcity and instead operate under different rationalities (e.g. leisure and mobility). Hunter-gatherers as ultimate uneconomic man!

While both Sahlins' and Polanyi's contributions in debunking the scarcity postulate have been immense, I should also briefly mention some of the problems with their work. They have tended to overly romanticise 'pre-modern' societies in ancient Greece, Mesopotamia and those of so called tribals and hunter-gatherers. They also have downplayed issues such as internal conflict, gender imbalances, acquisitiveness and so on. This notwithstanding, their work highlights the importance of focusing on non-economic rationalities that shape human behaviour and the embeddedness of economic action in social relations, history and culture.

Powerful critiques have also emerged from institutional perspectives. An impressive body of work by common property theorists has successfully discredited neo-Malthusian notions concerning population growth, resource availability and environmental degradation. Many empirical studies from Europe, Africa and Asia have shown how people cooperate in times of resource pressure and scarcity (Berkes, 1989; Bromley and Cernea, 1989; Ostrom, 1990). They have also shown how Hobbesian notions of anarchy, where states, regions and people fight over scarce resources, may not be an accurate or predictable scenario.

In his seminal study of starvation and famines, Sen (1981; 1983) argued that the fixation with the per capita food availability decline (FAD) is a misleading way to look at hunger and famine, since hunger is more about people not having access to food due to wider social and political arrangements as opposed to there not being enough food to eat. Thus, looking at per capita availability of a resource lacks relevant discrimination and is even more gross when applied to the population of the world as a whole (Sen, 1981). Water scarcity is also often misleadingly perceived as per capita water availability rather than inequality in access to water supply (see below).

Finally, socio-political perspectives and the focus on discourses by drawing on political ecology, science studies and Foucauldian analysis urge us to ask how scarcity is perceived at different levels and also to explore the nature of relations of power and production at global and local levels (see Peet et al., 2011). Within this approach, contestations take place at two levels: first, over meaning and text in the very conception of how we define water scarcity; and second, in competing claims and conflicts over resources. Here the focus is both discursive *and* materialist (cf. Escobar, 1996), where the nexus of power, ideas and social relations is the centrepiece of enquiry. Such an analysis tries to marry an ecological phenomenon (i.e. a shortage of food, water etc.) with political economy.

All these different approaches challenge the scarcity postulate through their focus on meaning and culture as well as specific institutional, economic and socio-political contexts. Rather than seeing scarcity as a phenomenon 'out there' over which humans have no control that consequently leads to standardised responses (e.g. either conflict or cooperation), it is important to look at local-specific contingencies in culturally-specific meanings and traditions and how these are mediated by power, politics and a wider political economy. These issues have a bearing on scarcity politics in the water domain to which I now turn.

## Conventional approaches to water scarcity

Water scarcity has emerged as one of the most pressing problems in the twenty-first century. Against a growing alarmism of 'water wars', several global agencies, national governments and non-governmental organisations (NGOs) have been concerned with emerging water 'crises' and the causality and solutions around water scarcity. International meetings around water are regular occurrences. Even though the water Millennium Development Goal (MDG) to halve the number of people without access to potable water was met in 2012, 700 million people around the globe still lack access to safe drinking water. This includes 18 per cent of the rural population worldwide, of which 47 per cent are in Sub-Saharan Africa. An estimated 2.4 billion people lack access to improved sanitation, with more than one billion defecating in the open (see HLPE, 2015).

While annual renewable fresh water resources are adequate at global levels to meet human water needs (HLPE, 2015), these resources are very unevenly distributed across the globe. Per capita, annual renewable water resources are particularly low in the Middle Eastern, North African and South Asian regions. There are also significant variations in water availability within regions and countries. Uneven water resource distribution can translate into uneven capacity to grow food and affect food availability and access. Poor access to water and access to water of poor quality also leads to adverse health outcomes leading to water-borne diseases that particularly affect babies and children in poor countries.

In recent years, think tanks and corporate players have argued that fresh water scarcity presents one of the most pressing crosscutting challenges in the future (Chatham House, 2012; SABMiller and WWF, 2014). The European Commission estimates that nearly one billion people globally have no safe water and that, at current rates, the demand for water will have grown by 40 per cent globally by 2030 (European Commission, 2012). The OECD predicts that globally more than 240 million people are expected to be without safe water access by 2050 (OECD, 2012). Amidst this projected increasing demand and the need for trade-offs among competing uses of water resources, climatic change means that rainfall and water availability are likely to become more uncertain (Steffen et al., 2015). Many of the solutions put forward concern resource management, infrastructure investment and technical improvements that increase production efficiency or substitutability as well as mitigation and policymaking for resilience.

From a nexus perspective, the use and management of water requires an integrated approach that takes into account both land and energy issues (European Commission, 2012). Since the 1990s, water sector reforms have been influenced by the concept of Integrated Water Resources Management (IWRM), which calls for 'co-ordinated development and management of water, land and related resources, in order to maximize welfare in an equitable manner without compromising the sustainability of vital ecosystems' (GWP, 2000: 22). IWRM is thus broadly in line with a water–energy–land (WEL) nexus perspective (European Commission, 2012). However, as a vast literature has revealed, IWRM has tended to be idealised, abstract and difficult to implement, especially in Sub-Saharan Africa where complex formal and informal rights, as well as customary land and water arrangements, prevail (see Mehta et al., 2016). IWRM implementation, in fact, may have resulted in an unwarranted policy focus on managing water instead of improving poor people's access to water. Furthermore, the newly created institutional arrangements have often been prone to elite capture and failed to address historically rooted inequalities (ibid).

Other dominant solutions to scarcity involve technical and market-driven approaches. As discussed, since the Dublin Declaration of 1992, water is increasingly seen as having economic value in all its competing uses. Accordingly, efficient resource management is equated with water having a price and the price signal is thus evoked as a way to solve water scarcity problems (see Finger and Allouche, 2002). Thus, in the past two decades, water has moved away from being viewed as a common good (however impure) and a public service to a commodity being managed according to economic principles (ibid). In part, this has to do with the growing influence of powerful players, such as the World Bank and transnational corporations that have paved the way for controversial water privatisations around the world. In the name of

28    L. Mehta

'efficiency' and 'scarcity', solutions have included water reallocation through water markets, water permits and different privatisation models. Private sector involvement in water provision was also imposed on many debt-ridden countries in the course of the economic restructuring of the 1990s. There are strong arguments claiming that poor people are willing to pay for water (Altaf et al., 1992) and, relatively speaking, poor people pay far more than the rich for water (see below). Still, experiences with privatisation of water have not always been poor friendly (see Bakker 2010; Finger and Allouche, 2002: McDonald and Ruiters, 2005; Dawson, 2010). One reason has to do with the nature of water markets. The high level of monopoly and low competition do not naturally lead to high responsiveness to user needs, and there is often no incentive to service non-profit-making sectors (such as rural areas and the urban poor) or to invest in unprofitable sectors (such as wastewater and sanitation) (see Finger and Allouche, 2002). Often prices have been raised beyond agreed levels within a few years of privatisation, and people who could not pay have been cut off (for South African examples, see McDonald and Ruiters, 2005; Dawson, 2010).

In this section, I have focused on the dominant portrayals of and 'solutions' to water scarcity and some of the negative impacts on poor people. I now turn to alternative framings and perspectives.

## The value of alternative perspectives on water access and scarcity

Water resources have particular characteristics that make them distinct from other natural resources. Water is fluid in nature and mostly a renewable resource. This means that the availability of water fluctuates in space and time and this is relevant when assessing water allocation and actual water distribution. Water scarcity is a complex phenomenon and can be analysed differently from social, political, meteorological, hydrological and agricultural perspectives (Falkenmark and Lannerstad, 2005). Scarcity of water is typically examined through two lenses. The first is 'physical water scarcity', which compares the amount of renewable water annually available per capita in a particular area with pre-determined thresholds to identify water-stressed and water-scarce areas, respectively (Falkenmark and Widstrand, 1992). The second lens is 'economic water scarcity' (CA, 2007). This refers to the fact that physical availability of water does not necessarily mean that water is available for use or is accessed. In some areas, while there may be abundant water available, the lack of infrastructure means that the water is not available where it is needed, or of an appropriate quality for use. For example, according to the United Nations Environment Programme (UNEP, 2011), an estimated 51 million people in the Democratic Republic of the Congo— around three quarters of the population—had no access to safe drinking water in 2011, even though the country is considered water rich, with more than half of Africa's water reserves. In such countries and regions, the challenge is economic water scarcity or lack of investment, appropriate infrastructure or management—rather than physical water scarcity—to provide for the needs of the population, including water for food security and nutrition. It must, however, be stated that both these portrayals of scarcity tend to direct attention to natural and economic forces rather than addressing human-induced land and water use practices, socio-political considerations and how scarcity can be socially mediated or constructed (Mehta, 2005; UNDP, 2006).

These lenses do not necessarily consider the way in which the distribution of and control over water is socially differentiated by gender, caste, race, occupation and other categories. Sen's (1981; 1993) entitlements approach, when applied to water, indicates that some people's lack of water does not necessarily imply that water is scarce. Instead, it has more to do with the fact that certain parts of the population are unable to gain access to water for one reason or another, be it that water is too highly priced, lack of infrastructure or due to social exclusion. Some groups may suffer from lack of water even when there is no decline in water availability in the region. Thus, water shortages (like famines) are entitlement failures.

Aggregate views of water scarcity can, therefore, be problematic because they could hide real inequalities in water access determined by property rights, social and political institutions, and cultural and gender norms. People's lack of access to water might have little to do with physical scarcity, per se, but may instead be due to exclusions arising from social positioning, gender or because of the way water is managed, priced and regulated (Mehta, 2014; UNDP, 2006). For example, deeply rooted traditional or historical inequalities can limit women's and other vulnerable groups' access to land and thereby to water for agricultural uses, which hampers livelihood strategies and negatively impacts food security.

Gender and other markers of identities continue to mould water allocation and access among users. Cultural norms in much of the developing world dictate that women and girls are responsible for water collection, and they may spend several hours per day collecting water. Unequal power relations within the household, and women's minimal control over household finances or spending, can force women into a daily trudge (taking precious time) for fetching cheaper or free untreated water, which may result in health problems or increased poverty and destitution. This time could instead be used to focus on livelihood and agricultural activities, attending school and improving maternal and infant health (Mehta, 2014; WHO/UNICEF Joint Monitoring Programme, 2012). This situation is worsened by the fact that women are often excluded from decision-making processes regarding water management projects or natural resource allocation (FAO, 2012).

According to the 2006 Human Development Report, which focuses in depth on water scarcity from a human development perspective, the global water crisis is overwhelmingly a crisis for the poor. The distribution of water access in many countries mirrors the distribution of wealth, and vast inequalities exist in both. The UNDP estimates that almost two in three people who

30    L. Mehta

lack access to clean water, and more than 660 million people without adequate sanitation, live on less than two dollars per day. Furthermore, not only do the poorest people get access to less water, and to water that is less clean and safe, but they also pay some of the world's highest water prices (UNDP, 2006: 7). It notes that 'the poorest 20 per cent of households in Argentina, El Salvador, Jamaica and Nicaragua allocate more than 10 per cent of their spending to water. In Uganda, water payments represent as much as 22 per cent of the average income of urban households in the poorest 20 per cent of the income distribution' (UNDP, 2006: 51).

In some severe situations, uneven power relationships and the absence of appropriately implemented water rights frameworks can open up the possibility of 'water grabs' (UNDP, 2006). According to Franco et al. (2013: 1653–1654), 'water grabbing is a process in which powerful actors are able to take control of, or reallocate to their own benefit, water resources used by local communities or which feed aquatic ecosystems on which their livelihoods are based'. They have shown how the land that is coveted by investors is often made out to be 'unproductive', 'scarce' or 'idle', thus justifying access rights to private companies and investors. These have usually led to the erosion of local people's rights to land and water, often nested in informal and customary systems.

These and other conflict situations can exacerbate unequal or lack of access to water, threaten provisions of water and divert attention from food production to other priorities. In such situations, the poor become the victims not only of the conflict itself but also of hunger and water-borne diseases. Water insecurities also persist in occupied areas such as Palestine when restricted water withdrawals enforce unequal access and use. For example, Israelis consume more than three times as much water per capita per day (300 litres compared to 73 litres), but strict military orders restrict water withdrawals and access for Palestinians living in occupied areas (Gasteyer et al., 2012).

Table 2.1 provides a summary of a typology to analyse and understand different portrayals of water scarcity (building on Wolfe and Brooks, 2003). It distinguishes between four kinds of scarcity: physical, economic, third order and socially constructed scarcity. Under each, the table provides the main characteristics, the disciplinary underpinnings and the accompanying solutions. Largely, global agencies draw on physical and economic characteristics of scarcity, which results in a focus on the relationship between supply and demand (1 and 2) rather than on scarcity arising due to problems of lifestyle or sociopolitical processes (3 and 4).

Problems arise when the solutions to the problems of scarcity lead to either simplistic supply or demand management kinds of solutions. Supply management results in augmenting water to various sectors, while demand management seeks to reduce demand or improve water management (see Lankford, 2010 and Molden et al., 2003). These are mostly required and appropriate interventions but may not get to the heart of the scarcity problem. Large-scale technical and engineering solutions are deployed

Table 2.1 Diverse ways to view scarcity

| | (1) Physical / first order scarcity | (2) Economic / second order scarcity | (3) Third order scarcity / adaptive capacity | (4) Scarcity arising through socio-political processes |
|---|---|---|---|---|
| Characteristics | Volumetric quantities<br>Population growth<br>Projection of future demand<br>Industrial growth | Inadequate development of water infrastructure<br>Poor management and institutional arrangements | Social, political and economic context of water management | Scarcity as a product of discursive and socio-political processes<br>Entitlements failures |
| Water management solution | Enhancing supply through storage (e.g. small v/s large dams debate)<br>Desalination<br>Extra basin transfer of water | Water reallocation through water markets<br>Water reform<br>Technological fixes<br>Pricing<br>Increasing efficiency | Social adaptive capacity through education, cultural change and lifestyle change | Deliberation<br>Decision making processes<br>Equity and reallocation |
| Access solution | MDGs<br>Lifelines | Water as an economic good<br>Pricing<br>Privatisation<br>Community management/PPPs | Social adaptive capacity through education, cultural change and Lifestyle change<br>Decision making | Redistribution/enhancing equity<br>Instituting entitlements to water (e.g. human right to water) |

Source: Mehta, 2014

## 32  L. Mehta

to augment water supplies (e.g. through storage systems, reservoirs and groundwater recharging). The solutions are largely concerned with the technical and economic aspects of scarcity. The assumption here is that scarcity is a 'biophysical' condition, which should be countered by 'wise management' practices. Instead, scarcity is a highly localised issue, subject to both local conditions and interpretations by different actors. It is also very much a political issue.

Further nuances are provided by political science and international relations literature that focuses on third order scarcity referring to the socio-political, technological and cultural changes that a society must undertake to deal with scarcity (see, for example, Ohlsson and Turton, 2000; Wolfe and Brooks, 2003). But these debates do not focus upfront on the social relations underlying resource use as discussed earlier in this chapter. They also lack the political ecology focus on how the 'problem' of scarcity is constructed and how a problematic framing might exacerbate scarcity conditions; on the need to disaggregate users and their entitlements; and on the politics of distribution within a frame of political economy. Finally, most debates ignore both the multiple aspects of scarcity and the appropriation of water by powerful actors. The resulting interventions, such as 'integrated water resource management' as discussed above, can intensify control over the resource and existing inequities (cf. Mehta et al., 2016).

This is why Nicholas Hildyard (2010) focuses on how scarcity often emerges as a political strategy. While numerous empirical studies locate the cause of deprivation in power imbalances and struggles over access to and control over resources, neo-Malthusianism has shifted focus to population growth as a cause of absolute scarcity in the future. Neo-Malthusianism is used to colonise the future to serve particular interests, be it to privatise the commons or water or promote biotechnology. The fear of unbridled population growth in the future is used to legitimise the present takeover of a range of resources. Projections and scares of future resource crises and a Malthusian world (witness, for example, current debates on climate change, mass migration and resource scarcity) are privileged over how local people live with and have adapted to scarcity conditions in specific contexts. In my own work, I have found it helpful to distinguish between 'lived/experienced' scarcity (something that local people experience cyclically due the biophysical shortage of food, water, fodder etc.) and 'constructed' scarcity (something that is manufactured through socio-political processes to suit the interests of powerful players—for example, the dam-building lobby and the interests of rich irrigators and agro-industrialists in Gujarat, India (see Mehta, 2005)). Official discourses portray scarcity as natural (rather than human-induced) and universal (rather than something that is cyclical). The external 'essentialised' notions of scarcity generated by state and donor discourses and programmes are often quite different from local people's knowledge systems and livelihood strategies that allow them to adapt to the unpredictability and temporary scarcity of water (ibid).

## Conclusions

By taking the case of water, I have demonstrated that scarcity is often seen to be a universal phenomenon in both academic and policy discourses. Scarcity is a bit of a dangerous idea. It seduces; it is appealing. It is a political strategy for certain powerful actors to appropriate resources and the future to their advantage.

Scarcity as a concept can provide meta-level explanations for a wide range of phenomena over which humans ostensibly have no control. Thus, scarcity emerges as a trope for the justification of need, it becomes a technical term that justifies certain action and solutions. Solutions usually lie in deploying markets, innovation, science and technology—for example, the new 'blue revolution' and more irrigation systems for Africa, controversial water privatisations or expansion into Mars, and so on—to meet earth's water needs. Technology is presumed to be neutral and its 'solutions' are supposed to transcend politics. But in reality, technology and techniques are deeply political, and contestations around technological solutions—be they around large dams, India's fantastical river interlinking project or water privatisation—are sites of politics (both in the cultural and material realm).

What are the ways forward? We need to link the discursive framings of what we mean by scarcity and how we determine what is scarce. Governmentality (i.e. the technologies and rationalities of the state) is key to understanding how issues of scarcity can legitimise policy and we need to be aware of wider political and economic forces that tend to aggravate and perpetuate scarcity. Clearly, simplistic portrayals of resource 'crises' must be challenged, and local realities need to be a part of policy responses to resource management and allocation processes.

I believe that there is sufficient food, water and energy on this planet to go around. Famines and water shortages are often the result of failures of allocation, especially to the poor and powerless. It is flawed to attribute these problems to 'nature' rather than humanity (see Rayner, 2010). Thus, it is important to shift away from a language of scarcity to the issues of resource allocation, access, entitlements and rights.

The global financial crisis of 2008 made it clear that the idea of a perfect and frictionless market system is a myth. As Polanyi in 1944 reminded us, the market is always embedded in culture, history and politics and scarcity is not something that is just the creation of market forces. The idea of stable markets around which scarcity is the norm is a myth. This needs to give way to approaches that acknowledge the role of the symbolic, the reciprocal, the substantive, the political, the uneconomic and maybe even the irrational. This means revisiting the ideas of John Maynard Keynes, Karl Polanyi, Ivan Illich and heterodox perspectives within economics, while also drawing on complementary anthropological and socio-political perspectives to scarcity. It also urges us to be more upfront about social and power relations as well as historical and cultural specificities around resources, which can ultimately help transcend the limited vision of *Homo economicus*.

Since notions of scarcity often lead to an erasure of issues of equity, scale, embeddedness and locality, there may be the need to recover different notions, for instance, of the 'good' and the 'commons'. This would mean rejecting processes that lead to the commodification and enclosure of resources and commons that undermine local people's rights and livelihoods (see Franco et al., 2013; Mehta et al., 2012). Regaining the commons is also about promoting just decision-making processes, and curtailing those who unseeingly and overbearingly exercise power over the weak and marginalised.

It is also important to critically engage with notions of limits. It is over 40 years since the Club of Rome funded the *Limits to Growth* (LtG) (Meadows et al., 1972) report which drew on now discredited doomsday predictions of resource use, production, pollution and population growth through computer simulation models. Despite all the problems with the work, the imperative to limit needs and consumption patterns cannot be denied because it is the drive for abundance that leads to never-ending needs, wants and desires. Here the degrowth movement, which is a political, economic and social movement that pushes for the downscaling of production and consumption with an aim of maximising happiness and human wellbeing through non-consumptive means, can provide some important lessons (Demaria et al., 2013; Kallis, 2015). While this is still more a movement in the Global North—and it is important to acknowledge that the satisfaction of needs, wants and desires in the North can sometimes lead to deprivation in the Global South (Sopher, 2006)—this movement and others are calling for new ways of being and living. For example, feminists have been calling for the recognition and value of care and social reproduction in green economy debates (e.g. Salleh, 2009; Vaughan, 2007). There are debates for replacing efficiency with sufficiency (Mehta, 2010; Salleh, 2009), and for a focus on communing and 'enough' as well as more fundamental 'green transformations' that restructure production, consumption and political–economic relations along truly sustainable pathways (Wichterich, 2012). These arguments link with growing narratives and action around alternative economies and solidarity economies (Unmüßig et al., 2012), and powerful examples of collective organising and social movement activism around the world.

To conclude: scarcity is not necessarily natural or universal. But universalised notions of scarcity have tended to evoke a standardised set of market/institutional and technological solutions as the (universal) fix, which have blocked out political contestation around access as a legitimate focus for academic and policy debates. It is time to write the obituary of the universal legacy of the scarcity postulate and develop new imaginaries of scarcity that are context bound and truer to local people's meanings and experiences.

## Notes

1 Some parts of this chapter draw on Mehta (2010). I am grateful to the editors for their very helpful comments and patience and to Alice Shaw for her help with copy-editing and formatting this chapter.
2 Jean-Paul Satre in Xenos (1989).

## References

Allouche, J., Middleton, C. and Gyawali, D. (2014) 'Nexus Nirvana or Nexus Nullity? A dynamic approach to security and sustainability in the water-energy-food nexus', STEPS Working Paper 63, Brighton: STEPS Centre.

Altaf, M.A, Jamal, H. and Whittington, D. (1992) *Willingness to Pay for Water in Rural Punjab, Pakistan. Water and Sanitation Report 4.* Washington, DC: The World Bank.

Baechler, G. (1999) *Violence through Environmental Discrimination: Causes, Rwanda Arena, and Conflict Model.* Dordrecht: Kluwer Academic Publishers.

Bakker, K. (2010) *Privatizing Water: Governance Failure and the World's Urban Water Crisis.* Ithaca: Cornell University Press.

Berkes, F. (1989) *Common Property Resource: Ecology and Community-Based Sustainable Development.* London: Belhaven Press.

Borras, S.M., Franco, J.C., Gómez, S., Kay, C. and Spoor, M. (2012) 'Land grabbing in Latin America and the Caribbean', *The Journal of Peasant Studies*, 39(3–4), pp. 845–872.

Bromley, D. and Cernea, M. (1989) *The Management of Common Property Natural Resources: Some Conceptual and Operational Fallacies.* Washington, DC: The World Bank.

CA (Comprehensive Assessment of Water Management in Agriculture) (2007) *Water for Food, Water for Life: A Comprehensive Assessment of Water Management for Agriculture.* London: Earthscan.

Chatham House (2012) *Resources Futures.* London: Chatham House.

Dalby, S. (2014) 'Security', in C. Death. (ed.), *Critical Environmental Politics.* London and New York: Routledge, 229–237.

Dawson, M.C. (2010) 'The cost of belonging: exploring class and citizenship in Soweto's 'water war'', *Citizenship Studies,* 14(4), pp. 381–394.

Demaria, F., Schneider, F., Sekulova, F. and Martinez-Alier, J. (2013) 'What is degrowth? From an activist slogan to a social movement', *Environmental Values*, 22(2), pp. 191–215.

Earth Security Group (2015) *The Earth Security Index 2015: Managing Global Resource Risks and Resilience in the 21st Century.* Stockholm: Earth Security Group.

Escobar, A. (1996) 'Constructing nature: Elements for a poststructural political ecology', in R. Peet and M. Watts (eds) *Liberation Ecologies: Environment, Development, Social Movements.* London: Routledge, pp. 46–68.

European Commission (2012) *The European Report on Development 2011/2012: Confronting Scarcity: Managing Water, Energy and Land for Inclusive and Sustainable Growth.* Belgium: European Union.

Falkenmark, M. and Lannerstad, M. (2005) 'Consumptive water use to feed humanity—Curing a blind spot', *Hydrology and Earth System Sciences* 9(1–2), pp. 15–28.

Falkenmark, M. and Widstrand, C. (1992) 'Population and water resources: A delicate balance', *Population Bulletin*, 47(3), pp. 1–36.

36 *L. Mehta*

FAO (2012) *Passport to Mainstreaming Gender in Water Programmes: Key Questions for Interventions in the Agricultural Sector.* Rome: FAO.

Finger, M. and Allouche, J. (2002) *Water Privatisation: Transnational Corporations and the Re-regulation of the Global Water Industry.* London and New York: Taylor & Francis.

Franco, J., Mehta, L. and Veldwisch, G.J. (2013) 'The global politics of water grabbing', *Third World Quarterly*, 34(9), pp. 1651–1675.

Gasteyer, S., Isaac, J., Hillal, J. and Hodali, K. (2012) 'Water grabbing in colonial perspective: land and water in Israel/Palestine', *Water Alternatives*, 5(2), pp. 450–468.

GWP (2000) *Integrated Water Resources Management.* Stockholm: Global Water Partnership (GWP).

HLPE (2015) *Water for Food Security and Nutrition.* Rome: High Level Panel of Experts on Food Security and Nutrition of the Committee on World Food Security (HLPE).

Hildyard, N. (2010) '"Scarcity" as political strategy: reflections on three hanging children', in L. Mehta (ed.) *The Limits to Scarcity: Contesting the Politics of Allocation.* London: Earthscan, pp. 149–164.

Hoff, H. (2011) 'Understanding the Nexus: Background Paper for the Bonn2011 Conference', in *Bonn2011 Conference: The Water, Energy and Food Security Nexus Solutions for the Green Economy.* Stockholm, Sweden, 16–18 November 2011. Stockholm: Stockholm Environment Institute.

Homer-Dixon, T.F. (2001) *Environment, Scarcity and Violence.* Princeton: Princeton University Press.

ICWE (International Conference on Water and the Environment) (1992) 'The Dublin Statement on Water and Sustainable Development, in *International Conference on Water and the Environment.* Dublin, Ireland, 26–31 January 1992. ICWE: Dublin, available: www.wmo.int/pages/prog/hwrp/documents/english/icwedece.html [accessed May 2017].

Kallis, G. (2015) 'The degrowth alternative', A Great Transition Initiative Viewpoint, February 2015, available: www.greattransition.org/images/GTI_publications/Kallis-The-Degrowth-Alternative.pdf [accessed May 2017].

Lankford, B. (2010) 'A share response to scarcity: moving beyond the volumetric', in L. Mehta (ed.) *The Limits to Scarcity: Contesting the Politics of Allocation.* London: Earthscan, pp. 195–214.

Le Billon, P. (2001) 'The political ecology of war: natural resources and armed conflicts', *Political Geography*, 20(5), pp. 561–584.

McDonald, D. and Ruiters, G. (eds) (2005) *The Age of Commodity: Water Privatization in Southern Africa.* London: Earthscan.

Meadows, D., Randers, J. and Behrens, W. (1972) *The Limits to Growth.* London: Earth Island Limited.

Mehta, L. (2010) 'The scare, politicization and naturalization of scarcity', in L. Mehta (ed.) *Limits to Scarcity: Contesting the Politics of Allocation.* London: Earthscan, pp. 13–31.

Mehta, L. (2005) *The Politics and Poetics of Water: Naturalising Scarcity in Western India.* New Delhi: Orient Longman.

Mehta, L. (2014) 'Water and human development', *World Development*, 59, pp. 59–69.

Mehta, L., Movik, S., Bolding, A., Derman, A. and Manzungu, E. (2016) 'Introduction to the special issue—Flows and practices: the politics of integrated water resources management (IWRM) in Southern Africa', *Water Alternatives*, 9(3), pp. 389–411.

Mehta, L., Veldwisch, G.J. and Franco, J. (2012) 'Introduction to the special issue: water grabbing? Focus on the (re)appropriation of finite water resources', *Water Alternatives*, 5(2), pp. 193–207.

Molden, D., Murray-Rust, H., Sakthivadivel, R. and Makin, I. (2003) 'A water productivity framework for understanding and action', in J. Kijne, R. Barker and D. Molden (eds) *Water Productivity in Agriculture: Limits and Opportunities for Improvement, Comprehensive Assessment of Water Management in Agriculture*. Wallingford: CABI Publishing in Association with International Water Management Institute (IWMI), pp. 1–18.

Nicol, A., Mehta, L. and Allouche, J. (2011). '"Some for all?" Politics and pathways in water and sanitation', IDS Bulletin, 43(2). Brighton: IDS.

OECD (2012) *OECD Environmental Outlook to 2050: The Consequences of Inaction*. Paris: OECD Publishing.

Ohlsson, L. and Turton, A. (2000) 'The turning of a screw: social resource scarcity as a bottle-neck adaptation to water scarcity', *Stockholm Water Front - Forum for Global Water Issues*, 1. Stockholm: Stockholm International Water Institute (SIWI).

Ostrom, E. (1990) *Governing the Commons: The Evolution of Institutions for Collective Action*. New York: Cambridge University Press.

Peet, R. and Watts, M. (1996) *Liberation Ecologies: Environment, Development, Social Movements*. New York: Routledge.

R. Peet, Robbins, P. and Watts, M. (eds) (2011) *Global Political Ecology*. Oxon: Routledge.

Peluso, N.L and Watts, M. (eds) (2001) *Violent Environments*. Ithaca and London: Cornell University Press.

Polanyi, K. (1944) *The Great Transformation: The Political and Economic Origins of Our Time*. Boston: Beacon Press.

Polanyi, K. (1957) 'The economy as instituted process', in K. Polanyi, C. Arensberg and H. Pearson (eds) *Trade and Market in the Early Empires: Economies in History and Theory*. New York: The Free Press, pp. 243–270.

Rayner, S. (2010) 'Foreword', in L. Mehta (ed.), *The Limits to Scarcity: Contesting the Politics of Allocation*. London: Earthscan, pp. x–xvi.

Robbins, L. (1932) *An Essay on the Nature and Significance of Economic Science*. London: Macmillan.

SABMiller and WWF (2014) *The Water-Food-Energy Nexus: Insights into Resilient Development*. London: SAB Miller and the Worldwide Fund for Nature.

Sahlins, M. (1972) *Stone Age Economics*. New York: Aldine Publishing Company.

Salleh, A. (ed.) (2009) *Eco-sufficiency & Global Justice: Women Write Political Ecology*. London: Pluto Press.

Sen, A. (1993) 'Capability and wellbeing', in M. Nussbaum and A. Sen (eds) *The Quality of Life*. Oxford: Clarendon Press, pp. 30–53.

Sen, A. (1981) *Poverty and Famines: An Essay on Entitlement and Deprivation*. Oxford: Clarendon Press.

Sen, A. (1983) Poor, relatively speaking', *Oxford Economic Papers*, 35(2), pp. 153–169.

Sopher, K. (2006) 'Conceptualizing needs in the context of consumer politics', *Journal of Consumer Policy*, 29(4), pp. 355–372.

Steffen, W., Richardson, K., Rockström, J., Cornell, S.E., Fetzer, I., Bennett, E.M., Biggs, R., Carpenter, S.R., de Vries, W., de Wit, C.A., Folke, C., Gerten, D., Heinke, J., Mace, G.M., Persson, L.M., Ramanathan, V., Reyers, B. and Sörlin, S. (2015) 'Planetary boundaries: guiding human development on a changing planet', *Science*, 347(6223): 736–746.

## 38   L. Mehta

Unmüßig, B., Sachs, W. and Fatheuer, T. (2012) 'Critique of the green ecology—Toward social and environmental equity', *Ecology Series*, 22. Berlin: Heinrich Böll Stiftung.

UNDP (2006) *Human Development Report 2006: Beyond Scarcity: Power, Poverty and the Global Water Crisis*. New York: Palgrave Macmillan.

UNEP (2011) 'Towards a green economy: pathways to sustainable development and poverty eradication—A synthesis for policy makers, available: www.unep.org/greeneconomy [accessed: May 2017].

Vaughan, G. (ed.) (2007) *Women and the Gift Economy: A Radically Difference Worldview is Possible*. Toronto: Inanna Publications and Education Incorporated.

WHO/UNICEF Joint Monitoring Programme (2012) *JMP Working Group on Equity and Non-Discrimination Final Report*. Geneva: WHO/UNICEF.

Wichterich, C. (2012) 'The Future we want. A feminist perspective', *Ecology Series*, 21. Berlin: Heinrich Böll Stiftung.

Wolfe, S. and Brooks, D.B. (2003) 'Water scarcity: an alternative view and its implications for policy and for capacity building', *Natural Resources Forum*, 27(2), pp. 99–107.

World Economic Forum (2014) *The Future Availability of Natural Resources: A New Paradigm for Global Resource Availability*. Geneva: World Economic Forum.

Xenos, N. (1989) *Scarcity and Modernity*. London: Routledge.

# 3 Cooperation in the power sector to advance regionalisation processes and sustainable energy flows

*Andreas Lindström, Kevin Rosner and Jakob Granit*

## Introduction

Regional development and growth, energy security, sustainable environmental systems and human prosperity are tied together (Söderbaum and Granit, 2014). Secure energy provision and healthy ecosystems capable of delivering life-supporting ecosystem services provide the basis on which our economic system functions (Granit and Rosner, 2012). Natural resources serve as a key input to power generation. Energy produced, increasingly in the form of electricity, enables economic and social system services. Transport, commercial, industrial, communication and information systems all depend on a secure and reliable supply of energy. Without adequate energy supply a modern economy cannot function and inadequacies in energy supply may be translated into the poor economic performance of specific regions or countries. This has been well documented in the recently concluded UNFCCC Paris Agreement on Climate Change (UNGA, 2015) and the UN 'Transforming our world: the 2030 Agenda for Sustainable Development'. Target 7 of the Sustainable Development Goals (SDGs), to 'Ensure access to affordable, reliable, sustainable and modern energy for all', highlights this relationship.

Because energy sources are unevenly distributed across different geographies, energy systems and markets typically span political borders thereby locking countries into trade relationships. If energy security is threatened it can become a threat multiplier contributing to state insecurity (Granit and Lindström, 2012). It is important to highlight that the sourcing and transformation of natural resources into electricity on a regional basis can help in evening out the peaks and valleys of physical resource availability. Transforming raw commodities into electric power in effect can address the issue of scarcity by transiting the end product, electricity, from resource rich areas where electricity can be generated to energy poor ones.

The formation of 'macro regions', defined loosely as a number of states that share a geographical relationship and levels of mutual interdependence, can be catalysed for several different reasons (Nye, 1968). Different countries might share joint ambitions to achieve specific targets of political, economic, environmental or social nature. No matter what the reason might be to initiate collaboration, expansion of cooperation at several different levels is often an outcome of initiated partnerships (Söderbaum and Granit 2014; Wilde, 2015). Most importantly, a regional conceptualisation of a market for generated power (electricity) may eclipse territorial boundaries, provide expanded access to energy commodities, and accordingly—and importantly—transform the vision of the market by tangibly expanding along trade and commercial pathways that already exist.

The concept of regionalism, which 'refers to the common objectives, values and identities that lead to region-formation and regional cooperation within a given geographical area' (Söderbaum and Granit, 2014: 7), is theoretically relevant when analysing energy and cooperation. Cooperating in different regional configurations to reach mutual benefit is not a new concept. However, the patterns and characteristics of regional cooperation have changed in step with globalisation and the existing world order. 'Classic' regionalism as defined in a post-World War II era was very much influenced by bi-polar Cold War logic and, as such, characterised by sector specific cooperation, protectionism as well as exclusiveness in terms of membership (Söderbaum and Granit, 2014). New order regionalism, however, is shaped by a multipolar world and is characterised by being more extrovert and inclusive in terms of membership and being more comprehensive and multipurpose in terms of focus (ibid).

The concept of governance is a key defining aspect in all types of regional formations. Governance can be defined as 'spheres of authority at all levels of human activity that amount to systems of rule in which goals are pursued through the exercise of control' (Rosenau, 1997: 145). A traditional concept of governance in terms of international relations defined by clear borders, separation and non-interference is becoming increasingly dysfunctional in a globalised world (ibid). Governance systems tailored to modern region building is therefore multi-layered and can include a range of actors, public and private, formal and informal, and they are not to be confused with government (Söderbaum and Granit, 2014). Though regional governance systems and connected institutions are positively recognised, they are most often characterised as 'nested systems' (ITFGPG, 2006). This means that different levels of governance (local, regional, national, macro regional, global) are intertwined in systems both competing with and complementing each other (Olsen, Page and Ochoa, 2009).

Nested systems have, among other reasons, evolved out of specific management needs not easily confined to one specific scale (ITFGPG, 2006). This is not least true for transboundary water management as well as for energy development. The degree of regional development and the progressiveness of incorporated governance systems will influence both natural resources management and economic and energy development in a globalised world. Likewise, heightened pressures on and demand for water and energy resources will serve as catalysts forming new regional dynamics and relationships.

Questions addressing resource scarcity, power generation technologies and choice in an era sensitised by climate change are approached differently by the world's energy regions. This chapter provides some initial insight into how cooperative actions on energy matters preceded, as one example, the effective creation and transboundary functioning of the European Union (EU) itself. Elsewhere, power pooling has allowed and facilitated EU member and non-member states, exemplified by Sweden and Norway respectively, to coordinate the dispatch of electricity across Europe's northern frontier to provide security, stability and certainty of energy access to members of the Nordic Power Pool. Finally, in Southern Africa power pooling, managed and coordinated by the Southern Africa Power Pool (SAPP), preceded as a direct result of the creation of the Southern Africa Development Community as a mechanism for binding Africa's front-line states together with post-apartheid South Africa. We argue in this chapter that regional peace and stability, economic growth and improved human security can be generated by and through the effective, competitive and rational sharing of electricity across national borders. Power pools provide a sum greater than their parts and, in doing so, establish cooperative methods of discourse and decision making that transcend the territorial boundaries of the nation state through a positive burst of tangible synergy allowing for sustainable energy choices.

## Case studies on cooperation in the power sector

### The EU

The EU is today one of the largest economies in the world when compared to individual countries as well as economic regions, and the largest trader of manufactured goods and services (European Commission, 2014). The impact of European cooperation on the EU has produced several interesting observations related to the development of regional cooperation on energy issues.

The evolution of what is today one of the world's most successful economic entities has not always been smooth; there have been several setbacks. It should also be mentioned that motivations for economic and energy cooperation were partially grounded in a will to reach political agreement and in doing so to minimise the risk of resumed violent conflict. Cooperation on coal, the main energy resource at the time, and steel as well as economic integration was identified as the path of least possible resistance to obtain this.

What was to become the EU was born out of conflict. Devastated by World War II, the 'Treaty of Paris', signed in 1951 by Great Britain, West Germany, Luxembourg, Italy, Netherlands and Belgium, marked the start of the European Coal and Steel Community (ECSC) and laid the foundation for what would eventually be the EU. Simultaneously, the treaty based on energy and natural resources trade formed the first ever organisation built on the concept of 'supranationalism' (Mason, 1955). This refers to a multinational political entity where an authority composed of member state governments is delegated agreed elements of power (Martin, 2004). The core purpose of the newly found collaboration was stated by the then French foreign minister, Robert Schuman, as being to make war 'not merely unthinkable, but materially impossible' (EU, 2015).

The vision to pursue unification through economic cooperation can be seen as a continuation of the inter-war period between World War I and World War II, when attempts were pursued to forge economic links through international trade cartels in order to prevent new conflicts. These early attempts were insufficient in preventing the outbreak of World War II. In spite of this failure, economic integration was again attempted in the post-World War II era. This is mainly because there were few other options that could be deemed realistic at the time (Gerbet, 1956). Interest in other forms of political cooperation was considerably low and the idea of a unified Europe was non-existent. The form of cooperation was negotiated and established through the so-called 'Schuman Plan', after the French minister, with the overall purpose to reach political cooperation through providing economic opportunity (Kiersch, 1963).

There are many reasons why the coal and steel sectors were selected to pursue regionalisation in Europe. In the aftermath of World War II, Europe's industrial infrastructure was shattered; collaboration was one way of addressing the reality that important natural resources were located in one part of the continent while industrial capacity was located in another (Schmidt, 1968). Collaboration in relation to coal and steel, central to warfare and defence, also made sense for a weakened Europe in order to protect it from other possible external threats emerging in the wake of the war. Though things would soon change, coal and steel were still considered basic industries hosting similar rationalisation, investment and organisational principles internationally (Haas, 1958). To support the overarching aim of the ECSC to usher in greater political stability in Europe, cooperation on coal and steel made sense on both symbolic and economic levels.

Favourable traits of the sectors, from political and symbolic standpoints, were that they were built on historical traditions, geopolitical realities and that they could generate relative consensus (Mioche, 1998). This might also explain some of the challenges experienced when trying to integrate coal and steel markets as no pre-feasibility studies on the suitability of these priorities were made prior to selecting these sectors (Gerbet, 1956).

The official opening of the common market for coal and steel was in February 1953 (EU, 2017). From the outset compliance with policies was problematic. Forms of subsidies and cartelisation as well as the lack of pricing transparency continued in the nations of the ECSC (Alter and Steinberg, 2007). The idea of supranationalism had not yet emerged among ECSC nations that sought growth and job protection mainly defined in strict 'national terms' (Alter and Steinberg, 2007). In this regard, the idea of increased competition through an integrated market did not necessarily align with perceived national objectives; at the outset ECSC policies were largely followed when deemed convenient. The ECSC did, however, provide other goods beyond the economic field in overall support of strengthening regional development. Investments aimed to increase welfare for coal and steel industry workers provided support to financing housing as well as redeployment costs related to lost jobs due to the decommissioning of coal mines and steel works (Mathieu, 1970).

The European Economic Community (EEC) can be seen as a continuation of the economic integration component of the ECSC. The EEC had in its mission for expanding economic cooperation the intention to create a single integrated market for all industrial goods and to facilitate the free movement of capital, services and people. Within ten years of signing the Treaty of Rome the value of trade quadrupled between member countries (Gabel, 2010). The EEC facilitated a merger with existing ECSC institutions as well as adding new ones. The EEC was a big and largely successful step towards an integrated European market. The key goals of the EEC in stimulating economic activity, promoting economic expansion and improving living standards in member countries were in many regards met. War torn economies were allowed to recover successfully. The EEC managed to rid barriers to internal trade and harmonise common policies supporting intra-trade relationships.

Positive outcomes from enhanced economic collaboration of the EEC paved the way to, again, push for the concept of European supranationalism. The 1992 Maastricht Treaty (also known as the 'Treaty of the European Union') unified the existing European treaties (ECSC, Euroatom, EEC/EC) in a new form of cooperation (Bradley, 2011). Energy cooperation has concurrently developed, resulting in more common regional energy policies. Though energy cooperation and integration has not evolved at the same pace as economic collaboration since the ECSC, EU nations are today bound by several common policy frameworks on energy (Maltby, 2013). A prominent example includes the EU 2020 policy with aims to reduce $CO_2$ emissions by 20 per cent and increase renewable energy by 20 per cent with a 20 per cent increase in energy efficiency by 2020 (ibid). A strategy towards 2030 has also been agreed boosting the targets from the 2020 policy to reach even more ambitious targets. These targets include a 40 per cent cut in greenhouse gas emissions compared to 1990 levels, a 27 per cent share of renewable energy consumption and 27 per cent energy savings compared with the business-as-usual scenario (Europe Documents, 1 January 2014). However, in February 2015 the EC announced a new project of exploring ways to form an energy union with a focus on reliable, affordable sustainable and competitive energy supply.

In February 2015, the EC launched a vision to form an energy union in response to increasing energy demand and interconnected challenges. The vision states that the EU shall achieve secure, affordable and climate-friendly energy (European Commission, 2015). The vision includes delivery in five key policy areas: the first area is to achieve energy security through better diversification of its energy sources and increase energy efficiency for internally produced energy; second the EU aims to remove all internal barriers (technical and regulatory) and enable free flowing energy across the region regulated by one fully integrated market; third is reducing imports by reducing energy consumption, which will also reduce energy related pollution; fourth is to encourage private infrastructure investments and to renew the European emissions trading scheme, and take strong action to reach a global deal for climate change; and the final policy area includes investing in science and low-carbon technologies supported by private sector investments.

The move towards a fully integrated energy region will harmonise what is presently 28 different national regulatory frameworks and ensure customer influence and adjusted, functioning infrastructure to better accommodate increased renewable energy generation (CICERO Group, 2015). The energy union adheres to the same principal understanding of a unified Europe as other EU bodies or functions. Greater interdependence between EU states to shore-up energy supply through further market integration and infrastructure development is a key motivation.

A second motivation is the EU's firm identification of the need to make a transition to a de-carbonised economy powered by a low-carbon energy future. The energy union, through the harmonisation of energy market functions and investments in clean energy technologies and science, will support the EU ambition of becoming the world leader in renewable energy. As the EU is currently making good progress on ambitious climate targets the energy union will help to stimulate the development of competitive renewable energy options and boost its implementation through adjusting market rules and by investing in smart grid energy demand response solutions.

Another objective is the identification of opportunities embedded in what can be perceived as shifts in the global economy. It is envisioned that the low-carbon transition will create new sectors, jobs and skill sets. By leading the curve, the EU is positioning itself to become a key actor, as other countries follow suit.

In short, despite temporary setbacks early payoffs from closer economic cooperation provided enough incentives to continue to deepen this type of relationship building. The case of Europe also seems to support the notion that trying to impose supranational structures too early will not be successful. Giving up decision-making power at early stages can be perceived as a threat to national sovereignty and self-determination.

When economic integration and other types of development cooperation have sufficiently evolved, trust in supranational institutions may become a reality; however, there needs to be a good balance with national decision-making powers to maintain the support for broad scale regionalisation processes such as the EU. A half century after the signing of the Treaty of Paris, the success of European integration is evident in most parameters examined. As for political stability, there have been no major interstate conflicts between member states since the signing of the treaty. Economic interdependencies undermine the fundaments of such conflicts.

Energy cooperation has been a central part of European development success from the beginning not least as an enabler and catalyst for overall economic integration, which has been at the core of region-building activities to date. The close connections between energy developments, sustained economic growth and emerging environmental challenges indicate a return of energy integration issues to the forefront of EU politics. The possible emergence of a European energy union would be a sensible and credible step along the lines of stronger integration, tackling challenges through eliminating barriers in the energy sector and by pooling energy resources to an even higher degree than is presently the case.

This EU case study provides several noteworthy takeaways. First, cooperation on energy (i.e. coal and energy economics) offers one of a limited number of avenues available to stabilise relations in regions severely affected by conflict. Second, energy security and economic integration go hand in hand where integration of markets for trading energy resources offer a platform for strengthened economic integration and progress. Third, political unification can be a positive spin-off from cooperation on energy and economic exchange. Fourth, receptivity to supranational structures increases as a consequence of other successful types of cooperation and integration.

### The Nordic sub-region

As the first deregulated and fully integrated electricity market in the world, the Nordic power market known as Nord Pool is in many respects the most mature and developed power pool by any standard (Carlsson, 1999). Several others are found in Continental Europe, North America and in parts of Africa ranging in levels of development from mature to underdeveloped (Musiliu and Pollitt, 2014). Electricity transfers and trade started between the Nordic countries in the 1960s in order to meet variations in demand on daily to yearly basis. By the mid-1970s all Nordic countries (with the exception of Iceland) were interconnected through a shared power grid (earlier connections between Finland and Russia already existed) (Grönkvist, Stenkvist and Paradis, 2008). More recently, concrete expansion plans include extensions (either new links or improved existing ones) to the Netherlands, Lithuania, Estonia and possibly Great Britain.

Hydropower is a dominant source of electricity among most Nordic countries. On average, hydropower supplies 45 per cent of electricity to the Nordic region and is the main supplier of renewable electricity, comprising close to 100 per cent of all power production in Norway and approximately 50 per cent in Sweden (IEA, 2008). In the latter country, hydropower has been developed for over a century with major investments taking place in the early to mid-twentieth century as a key component enabling Sweden's rapid industrialisation and subsequent economic growth trajectory. Today most rivers in Sweden with an exploitable hydropower potential have been developed with hydropower plants, amounting to approximately 2100 plants, most with a capacity of less than 10 MW. Sweden has implemented environmental legislation in different stages while preventing hydropower construction on some major rivers. Hydropower is currently the main option for energy storage in the Nordic electric system providing regulatory services in the energy system for meeting peak demand and also by enabling deployment of other renewable energy sources such as wind power.

Norway was the first Nordic country to deregulate its electricity market in 1991. Principal reasons for this were a deepening dissatisfaction with sector performance and particularly with regard to demand forecasting, which repeatedly projected capacity that greatly exceeded demand (Bye and Hope, 2005). Moves to facilitate deregulation had already begun in Norway in the 1970s. Electricity was predominately sold on long-term contracts between consumers and producers. The contractual arrangements between different producers safeguarded that quotas could be met within respective concessional areas. Combined with the irregularity of hydropower production, the formation of a power exchange among power producers was organised as a spot market in 1972 and emerged as an effective response (ibid). In similar fashion deregulation occurred in Sweden (1996), Denmark (1999) and Finland (1999). Other Nordic countries subsequently joined the Norwegian power exchange, which was then expanded to include transmission systems as well. Today the Baltic states are also part of Nord Pool.

To understand how electricity trading functions in the Nordic power pool one must be aware of different distribution systems along with their associated ownership structures. The Swedish electricity grid is approximately 555,000 kilometres long with 360,000 kilometres of ground lines and 195,000 kilometres of overhead lines with average system delivery reliability at 99.98 per cent (Svensk Energi, 2017). As part of the Swedish 'zero-vision' strategy regarding power delivery, weather-proofing the system has played a central role in reliability. This has primarily focused on replacing especially sensitive overhead lines with underground lines for better protection during occasional storms, which constitute the biggest threat to supply disruptions.

There are essentially three organisational structures for transmission networks. The national grid, owned by the state-run authority 'Svenska Kraftnät', spans the country and consists of 15,000 kilometres of cables enabling long distance transport (Nordic Electricity Exchange and the Nordic Model for a Liberalized Electricity Market, n.d.). These cables connect production sites to other countries at 16 different points in addition to regional (intrastate) grids within the country enabled by 160 transformation and junction stations (Svensk Energi, 2017). Most cables on the national grid have a capacity of 400 kV while a smaller proportion has a capacity of 220 kV, both using alternating current (AC) (ibid). Svenska Kraftnät is also responsible for making sure that power production and consumption are evenly matched. However, this does not include responsibility for production, which rests with the electric power generating companies themselves. They in turn predicate electricity output on cyclical demand forecasts and trade volumes from the common spot market.

Another important task for Svenska Kraftnät is to maintain sufficient power reserves when demand periodically eclipses supply. Regulated by Swedish law, Kraftnät is responsible for maintaining approximately 2000 MW of spare capacity during the winter season (Miljö- och energidepartementet, 2003). The regional grid(s) has the primary purpose of transferring electricity between the national and local grids. Regional grids are consequently operated by distribution companies affiliated with major power producing companies through so-called 'line concessions'. These concessions are awarded for power lines of certain specified capacities and are normally reserved for higher voltages. Line concessions are authorised for 40-year increments and are renewable (ibid).

Nord Pool is divided into two physical markets and one financial market (Nord Pool Spot, 2017). The spot market or the market for trading electricity for physical delivery is organised to accommodate short-term trades. Approximately 85 per cent of power trade takes place on the spot market (Energimarknadsinspektionen, 2015). The spot market (exchange) is owned by the major, normally state-owned, national transmission system operating entities in each country. There are several different actors on the electricity market.[1] Entities send their buy or sell orders to the exchange and based on this activity a system price or so-called 'spot price' is calculated on an hourly basis. The other physical market is called Elbas, which is an 'adjustment market' where entities can trade up to an hour before actual delivery. This market adjusts for imbalances that might have otherwise occurred after the closing of the spot market. The financial market component is organised for longer-term trade based on future delivery (ibid). The financial marketplace accommodates standardised financial contracts for time periods up to several years so that participating entities can compensate for fluctuations in the spot price to limit risk.

The functionality of an energy region is determined by the status of the region's infrastructure and the level and degree of market integration. The integrated power supply network among the Nordic countries has made the region energy resilient and therefore secure from an electricity supply standpoint. A major value of an energy region is the ability to integrate renewable energy into the regional grid. The vast amount of renewable energy available in some Nordic countries has become largely accessible to the entire region. This has enabled the region to set ambitious targets towards decreasing the carbon footprint of its energy mix. Total decarbonisation of Nordic electricity generation might be possible by 2050 according to the International Energy Agency, and the common electricity market and the availability of flexible power are key contributing factors to this end.

This case study on Nordic power cooperation provides the following important takeaways worth noting. First, a common market and integrated energy and electricity systems have seemingly generated several advantages for the Nordic region. This includes providing flexible, resilient and reliable supply systems. This in turn enables a substantial share of renewable energy to become available to the entire region, making it well positioned to meet targets for full decarbonisation. The common electricity market in the Nordic region strongly contributes to binding nations together enabling cooperation on many levels.

Second, with regard to electricity market deregulation there are several noteworthy issues related to pricing. In Norway, deregulation saw electricity prices decrease and become more consistent between consumer groups (Bye and Hope, 2005). Contrarily, Sweden experienced continuous increases in electricity prices following deregulation. However, recent studies have indicated that deregulation in itself has not been the reason for this and that other

## 48   A. Lindström, K. Rosner and J. Granit

factors such as fluctuating generation capacities in mainly hydro and nuclear power and, possibly foremost, increased tax levels have played a more significant role in higher price levels (CERE, 2012).

Third, issues of market concentration have also been identified as a result of deregulation. Large market shares, both in terms of production and network operations, are controlled by a small number of actors. Though there could be a potential risk in the exercise of market power by a few dominant actors, studies have shown that this has not occurred to any measurable extent (Nordic Competition Authorities, 2003).

### Southern Africa

An example of pooled energy cooperation outside the EU region is found in southern Africa through the SAPP.[2] The SAPP consists of 12 member states represented by 14 (combined) national utilities, independent power producers and independent transmission companies from member states of the Southern Africa Development Community as of September 1994 (SAPP, 2016). Each country can designate one national utility to the power pool as a full member although the list of participating companies in some cases counts more than one company per country. For example, in the case of Zambia, Zesco Limited is listed as an operating entity and Zambia Electricity Supply Corporation as a non-operating entity. In addition, the independent power producer Lunsemfwa Hydro Power Company (Zambia) and the independent transmission system operator Copperbelt Energy Corporation (Zambia) are also listed as participating companies in the SAPP.

The SAPP is linked to the evolution of the establishment of the South African Development Community (SADC) and was realised through the signing of an Intergovernmental Memorandum of Understanding in August 1995. In a 2015 report titled 'SADC Industrialisation Strategy and Roadmap 2015–2063' the organisation clearly highlights the link between provision of energy and prosperity. The strategy states that, 'Cheap energy is a necessary condition for industrial competitiveness and to that end, Member States should draw on lower cost regional supplies where practicable, rather than focusing on national self-sufficiency' (SADC, 2015: 23).

SAPP's (self-described) primary aim is, 'to provide reliable and economical electricity to supply to the consumers of each of the SAPP members, consistent with reasonable utilisation of natural resources and the effect on the environment' (SAPP, 2016). Initially designed to provide a basis for cooperative electricity exchange, the SAPP is evolving towards embracing and facilitating a more competitive energy market through three mechanisms: the STEM (short-term energy market), the post STEM, and the DAM (day ahead energy market). As of 2014 other products are to be developed such as a FPM (forward physical market) and an IDM (intra-day market) (SAPP, 2016).

Accordingly, '[b]y empowering SAPP, SADC has contributed to regional integration through the implementation of [a regional electricity market] REM'

(Maupin, 2013: 2). The SAPP can therefore be interpreted as a mechanism for regional integration catalysed by SADC as a key aspect of the southern Africa vision of an integrated development community. At the same time, control over a nation's power production is viewed in Africa, as elsewhere throughout the world, as an issue of national security and sovereignty (even if left unsaid). There is therefore an uneasy balance to be struck by SAPP/SADC members between deeper electricity market integration, which is probably the least costly way of providing additional electricity capacity to countries throughout the region, and maintaining adequate generating capacity to meet a nation's needs.

SAPP's activity is largely and proportionally reflective of the economic composition (weighted by country as a measure of gross domestic product (GDP)) of SADC itself. This is to say that the character of SAPP power trade is heavily weighted towards South Africa as the region's largest economic power, largest producer of electric power and the SAPP's most active trading partner. South Africa's weighted GDP within SADC averaged 67.9 per cent of this regional economic community's overall GDP over the period 2002–2012 (ReSAKSS, 2015). In 2009, for example, South Africa also generated approximately 80 per cent of all available power in the SAPP and, in 2008, accounted for the vast majority of its bilateral contracts. This reality, however, over-shadows the potential for other SAPP members to become more active generators of electric power themselves and potentially more active power traders. In order for individual SAPP/SADC member states to invest and upgrade their power generating capacity, a percentage of which could be *regionally* intended for export, it is essential that the power be competitively priced and sold with a return on investment that is competitive relative to other investment options.

The SAPP is increasingly providing a competitive electricity market, but the departure point for measurement is exceedingly low. Energy choice, which is an important question looming over SADC's energy future in light of significant (potential) nuclear power development in South Africa and new coal-fired thermal power generation in Maputo, South Africa or Botswana, will shape the future of energy in SADC for decades to come.

Overall the generation mix can largely be sketched as hydropower in the north of SADC dominated by the Democratic Republic of Congo and the Zambezi states, and coal-fired thermal power generation in SADC's southern tier dominated by South Africa. Renewable energy, given Sub-Saharan Africa's amount of available and exploitable wind and solar power, is making inroads into the SAPP's energy mix but it will take decades of development and dedication by policymakers before it takes its rightful place alongside King Coal and hydropower. Having said this, the SAPP, like the EU, seeks to capitalise on its vast renewable energy resources. Climate change is identified as a threat to overall development opportunities as well as a challenge to capitalising on future energy resources. SAPP holds major renewable energy potentials primarily in hydropower, wind, solar and biomass. Capacity increases of 13,719 MW, 10,345 MW and 8,243 MW in 2017, 2022 and 2027 respectively are planned with the largest contributions to come from hydropower (SADC, 2012).

As an emerging macro regional economic development community, partially established around cooperation and trade of energy as a key resource for integration, SADC shows both common and unique features. First, not unlike other regions and regional economic communities, SADC illustrates a range in the composition of its member states from island communities to small, landlocked states. The SAPP includes only landed (versus island) member states, many of which have low levels of economic activity. This makes it difficult for countries like Swaziland, Lesotho or even Malawi to invest in new generating capacity. However, if the SAPP service area is viewed as a market, then ostensibly these small economies could be participants in, and better served by, larger-scale electricity supply generated cost competitively in neighbouring or regional states. This is one of the exciting dimensions of addressing resource scarcity at the regional level, but which must confront the traditional and historic challenge of insisting on control over electric power at the scale of the nation state.

Second, power generation on a regional scale should provide at least some economy-of-scale cost–benefit advantages, although this always needs to be defined within the context of a project's specific parameters. If it holds true that larger power projects can provide electricity at or below smaller scale generation projects, then the least-cost affordability threshold for SAPP/SADC could be met.

The third, and perhaps most innovative is the demonstration that a 'regional approach' to the provision of power to rural communities could also be tackled by the development of rural mini-grids, which may or may not traverse official territorial boundaries. Where territorial boundaries are in play, such a regional decentralised provision of electric power could have a transboundary, cooperative effect on relations among and between citizens of different countries.

Finally, the only way that SADC will come even close to approaching success with its Industrialisation Strategy and Roadmap (2015–2063) is through the large-scale provision of new electric power. Hence the strategy stresses the concurrent introduction of new, low cost energy supply with a move away from a national energy security strategy to the newer and decidedly visionary regional approach to energy provision from which economic development, and hence industrialisation, can proceed. This puts the SAPP at the centre of SADC's, and therefore Sub-Saharan Africa's, energy and economic future.

In conclusion, it may be that too much lip service has been paid to the *perceived* relationship between trade, economic growth and electricity consumption and too little effort to *demonstrating* this relationship in a regional SADC context. This relationship needs to be underpinned by relevant data that can be used to catalyse energy and economic development across the region if put in the hands of the SAPP or energy experts within SADC itself.

## Discussion

This chapter links a number of theoretical concepts that are rooted in natural resources management and function as the basis for sustainable growth,

Cooperation in the power sector 51

reduced conflict risk and economic success by building on cooperation in the power sector. These concepts are strongly interlinked and depend on the functionality of one another in order to render positive outcomes.

The concept of regionalisation describes how two or more countries (or other units) choose collaboration to reach common goals. The experience of European collaboration, which eventually led to the establishment of the EU, shows that this process can often start in spite of (or possibly because of) the lack of trust, order and infrastructure preconditions (post-World War II Europe lacked all of these components). When conflict—or a return to it—is rejected, cooperation can begin. In the case of Europe and other regions, this happens first along lines of least possible resistance, and/or by focusing on objectives that all parties wish to achieve and that are not contested among cooperative parties.

The case of the EU shows how motives for collaboration might change over time. In the beginning, cooperation with regard to natural resources was pursued not only to gain political control and limit risks to the resumption of violent conflict, but also for economic gain. However, as economic collaboration matured and resulted in economic growth for all concerned, the drivers of conflict diminished and broader partnerships matured as a result. Over time macro regions may emerge when certain aspects of power are delegated to common governing institutions.

A similar development can be witnessed in southern Africa and the regionalisation process of SADC. Though less mature compared to the EU, positive effects of regional cooperation have been identified and progress towards full integration in SADC is on the way. Economic gains and political stability have been early positive deliverables, similar to those of early European integration. Also in the case of SADC, energy and water are central themes in which the region sees strong development potential for integrating the region and thereby bolstering its energy security.

Regionalisation processes result when different entities strive to reach common beneficial goals through integration and cooperation on one or more levels. The need to satisfy increasing energy demand, including the escalating rate of electrification, makes energy cooperation and power pooling a cornerstone in contemporary regionalisation efforts.

The concept of 'energy unions' is discussed as a departure point for achieving energy security and broader regionalisation objectives. This is evident in the continued strengthening and expansion of already existing and mature energy sharing systems such as the Nordic energy market. Nordic power cooperation exemplifies how advanced power trade can constitute a backbone of overall cooperative structures in a region, while simultaneously positioning all participating countries in pole position to meet new challenges in the most sustainable manner. The ability to become a region fully reliant on renewable energy is one example where the Nordic region, through cooperation on its energy resources, can face global challenges such as climate change and at the same time be at the forefront of realising a transition towards a 'greener' economy.

52  *A. Lindström, K. Rosner and J. Granit*

The same ambitions are also evident in the EU and the creation of a unified European energy union in which the share of renewable energy is set to grow substantially.

In regions undergoing rapid development such as SADC and through institutions such as the SAPP, which consolidate partnerships to secure development goals, the strong link between energy access and development can and should accelerate collaboration and economic integration. The fast rate of global electrification and the need to meet climate challenges through faster deployment of renewable energy types makes trade in electricity and the establishment of power pools ever more important. Energy regions bound together by common grid networks and systems for electricity trade/exchange open new doors for reaching energy security objectives particularly for those countries which themselves lack significant energy resources of their own. Sustainable energy can make a significant improvement to the quality of life in SADC largely by narrowing the increasingly widening gulf between energy supply and demand in the SAPP/SADC region, while concurrently providing clean and environmentally sustainable energy for all. Major challenges to achieving such outcomes in the SADC region are, inter alia, access to sufficient finance, regulatory policies and protocols providing probably preferred access to the grid for renewable energy. All of these challenges point to the efficacy of regionalism as a way forward to addressing the SAPP/SADC's energy challenges.

## Notes

1 The Swedish Smart Grid Coordination Council describes four market actors as follows Electricity producers: produce electricity in power plants and feed it to the grid. Most power is produced by a couple of major energy producing companies. They can determine if produced power should be sold to trading companies, consumers or if it will be allocated to the exchange or consumed for other purposes. Transmission System Operators (TSOs): the entities operating different portions of the grid either at national, regional or local levels (as described earlier). Electricity trading companies: trading companies buy electricity through the exchange or from other trading companies. They sell to consumers in competition with other trading companies. These companies can offer a variety of services beyond retail electricity including as a balancing power operator and energy portfolio management function. They host of wide variety of ownership forms. Consumers: they are comprised of a variety of end-user groups such as residential households and industries. Consumer groups are bound by agreements with a TSO with regards to electricity transfer and a similar agreement regarding the purchase of electricity either directly with a producer or trading company. Consumers can also buy electricity through the exchange.

2 An examination of the SAPP's objectives provides some perspective on where this power pool is in relation to its overall vision. According to the SAPP 2015 Annual Report, the SAPP vision is to: facilitate the development of a competitive electricity market in the SADC region; give the end user a choice of electricity supplier; ensure that the southern African region is the region of choice for investment by energy intensive users; ensure sustainable energy developments through sound economic, environmental and social practices.

# References

Alter, K.J. and Steinberg, D. (2007) 'The theory and reality of the European coal and steel community', in S. Meunier and K. McNamara (eds) *Making History: European Integration and Institutional Change at Fifty*. Oxford: Oxford University Press, pp. 89–107.

Bradley, K. (2011) 'Powers and procedures in the EU Constitution: Legal bases and the court', in P. Craig and G. de Búrca (eds) *The Evolution of EU Law*. Oxford: Oxford University Press, pp. 85–110.

Bye, T. and Hope, E. (2005) 'Deregulation of electricity markets—The Norwegian experience', Discussion Papers No. 433, September, Research Department Statistics Norway, available http://www.ssb.no/a/publikasjoner/pdf/DP/dp433.pdf [accessed 11 May 2017].

Carlsson, L. (1999) 'International power trade—the Nordic Power Pool', available: http://www.decisioncraft.com/energy/papers/ecc/ps/rem/npt.pdf [accessed 11 May 2017].

CERE (2012) 'Elmarknaden och elprisets utveckling före och efter avregleringen: ekonometriska analyser', Working paper, available: http://www-sekon.slu.se/~gbost/CERE_WP2012–14.pdf [accessed 11 May 2017].

CICERO Group (2015) 'EU Energy Union. A CICERO Group analysis: towards an energy union', available: http://cicero-group.com/wp-content/uploads/2015/02/EU-Energy-2.pdf [accessed11 May 2017].

Energimarknadsinspektionen (2015) 'Handel med el Energimarknadsinspektionen', available: http://www.energimarknadsinspektionen.se/sv/el/elmarknader-och-elhandel/handel-med-el/ [accessed 11 May 2017].

European Union (EU) (2017) 'EUROPA—The history of the European Union—1953', available: http://europa.eu/about-eu/eu-history/1945–1959/1953/index_en.htm [accessed 11 May 2017].

European Union (EU) (2015) 'Europa—the Schuman declaration—9 May 1950', available: http://europa.eu/about-eu/basic-information/symbols/europe-day/schuman-declaration/index_en.htm [accessed 11 May 2017].

European Commission, Trade (2014) 'EU position in world trade', available: http://ec.europa.eu/trade/policy/eu-position-in-world-trade/ [accessed 11 May 2017].

European Commission (EC) (2015) 'Communication—Energy union package: a framework strategy for a resilient energy union with a forward-looking climate change policy, COM(2015) 80 final', available: http://eur-lex.europa.eu/resource.html?uri=cellar:1bd46c90-bdd4–11e4-bbe1–01aa75ed71a1.0001.03/DOC_1&format=PDF [accessed 11 May 2017].

Europe Documents (2014) (SN 79/14) (1 January), European Council.

Gabel, M.J. (2010) 'European Community (EC)—European economic association', available: http://www.britannica.com/topic/European-Community-European-economic-association [accessed 11 May 2017].

Gerbet, P. (1956) *La Genèse du Plan Schuman: Des Origines à la Déclaration du 9 Mai 1950*. Paris: Presses Universitaires de France.

Granit, J. and Lindström, A. (2012) 'Constraints and opportunities in meeting the increasing use of water for energy production', in proceedings of the ESF strategic workshop on accounting for water scarcity and pollution in the rules of international trade, 17–22 March 2013. Value of Water Research Report, Series No. 54. Delft: UNESCO-IHE.

## 54 *A. Lindström, K. Rosner and J. Granit*

Granit, J. and Rosner, K. (2012) 'The water-energy-security nexus: regional approaches to a global challenge—Integrating water and energy planning', International Policy Analysis, Friedrich Ebert Stiftung, available: http://www.gwp.org/globalassets/global/toolbox/references/the-water-energy-security-nexus_regional-approaches-to-a-global-challenge-fes-2012.pdf [accessed 11 May 2017].

Grönkvist, S., Stenkvist, M. and Paradis, H. (2008) 'Energy map of northern Europe. (In Swedish: Nordeuropeisk energikarta)'. Unpublished technical report, available: https://www.researchgate.net/publication/273118388_Energy_map_of_northern_Europe_In_Swedish_Nordeuropeisk_energikarta?channel=doi&linkId=54f7056d0cf28d6dec9c77e2&showFulltext=true [accessed 2 July 2017].

Haas, E.B. (1958) *The Uniting of Europe: Political, Social, and Economic Forces, 1950–1957*. Notre Dame, IN: University of Notre Dame Press.

IEA (2008) 'Nordic country report: Innovative electricity markets to incorporate variable production', International Energy Agency, available: http://iea-retd.org/wp-content/uploads/2011/10/Nordic-Country-Report.pdf [accessed 11 May 2017].

ITFGPG (2006) 'Meeting global challenges: international cooperation in the national interest', Final report, available: http://www.policyinnovations.org/ideas/policy_library/data/01431 [accessed 11 May 2017].

Kiersch, G. (1963). 'Die internationalen Stahlkartelle zwischen den beiden Weltkriegen', in L. Kastl (ed.) *Kartelle in Der Wirklichkeit*. Köln, Berlin, Bonn: Carl Heymanns Verlag KG.

Maltby, T. (2013) 'European Union energy policy integration: a case of European Commission policy entrepreneurship and increasing supranationalism', *Energy Policy*, 55, pp. 435–444.

Martin, S. (2004) 'Coal and steel: first steps in European market integration', Working Paper, available: http://www.krannert.purdue.edu/faculty/smartin/vita/EI5060D.pdf [accessed 11 May 2017].

Mason, H.L. (1955) *The European Coal and Steel Community: Experiment in Supranationalism*. The Hague: Nijhoff.

Mathieu, G. (1970) 'The history of the ECSC: Good times and bad', *Le Monde*, 9 May, available: http://www.cvce.eu/content/publication/1997/10/13/54f09b32-1b0c-4060-afb3-5e475dcafda8/publishable_en.pdf [accessed 11 May 2017].

Maupin, A. (2013) 'PERISA case study 4: building a regional electricity market—SAPP challenges', available: http://ecdpm.org/wp-content/uploads/2013-PERISA-CaseStudy4-Public-Goods-Regional-Electricity-Market-SAPP-Challenges.pdf [accessed 2 July 2017].

Miljö- och energidepartementet (2003) 'Lag (2003: 436) om effektreserv', available: https://lagen.nu/2003:436 [accessed 11 May 2017].

Mioche, P. (1998) 'The European coal and steel community in historical perspective', in R. Ranieri and E. Gibellieri (eds) *The Steel Industry in the New Millennium*, Vol. 2. London: IOM Communications Ltd.

Musiliu, O.O. and Pollitt, M. (2014) 'Institutional arrangements for the promotion of regional integration of electricity markets: International experience', Policy Research Working Paper No. 6947. Washington, DC, World Bank, available: https://openknowledge.worldbank.org/handle/10986/19376 [accessed 11 may 2017].

Nordic Competition Authorities (2003) *A Powerful Competition Policy: Towards a More Coherent Competition Policy in the Nordic Market for Electric Power*. Copenhagen, Oslo, Sweden, Konkurrencestyrelsen.

Cooperation in the power sector 55

Nord Pool Spot (2017) 'The power market', available: http://www.nordpoolspot. com/How-does-it-work/ [accessed 11 May 2017].

Nye, J. (1968) *International Regionalism*. Boston: Little, Brown and Company (Inc.).

Olsen, S.B., Page, G.B., and Ochoa, E. (2009) 'The analysis of governance responses to ecosystem change: a handbook for assembling a baseline', LOICZ Reports & Studies No. 34. Geesthacht: GKSS Research.

ReSAKSS (2015) SADC | ReSAKSS (July). Retrieved from http://www.resakss.org/ region/sadc

Rosenau, J. (1997) *Along the Domestic-Foreign Frontier: Exploring Governance in a Turbulent World*. Cambridge: Cambridge University Press.

SADC (2012) 'SADC regional infrastructure development master plan', Executive summary, SADC, available: http://www.sadc.int/files/7513/5293/3530/ Regional_Infrastructure_Development_Master_Plan_Executive_Summary.pdf [accessed 11 May 2017].

SADC (2015) 'SADC Industrialisation strategy and roadmap 2015–2063', available: http://www.ilo.org/wcmsp5/groups/public/---africa/---ro-addis_ababa/---ilo-pretoria/documents/meetingdocument/wcms_391013.pdf [accessed 2 July 2017].

SAPP (2016) Annual Report, available: http://www.sapp.co.zw/areports.html [accessed 30 Jun 2017].

Schmidt, R.J. (1968). *Versailles and the Ruhr: Seedbed of World War II*. The Hague, Martinus Nijhoff.

Svensk Energi (2017) Elnätet–Distribution, available: https://www.energiforetagen. se/sa-fungerar-det/el/distribution/ [accessed 17 July 2017].

Söderbaum, F. and Granit, J. (2014) 'The political economy of regionalism: the relevance for international waters and the global environment facility: A STAP Issues Paper, Washington, D.C.: Global Environment Facility, available: https://www.thegef.org/ publications/political-economy-regionalism-relevance-international-waters-and-global-environment [accessed 11 May 2017].

UNGA (2015) 'Adoption of the Paris Agreement', 21st session of the Conference of the Parties, FCCC/CP/2015/L.9/Rev.1, available: https://unfccc.int/resource/ docs/2015/cop21/eng/l09r01.pdf [accessed 11 May 2017].

Wilde, R. (2015) 'History of the European Union', available: http://europeanhistory. about.com/od/governmentandlaw/a/europeanunionhist.htm_[accessed 11 May 2017].

# Part II

# Resource scarcity and tensions in international relations

# 4 Phosphorus security

## Future pathways to reduce food system vulnerability to a new global challenge

*Stuart White and Dana Cordell*

## Introduction

Phosphorus is an element that has significant interdependence with global food security. It is essential for plant growth, and the demand for phosphorus from fossil resources (phosphate rock) has grown rapidly in the last 100 years. This mirrors many other resources; however, the implications of a peak in production may be more profound in this case due to the lack of substitutability, the geopolitical concentration of known reserves and the implications for farmers across the world. Another factor that makes phosphorus important in global environmental terms is the impact of increased phosphorus use on downstream environments due to eutrophication of waterways.

Growth in global per capita demand for phosphorus has been stimulated by global changes in diet with increased consumption of animal products, as well as the accelerated production of biofuels, both of which significantly increase demand for phosphorus fertilisers. Global population growth has also contributed to absolute levels of demand. There are, however, significant opportunities for improvement in the use of phosphorus, with over 80 per cent of phosphorus lost between mine and fork.

This chapter describes the key issues regarding this resource, outlining some of the institutional and global security aspects, and provides a description of a path forward. Despite the strategic significance of this resource, and the increasing interest in it, there is no current framework for global governance. At the national and regional levels, there are emerging initiatives to improve institutional arrangements, including at the EU level, and in the UK, Netherlands and the US.

## Phosphorus and its geopolitical context

Phosphorous is unique in its role in global sustainability and geopolitics. It is an essential element for all living organisms and, in relation to food production, it is one of the three main ingredients of commercial 'NPK' fertilisers, which contain the primary macronutrients (nitrogen, phosphorus, potassium) essential for plant growth. In its natural state phosphorus exists only as a solid and, unlike nitrogen, it cannot be obtained from the atmosphere or through the use of nitrogen fixing crops.

Chemical fertilisers have contributed to feeding billions of people by boosting crop yields. In the 1960s and 1970s the use of phosphate from guano mined on the island of Nauru was the most significant factor in boosting agricultural yields in Australia and New Zealand. Similar deposits were mined from islands off the South American coast for use in European agriculture. Worldwide, sustained high agricultural yields are now almost totally dependent on the phosphate rock reserves used to produce phosphate fertilisers.

There will always be a global demand for phosphorous for the production of food and fibre. However, phosphate rock itself is a finite and non-renewable resource, and the world's high-quality reserves are becoming scarce. Over 90 per cent of mined phosphate rock is used for food production, while the remaining 10 per cent is used for other industrial purposes, primarily in the production of some detergents and increasingly in lithium ion phosphate batteries.

Despite phosphorus being integral to human existence, the awareness of global phosphorus supply and demand as an issue worthy of policy discussion has been relatively recent. Prior to 2008 environmental and regulatory concerns about phosphorus principally arose because of the eutrophication of lakes and water bodies. This process involves the increase in nutrient runoff from agriculture and poor land management, which causes excessive growth of plants and algae in water, resulting in depletion of oxygen and fish kills. Eutrophication has been a major problem in the Great Lakes in North America and the Baltic Sea in Northern Europe. In Australia, the Murray-Darling and Western Australia's Peel-Harvey estuarine systems have been major sites of eutrophication. It is only more recently, and principally since the spike in rock phosphate price in 2008, that there has been a major focus on long-term phosphorus security as a policy issue, including a foreign policy and security issue for phosphate importing countries.

The significant global growth in demand for phosphate rock as a source of fertiliser is depicted in Figure 4.1. The spatial pattern of global consumption of phosphorus fertiliser has changed dramatically over the last 40 years. In the 1970s, for example, low-income countries were responsible for less than 20 per cent of phosphorus fertiliser demand and 40 years later they accounted for over 75 per cent of demand (IFA, 2009), and are responsible for the growth in global demand. Future growth in global phosphorous fertiliser consumption is similarly expected to occur predominantly in low-income countries and emerging economies. This is for two main reasons. The first is the economic development in those countries and the accompanying shift to diets containing more animal products, which have an intrinsically higher phosphorus burden due to the losses in conversion of plant protein to animal protein. Diets that are high in animal products can require between two and ten times more phosphorus than plant-based diets. The second is that in high-income countries, where phosphorus fertiliser has been applied for many years, soils have tended to become saturated with phosphorus and so the need to boost soil phosphorus content has lessened. Worldwide, the distribution of phosphorus in soils is uneven, with strong surpluses in Europe and parts of the US, and significant underlying deficits in other regions—particularly Sub-Saharan Africa—with older, weathered soils and less historical application of chemical fertilisers.

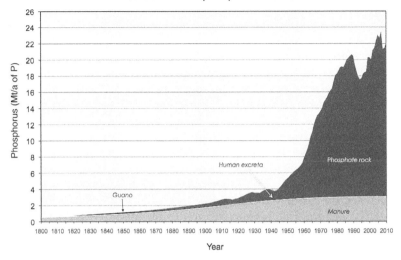

*Figure 4.1* The growth in production of phosphorus fertilisers by source
Source: Adapted from Cordell et al., 2009

In 2008 the price of phosphate rock, which had been stable for many years at approximately US$50 per tonne, spiked at US$430 per tonne. This dramatic price increase coincided with significant hikes in food and oil prices, and contributed to major disruptions worldwide, including rioting in several countries. For the first time, the notion of peak phosphorus, as in a peak in production due to constraints on resources of sufficient quality, was discussed in the media and in public policy discourse. A vigorous debate about when phosphorus production might peak ensued. Estimates have ranged from 30 years' time to 300 years' time (Cordell and White, 2014).

## The dimensions of phosphorus scarcity

The issue of the scarcity of phosphorus needs to be understood in broader terms than just the physical availability of rock phosphate. The total amount of phosphorus in the earth's crust, approximately $4 \times 10^{15}$ tonnes, is relatively high compared to most elements, and does not itself reflect scarcity. Instead, the scarcity issue is one that is reflected in a number of different dimensions, and also the fact that transferring phosphorus from the earth's crust to farmers' crops is a complex process involving a number of steps (Cordell and White, 2011).

Firstly, in terms of the dimension of the availability of phosphorus, the estimated phosphate rock reserves are $2 \times 10^9$ tonnes, a value which is limited by the phosphate rock deposits of sufficient concentration that the energy, waste generation, cost and geopolitical issues enable it to be mined. Like oil, phosphate rock is anticipated to reach a production peak due to these constraints. The estimated timeline for this peak production is highly contested. Our prognostication, based on the most recent estimates of reserves, and taking appropriate consideration of projected demand levels is that the peak in phosphorus production may occur between 2025 and 2084 (Cordell and White, 2014).

A major constraint on the expansion of mining of phosphate rock deposits, particularly as the concentration of deposits diminishes, is the resultant increase in waste product generation. The waste products from extraction, including radioactive wastes, are increasing. The production of one tonne of phosphate gives rise to five tonnes of radioactive phosphogypsum waste, which is stockpiled and contains heavy metals including cadmium, uranium and thorium, which are naturally present in phosphate deposits and can transfer to soils.

The second dimension is managerial scarcity, which arises due to inefficient phosphorus use in the global food system. While 15 million tonnes of phosphate rock are mined each year, only three million tonnes are available to humans through the food produced from that phosphorus. This means that 80 per cent of the phosphorus is lost between the mine and the fork (Cordell et al., 2009). There are significant losses in the mining and processing of phosphate rock to make fertiliser, with generation of waste containing heavy metals including cadmium, and radioactive elements. There are also major inefficiencies in application of fertiliser in agriculture, including whether the phosphorus is in a plant available form or bound to the soil, and on-farm losses, which are often the cause of nutrient runoff into waterways. In addition, there are the losses that occur in the food cycle, including the inefficiency of conversion of plant protein to animal protein, and the waste of food itself both before and after reaching the consumer.

The third dimension of scarcity is economic scarcity for consumers, or lack of access to phosphorous for those who need it, particularly farmers. They need both short- and long-term access to fertilisers, in terms of meeting immediate crop needs and planning for building up soil fertility in the longer term. Almost a billion farmers lack the purchasing power to access fertiliser markets. Farmers in some land-locked African countries can pay two to five times more than European farmers for fertilisers due to high transport costs, handling duties and corruption (IFDC, 2008).

The African continent is a key location for global phosphorus inequity. There is significant 'silent' demand from farmers with low purchasing power in Sub-Saharan Africa where soil fertility is low and food insecurity is high. Sub-Saharan Africa has the following characteristics:

- It is adjacent to the largest source of high-quality phosphate rock, in the north including Morocco and Western Sahara, Tunisia and Algeria.
- Soil fertility is low, due to old, weathered soils, which means that it will require significant phosphorus inputs to build this up, impacting global phosphorus demand.
- Despite the low soil fertility levels, it has the lowest phosphorus fertiliser application rates globally.

- It has the world's poorest farmers; therefore the equity issues associated with access to phosphorus fertilisers is amplified.
- It has high levels of food insecurity, indicating a need for greater and more reliable food production supported by access to fertilisers (Cordell et al., 2009).

The fourth dimension of scarcity is the geopolitical scarcity associated with the remaining reserves. Farmers in all countries need phosphorus, yet just five nations control around 85 per cent of the world's remaining phosphate rock reserves (Morocco and Western Sahara, China, Algeria, Jordan and Syria). Morocco controls 75 per cent of available reserves, because it controls the resources in Western Sahara; a region that it occupies in defiance of UN resolutions. China is a major producer, but imposed a 135 per cent export tariff in 2008. The US, which was once the world's largest producer, consumer and importer of phosphate rock and exporter of phosphorus fertiliser now has approximately 25 years left of its own reserves. India, Australia and the EU are dependent on imports and are therefore vulnerable to price fluctuations and supply disruptions.

One of the key reasons for geopolitical vulnerability is that a number of major producers are in politically unstable regions. This creates a serious risk of disruption to supply and price fluctuations (HCSS, 2012). In addition, Morocco's control of the phosphate reserves in the Western Sahara means that there is a significant supply disruption risk as well as human rights violations associated with the displacement of the Sahrawi people (Smith, 2011). There is also a reputational risk for phosphate companies importing phosphate from the region. Trade in phosphate from the Western Sahara has been termed, 'blood phosphate' (Pecquet, 2015), which—much like the revelations around Africa's 'blood diamonds'—implies that phosphate companies, agri-businesses, farmers and food consumers are knowingly or unknowingly contributing to the oppression in this region.

The final element of scarcity is institutional scarcity, which revolves around the question of whose responsibility it is to provide governance of this scarce resource. There is a lack of effective global governance as there are currently no international or national policies, guidelines or organisations responsible for ensuring the long-term availability and accessibility of phosphorus for food production. The market for phosphorus, both in terms of mining and manufacturing, is dominated by a few major companies, the largest of which is the OCP Group (formerly the *Office chérifien des phosphates*), which is wholly owned by the Government of Morocco, essentially meaning that it is 100 per cent owned by the King of Morocco. Similarly, the second largest phosphate mining company in the world, based in China, is state owned.

The history of phosphate rock mining has been a history of colonial relationships and oppression, with the displacement of entire populations in Banaba (Ocean Island) in Kiribati and lengthy court cases to obtain compensation for locals (Binder, 1978). Nauru, a small Pacific island nation and the major source of phosphate rock for the expansion of agriculture in Australia and New Zealand, has been the subject of economic and political exploitation for most of the last 100 years (Garrett, 1996). The British Phosphate Commission, formed in 1920 by the governments of the UK, Australia and New Zealand and operating until the 1980s, was a powerful force to ensure the growth of the industry (Williams and MacDonald, 1985). Phosphorus is one of the world's most traded commodities, with transport comprising a major proportion of the costs of delivered fertiliser.

Throughout the history of phosphate production, as with many commodities, there has been a combination of national interests, colonialism and economic exploitation, against the backdrop of a global commodity market. While there have been national and even regional (e.g. European) policy initiatives to consider the strategically significant role of phosphorus fertilisers, there has been no equivalent international policy discussion or initiative. There is a prevailing assumption that 'the market will take care of it', but the market alone is not sufficient to ensure equitable, timely and sustainable management of this highly important resource.

The phosphorus system is therefore a vulnerable system, and can be analysed as such, at a global, regional, national or even a local level. Figure 4.2 shows the outcome of a phosphorus vulnerability assessment in relation to a national food system, including external and internal factors (Cordell and Neset, 2013). This vulnerability assessment was undertaken in Australia, and shows that, while Australia is a net food exporter, it is also a net phosphorus importer. In fact, Australia is the world's fifth largest importer. Australia's soils are naturally phosphorus deficient and its agriculture is heavily invested in phosphorus-intensive exports (beef, live animals, wheat and dairy). Australia also has declining investment in agricultural research and development, leaving it vulnerable to future phosphorus insecurity.

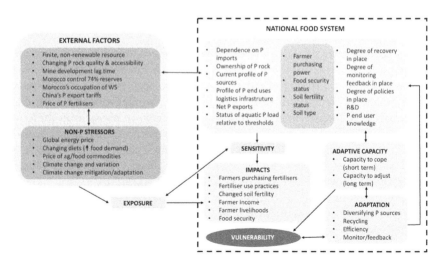

*Figure 4.2* Outcomes of a vulnerability assessment for phosphorus in Australia
Source: Adapted from Cordell et al., 2014

This vulnerability assessment identified four potential adaptive pathways, which could buffer farms and farmers against fertiliser price increases. First, national stakeholders identified multiple pathways that could lead to phosphorous vulnerability in the Australian food system by exploring a range of 'what if' scenarios or perturbations in the system. Second, the potential adaptive pathways to increase the resilience of the food system (e.g. investing in phosphorus recycling from excreta and food waste, or improving farm practices such as soil testing these adaptive pathways) were then mapped, and the trade-offs explored. It was clear that if the current trajectory is not altered, then phosphorus scarcity is likely to have serious consequences for food security. These consequences would include reduced agricultural productivity and reduced smallholder farm access to fertilisers and food, particularly in developing countries. Moreover, vulnerability and adaptability to phosphorus scarcity is context specific and there is no single key to phosphorus security. Third, future-oriented system frameworks can guide identification of priorities to increase the resilience of foods systems. Conversely, a failure to adopt such frameworks will result in perverse outcomes, and investment in ineffective phosphorus strategies. Fourth, integrating phosphorus security into development goals has great potential to improve outcomes.

## A sustainable future for phosphorus use

There is a key question arising from this situation: where does responsibility rest for ensuring long-term phosphorus security, and how would that be achieved? The governance of phosphorus production and use is fragmented and there is little coordination between the industry's many different sectors and stakeholders. These stakeholder groups range from mining of phosphate rock, manufacturing and sales of fertiliser, agriculture, food production, nutrition and the sanitation and wastewater industry. It is unusual for such a diverse group of stakeholders to recognise the common interest that they have in such an issue and to come together to address it without the auspices of, or facilitation by, an appropriate, international group. For example, in terms of UN agencies, the Food and Agriculture Organization (FAO) would be a suitable candidate agency, yet it has not prioritised this issue. The UN Environment Programme (UNEP) has co-ordinated the publication of key global reports on the issue, mostly regarding the environmental aspects, but has stopped short of further action.

It is possible to distinguish between a hard landing and a soft landing in terms of how the phosphorus scarcity problem could play out in geopolitical terms. First, imagine a business-as-usual future: if it proves impossible to change the current phosphorus use trajectory, a hard landing appears likely. This will mean increasing energy use costs and increased waste associated with phosphorous production and use, as well as volatile prices, geopolitical tensions, reduced farmer access to fertilisers, reduced crop yields and lower food security. Unless there is some recognition of the risks associated with the current trajectory and how to address these risks, then these are possible and probable outcomes.

On the other hand, imagine a sustainable future, or soft landing, in which phosphorus security enables all farmers to have short- and long-term access to sufficient phosphorus to grow enough to feed the world while maintaining ecosystem integrity and sustainable livelihoods. These two visions of the future are in very stark contrast. In the case of the soft landing, there would need to be concerted action to ease the demand for phosphorus, in order to reduce over-reliance on rock phosphate through improved efficiency of production and use and through the reuse of local sources including crop, animal, human and municipal wastes.

Averting a crisis and securing a sustainable future is possible, but no single action will achieve that end. As summarised below, substantial policy changes and investments in a range of areas will be required. Figure 4.3 shows an approach for reducing the annual consumption of phosphate rock compared to a business-as-usual trajectory. A combination of demand side measures is shown at the top of the diagram and supply side measures involving the reuse of phosphorus are shown at the bottom of the diagram.

There are several intervention points, in the agriculture and food systems in particular, which can make a major difference to the likelihood of a soft landing. These have been outlined in a separate paper (Cordell and White, 2014) and are summarised below. Interventions in the agricultural sector include measures that reduce the overall demand for fertilisers through improved efficiency of application. This has the advantage of reducing the demand for phosphate fertiliser, while also reducing the runoff of soil phosphorus into waterways, which is the major cause of algal blooms and aquatic degradation. These interventions, in the case of the agricultural use of phosphorus fertilisers, include:

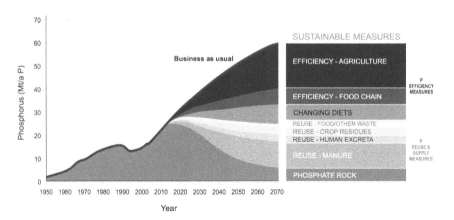

*Figure 4.3* Illustration of methods by which rock phosphate consumption could be reduced using a combination of supply side and demand side measures

Source: Adapted from Cordell and White, 2013

- Placement of fertiliser in the soil close to plant roots to ensure that phosphorus is absorbed.
- Choice of application time relative to growing season and plant stage to maximise phosphorus uptake.
- Adapting the rate of fertiliser application to better meet soil and plant needs.
- Ensuring comprehensive soil testing is in place to enable farmers to match fertiliser applications with plant needs using precision agriculture, remote sensing or low-tech testing.
- Erosion reduction through buffer strips to maintain root soil structure.

Additional measures can include the selection of appropriate plant types. For example, the use of natives, perennials or particular crop types can reduce the need for phosphorus. Other measures include the use of microbial inoculants and enzymes to increase phosphorus uptake by roots. In addition, it is possible to increase the amount of phosphorus available to roots by changing soil pH, and by altering levels of moisture, carbon and organic matter.

These measures, or technical interventions, can be achieved through the application of a broad set of three types of instruments, as described below, including: communication (farm extension services); economic instruments including direct investment in soil testing, information provision and advisory support possibly funded through a levy on fertiliser; and regulatory instruments including requirements for farm management plans and soil improvement practices. The best strategy is one that combines all three instruments to support the implementation of a suite of measures.

Perhaps one of the most effective, but contested and complex, areas relates to dietary change. In low-income and emerging economies, the demand for meat and dairy products is increasing as consumers imitate the diets of high-income countries. This is one of the major factors putting upward pressure on phosphorus use. By 2050, global meat production is projected to double from 2006 levels to 465 million tonnes per year, and milk production is also expected to double to 1043 million tonnes per year (FAO, 2006). If this trend persists, it will be one of the major factors contributing to an increase in phosphorus consumption globally, and it is likely to also be associated with greater eutrophication of waterways and compromised water quality.

In order to address these issues, and to ensure a soft landing, an integrated approach is required. There is no single step that will enable us to meet future phosphorus demand. The strategies that we put in place need to respond to global issues and at the same time they need to be context specific. The situation in Ethiopia will be very different to the situation in Australia, New Zealand or Cambodia, for instance. In addition, it will be essential to determine the most cost effective, energy efficient, equitable and environmentally compatible means of using and reusing phosphorus in a given context.

## Insights to phosphorus scarcity from other resources

In identifying key solutions to the global phosphorus security situation, and in aiming to increase the likelihood of a soft landing, we can learn a lot from responses to other resource issues. For example, responses to problems associated with climate change can provide clues to possible pathways for phosphorus. In the case of global responses to climate change, there is an implicit understanding in principle, and partially implemented in practice, that high-income countries have undergone development and built wealth through their use of the global atmospheric commons. Therefore, in addressing the issue now and in the future, a greater relative reduction in per capita emissions is warranted from these nations, to enable low-income countries to increase per capita emissions. This is the basis of the principle of *contraction and convergence*, which, while contested in the details of implementation, provides a foundation for climate negotiations, including the recent Paris Agreement (GCI, 2016).

The applicability of the framework of contraction and convergence to the phosphorus issue is quite strong. High-income countries have been responsible for the mining and processing of the highest concentration deposits to build up soil phosphorous concentrations and develop their agricultural production. As time goes on, low-income countries become more dependent on phosphate rock deposits and imports, just when the concentration of deposits decreases. High-income countries, as in the case of the greenhouse gas emissions issue, have a greater capacity to employ technical means to improve efficiency of application, for example, through precision, or smart farming. There is therefore a significant global benefit to be gained from the transfer of knowledge, technical capacity and investment from high-income to low-income countries with the objective of improving phosphorus use efficiency. At the same time, deep cuts in phosphorus use in high-income countries, especially through dietary change, would be appropriate to ensure greater equity in its use.

Similarly, an analysis of barriers to improving resource efficiency in the domains of energy and water resources can be equally well applied to the phosphorus domain. In many instances, solutions such as improved energy and water efficiency and the management of demand are highly cost effective relative to the increased capital and operating costs of increasing supply to support increased demand for energy and water resources. This is also true in the case of phosphorus fertiliser, where investments in improving efficiency often provide a net economic benefit relative to increased supply.

The main barrier to more sustainable approaches to phosphorus use is the result of market failure stemming from inappropriate pricing signals, payback gaps and lack of information. For example, failure to factor in the costs of externalities, such as the impacts of resource use that do not manifest as private costs, is a key market failure. The impact on waterways of phosphorus runoff, arising from over-application is a classic case of an externality, often a 'tragedy of the commons' (Hardin, 1968). Payback gaps relate to a difference between expectations of rate of return on investment between actors. For example, a tenant farmer may want to apply more phosphorus to get an immediate gain, expecting a one- to two-year payback, whereas a landowner, in principle, could afford to install equipment and systems to reduce the need for phosphorus fertiliser that may have a payback of four to five years.

Therefore, it is useful to learn from the experience in developing policy tools to overcome these market barriers, including the use of financial incentives, provision of information and extension services, appropriate regulations, supplemented by targets, facilitation, pricing and coordination. These policy tools are illustrated in Figure 4.4 and described in more detail by Dunstan et al. (2009).

The policy tools, in each of the different categories are designed to match the various policy barriers to implementation of sustainable initiatives. For example, one key barrier to phosphorus efficiency is the low cost of fertiliser, in many countries directly subsidised, which can lead to inefficient use. In that case, a solution can be to set a levy on the phosphorus content of fertiliser, as indicated in the example in Figure 4.4. To supplement the impact of the levy, and to some extent mitigate its impact, the proceeds from such a levy could be allocated, or hypothecated, to support farmers in improving the efficiency of phosphorus fertiliser application. This could be in the form of incentives for farmers to undertake soil testing, to ensure that excess phosphorus fertiliser is not applied.

An example of the use of a regulatory instrument for improving phosphorus fertiliser use would be to have a cap on the use or extraction of phosphate rock, similar to a ceiling on greenhouse gas emissions in a 'cap and trade' scheme, or caps on water extraction. This has the effect of recognising, by direct regulation, the limitations imposed by the biophysical reality of the resource base, or the biophysical limits to overuse of the resource.

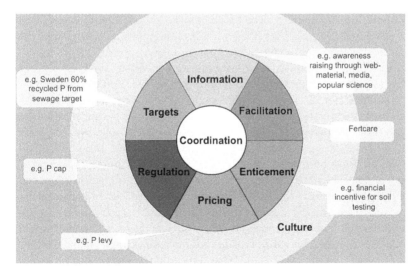

*Figure 4.4* Examples of policy tools

Source: Adapted from Dunstan et al., 2009 and applied to the phosphorus domain

An example of the application of targets that also have the effect of supporting new industries and innovation includes Sweden's target for recycling of phosphorus from sewage. This target was driven by the impacts of discharge of sewage into the Baltic Sea, and the algal blooms that result, and it has encouraged the wastewater and sanitation industry to innovate to capture and recycle nutrients from municipal and industrial wastewater.

The 'policy palette' depicting and categorising the policy tools provides a useful framework for ensuring that there is not too great a focus on different types of instruments. For example, an overemphasis on regulatory instruments can result in a backlash from farmers or industry, unless balanced by information and communication, or incentives or other support. Conversely, a reliance on information provision alone will often fail to make a sufficient difference, as it does not have strong enough impact to overcome structural barriers. Using incentives alone can increase costs of programmes, and risks attracting 'free riders' who benefit from incentives, even if they would have been prepared to act without them.

Coordination is a key aspect in addressing phosphorous security. There needs to be a responsible agency, which is tasked with developing a plan for which policy tools are appropriate and where they should be applied. Moreover, the engagement of a broad range of stakeholders is a very important requirement for the institutional response to the phosphorus security issue. Phosphorus security, like many issues, involves a great diversity of stakeholders. They range from farmers and those involved in the food and nutrition industry through to water and wastewater utilities as well as the mining and extractive industries. This means that extra efforts must be made to engage stakeholders and to stitch together the narrative around the range of solutions. The Global Phosphorus Research Initiative and the Australian National Strategic Phosphorus Advisory Group are two examples of initiatives to develop an integrated approach to phosphorus scarcity and security. The Global Phosphorus Research Initiative, combining the efforts of key research organisations working on many aspects of the issue, was the first platform of its kind, and aims to facilitate quality interdisciplinary research on global phosphorus security for future food production, and to provide networking dialogue and awareness raising among policymakers, industry scientists and the community on the implications of global scarcity and possible solutions.

We are now seeing the emergence of a range of policy initiatives in North America and Europe. In particular, the European sustainable phosphorus platform has been developed, which provides a forum to inform policy for European countries, and has already led to significant advances in institutional arrangements including for phosphorus recycling. There have also been five bi-annual global summits, which are unusual in bringing together researchers, practitioners, industry and non-governmental organisations (NGOs) across the many different aspects of the phosphorus issue, rather than dealing with only, for example, the agricultural aspects. These and similar initiatives provide some hope that there is an increasing awareness, and the potential for action for this major global security issue.

# References

Binder, P. (1978) *Treasure Islands: The Trials of the Ocean Islanders*. Sydney: Angus and Robertson.

Cordell, D. and Neset, T.-S.S. (2013) 'Phosphorus vulnerability: a qualitative framework for assessing the vulnerability of national and regional food systems to the multi-dimensional stressors of phosphorus scarcity', *Global Environmental Change*, 24, pp. 108–122.

Cordell, D., Neset, T.-S.S., White, S. and Drangert, J.-O. (2009) 'Preferred future phosphorus scenarios: a framework for meeting long-term phosphorus needs for global food demand', in D. Mavinic, K. Ashley and F. Koch (eds) *International Conference on Nutrient Recovery from Wastewater Streams Vancouver*. London: IWA Publishing, available: http://dx.doi.org/10.1016/j.gloenvcha.2013.11.005 [accessed 10 August 2016].

Cordell, D. and White, S. (2011) 'Peak phosphorus: clarifying the key issues of a vigorous debate about long-term phosphorus security', *Sustainability*, 3(10), pp. 2027–2049.

Cordell, D. and White, S. (2013) 'Sustainable phosphorus measures: strategies and technologies for achieving phosphorus security', *Agronomy*, 3(1), pp. 86–116.

Cordell, D.J. and White, S. (2014) 'Life's bottleneck: sustaining the world's phosphorus for a food secure future', *Annual Review of Environment and Resources*, 39, pp. 161–188.

Cordell, D., Mikhailovich, N., Mohr, S., Jacobs, B. and White, S. (2014) 'Adapting to future phosphorus scarcity: investigating potential sustainable phosphorus measures and strategies', Phase II of the Australian Sustainable Phosphorus Futures project, prepared for the Rural Industries Research and Development Corporation. Canberra: Australian Government, available: https://rirdc.infoservices.com.au/items/14–039/ [accessed 10 August 2016].

Dunstan, C., Langham, E. and Ison, N. (2009) 'Policy tools for developing distributed energy', Working Paper 4.2, CSIRO Intelligent Grid Research Program by the Institute for Sustainable Futures, University of Technology Sydney, available: http://www.igrid.net.au [accessed 10 August 2016].

FAO (2006) *Livestock's Long Shadow: Environmental Issues and Options*. Rome: Food and Agriculture Organisation, available: http://www.fao.org/docrep/010/a0701e/a0701e00.HTM [accessed 10 August 2016].

Garrett, J. (1996) *Island Exiles*. Sydney: ABC Books for the Australian Broadcasting Corporation.

GCI (2016) 'Contraction and convergence: climate truth and reconciliation', Global Commons Institute, London, UK, available: http://www.gci.org.uk/ [accessed 10 August 2016].

Hardin, G. (1968). 'The tragedy of the commons', *Science*, 162(3859), pp.1243–1248.

IFA (2009) *Production and International Trade Statistics*. Paris: International Fertiliser Industry Association, available: http://www.fertiliser.org/ifa/statistics/pit_public/pit_public_statistics.asp [accessed 12 August 2016].

IFDC (2008) 'World fertiliser prices drop dramatically after soaring to all-time highs'. International Fertiliser Development Center, Muscle Shoals, AL, available: http://www.eurekalert.org/pub_releases/2008–12/i-wfp121608.php [accessed 10 August 2016].

Heffer, P. (2011) 'Assessment of fertiliser use by crop at the global level', International Fertiliser Industry Association (IFA), Paris, available: http://www.fertiliser.org/imis20/images/Library_Downloads/AgCom.13.39%20-%20FUBC%20assessment%202010.pdf [accessed 10 August 2016].

HCSS (2012) 'Risks and opportunities in the global phosphate rock market: robust strategies in times of uncertainty', Rep. No. 17/12/12, Hague Centre for Strategic Studies, The Hague, available: http://www.hcss.nl/reports/download/116/2053 [accessed 12 August 2016].

Pecquet, J. (2015) 'Is Hillary Clinton taking "blood phosphate" money from Morocco?' *Al-Monitor*, 10 April 2015, available: http://www.al-monitor.com/pulse/originals/2015/04/hillary-clinton-morocco-blood-phosphate-money-donation.html [accessed 10 August 2016].

Smith, J.J.P. (2011) 'The plundering of the Sahara: corporate criminal and civil liability for the taking of natural resources from Western Sahara', available: http://arso.org/PlunderingoftheaharaSmith.pdf [accessed 10 August 2016].

Williams, M. and MacDonald, B. (1985) *The Phosphateers*. Melbourne, Australia: Melbourne University Press.

# 5 Peasant mineral resource extractivism and the idea of scarcity

*Kuntala Lahiri-Dutt*

## Introduction

In the Post-Washington Consensus era, many poorer countries underwent structural reforms, or 'adjustment programs' as they came to be known. Collectively, these suites of new neoliberal economic policies created more market-oriented economies. Integral to this neoliberal shift is the view that natural resources, such as land, its mineral resources and water, are tradable commodities that are subject to market forces. Consequently, most states have—with varying eagerness—exposed their mineral resources to investments by local as well as foreign entrepreneurs, resulting in the exploitation of resources at unprecedented rates. This strategy of exploiting resources for quick economic growth—supposedly in pursuit of human development, or at least to benefit people living in resource-rich areas—is known as extractivism. One can describe the process as a commodities consensus because of its complete disregard for the dispossession of people, resources and territories, while simultaneously creating new forms of dependencies.

The logic and practice of extractivism under neoliberal economic policies are often framed and legitimised by notions of scarcity and crisis. In recent years, after a protracted period of what Bridge (2001) calls 'resource triumphalism', predictions of scarcities of key resources (including petroleum, water and food) have been revived. Following the 2008 hike in food and oil prices, *The Wall Street Journal* published an article titled 'New Limits to Growth Revive Malthusian Fears'. It drew special attention to the improving wellbeing of the billions of Indians and Chinese who are 'stepping up to the middle class' and raising global demand (Lahart, Barta and Batson 2008: A1). In such a Malthusian scenario, resource scarcities lead to conflict and war; at the domestic scale, such conflict may involve the extraordinary phenomenon of ordinary peasants (defined here broadly as rural populations directly dependent and subsisting on land and water resources) who extract and degrade the very environment that supports them through small-scale mining activities.

Graulau (2001) maintains that instead of being a 'survival strategy', informal mining by peasants should be seen as a more considered strategy for increasing their odds of escaping poverty. A theoretical challenge is to interpret these livelihood choices and compulsions of extractive peasants within a singular frame,

74    *K. Lahiri-Dutt*

beyond the binaries of resource wars, victims and victors, and scarcity and abundance to understand the lives of those who are actively engaged in the capitalist processes of mineral resource extraction and surplus generation, yet whose livelihoods are not much better than the worst forms of labour. This chapter is a response to this challenge. It argues that peasant production and labour processes characterise an array of mineral extractive practices found in the mineral-rich tracts of the countries of the Global South today. These practices, and the organisation of labour and production in what is widely known as informal, or artisanal and small-scale mining (ASM), reconfigure the ways in which we have thus far conceptualised the extractive industries. The practices of these peasants cut across the spectrum of mining, ranging from the most artisanal individual and opportunistic enterprises to the work as hired labourers in licensed small-scale firms, while often engaging with markets located well beyond their immediate vicinity. These rural labourers undertake a wide array of tasks in the extractive industries, broadening the meaning of 'mining' as a human industry, and inhabiting the complex intersection of a number of social niches, contributing to new directions in scholarly research on resource extractivism in the contemporary world.

## Does scarcity push extractivism?

Experts believe that the processes of global resource scarcity will consolidate a model of development founded on an economy that extracts and over-exploits mineral resources—most of them non-renewable. One essential aspect of this extractive economy is the sense of urgency and crisis, which persists in an interesting association with scarcity, primarily in terms of the adequacy of natural resources to meet human needs.

Crisis and scarcity are different ideas, but both are inherently political in nature and closely interlinked. One can say that both are based on a materialist philosophical view of resources that is rooted in a functional or utilitarian view buoyed by positivism: that resources exist because they fulfil human needs, and that they can be measured as absolute amounts. The first view was proposed soon after World War II by an American economic geographer, Erich Zimmerman. His book, *World Trade and Resources*, is famous for its aphoristic comment, 'resources are not, they become' (1951: 814). Zimmerman's ideas heralded a new era in thinking about resources. They introduced, for the first time since the Scientific Revolution and the era of Enlightenment, that resources are a matter of appraisal, that is, what counts as a resource depends on the interaction between biophysical heterogeneity, technology and social institutions. In Zimmerman's words, resources 'evolve out of the triune interaction of nature, man, and culture, in which nature sets outer limits, but man and culture are largely responsible for the portion of physical totality that is made available for human use' (1951: 814–15). These ideas entrenched a functional utilitarianism that came to assume hegemony in the wider thought processes about resources. More importantly, the utilitarianism was apparently apolitical; Zimmerman's human society was a homogeneous category, discovering nature for its use-value, and putting it to use. For example, there was no consideration of the inequities in the end use of resources derived from nature.

The second dimension of this positivist view of resources, namely that the matter constituting nature can be measured in absolute amounts, assumes that 'stuff in nature' is unknown until we have extracted it and assessed its use-value. Therefore, the philosophy comes with its own epistemology of elaborate processes of accurate measurement. Many experts in the mainstream sustainability sciences were impressed by this approach, and took up the methodological tools to measure, assess and evaluate nature and the resources it offers to us. Once measured, they can be placed against other numbers and amounts. Approaches to resources adopted in the period since World War II, which was characterised by a remarkable phase of material prosperity and accumulating surpluses in the West, were primarily founded on this view. Each material, irrespective of whether it was water or a mineral, was regarded as a constituent of an environment, and its properties were identified and considered to be fixed, essential attributes of these things. No consideration was given to processual, relational or political dimensions. The matters of nature were objectively determined and practically experienced. The implications of such views were catastrophic for thinking about mineral extractive industries; the binary of 'supply and demand' became fully entrenched, as the more powerful and richer nations began to expand their extractive interests into the countries of the Global South where they assumed disproportionate controls over mineral resources. The earliest example was the far-reaching fall-out from the 1973 oil price hike by the OPEC (The Organization of the Petroleum Exporting Countries) countries, which, according to Brown (1974: 5), one of the earliest proponents of the scarcity agenda, was a 'fundamental' change from traditional buyers' markets to global sellers' markets for commodities. The ensuing sense of crisis added a crucial impetus to the structural reforms, changing economic policies to put economic growth on the foundation of extractivism. This turn of events is exemplified in Huber (2014: 816), who says: 'Resource scarcity is a fact likely to produce concerning effects.' In this paradigm, scarcity is described as a fundamental, economic problem: because of scarcity of resources, goods and services are limited, forcing the consumers to make choices. Therefore, the concept sounds like a schoolbook primer on 'unlimited wants, but alas, limited means'. A wider problem arises when resource scarcities are related to conflicts and wars (such as in Le Billon, 2004); invariably, one suggests an economic or a political system that allows the market to allocate these scarce resources, subsuming the possibilities of alternative imaginations of how resources can be redistributed. Then, the idea of crisis comes in handy to connote the sense of urgency; a compulsion that *forces* those in power to choose certain paths.

In the developing world, one response to perceived scarcity has been the emergence and consolidation of extractivism. Latin American scholar-activists distinguish between 'old extractivism' and 'new extractivism', observing that under the former, pursued by imperialist countries located at the global centres, resources were exploited ruthlessly without concern for the destruction caused

76   *K. Lahiri-Dutt*

in peripheral areas. Therefore, under old extractivism, open-access areas were over-exploited and radically depleted by coerced, underpaid and unquantified workers using outdated technologies to supply volatile external markets. Classic examples of such extractivism are the rubber economies of South America that destroyed the biodiversity of extensive areas by establishing monocultures (Svampa, 2011) and 'slaughter' coal mining that was followed by ruthless landlords seeking profits during the 1950s and 1960s in India (Lahiri-Dutt, 2014).

Veltmeyer and Petras (2014: 61) propose the emergence of a 'new extractivism' that operates differently. According to them, 'extractive imperialism' sees states actively support the operations of extractive corporations overseas. An example would be Canadian or Australian mining companies operating in poorer countries with implicit state support. In contrast, post-neoliberal governments formed over the past decades in many countries have opted for a strategy of resource extraction and export primarisation by striking deals with global extractive capital to promote coinciding economic interests. Throughout the Global South, states in economically poor but mineral-rich countries are now seeing revenues from natural resources as providing an easy path to buoy their exchequer. These states present themselves as 'resource frontiers'—a kind of virgin territory that offers the opportunity for acquiring huge quantities of hitherto untapped natural resources.

A key characteristic of new extractivism is that it typically operates in active collaboration with the state, but at the same time relies on mainstream science, particularly the expertise that has developed around sustainability (Hogenboom, 2012). This is done within 'triple bottom line' rubrics in which environmental indicators are incorporated alongside economic and social indicators, ideally to ensure sustainability. Therefore, 'new extractivism' appears to preserve natural resources (or at least, in the case of mining, attempts to care for the environment), while achieving a reasonable income via 'nature's subsidy'. All key players, the international agencies, governments and corporations, propagate the 'good extractivism' discourse. This is where the crucial tactics of invoking scarcity and crisis assume significance. Nature is still seen and utilised as the reservoir of resources from which to extract, but a rapid rate and massive scale of extraction are enabled by the sense of urgency that these two ideas convey.

## Extractive response of peasants to ideas of scarcity

The discourse of scarcity and crisis that fuels the current processes of extractivism has also stimulated shifts impacting on the internal social and political structures of extractivist states. Notably for the case of small-scale mining, the scale and extent of the contemporary occupational shift to mining arguably comprises one of the largest in human history. For example, the extraordinary rush of peasants for gold in Brazilian Amazonia attracted unprecedented numbers of people and extracted vast quantities of gold and other precious metals. The Brazilian story is not exceptional; variations can be seen throughout the mineral-rich tracts of the Global South, where the scramble for resources has reached a crescendo, as rural workers compete with multinational mining companies that funnel capital into remote locations.

The broad picture is one of innumerable people toiling on mineral-rich tracts, extracting enormous quantities of minerals. An exact number is difficult to establish for a number of reasons, chief among them being that the definitions of what constitutes a mine and what constitutes mining work vary from one country to another. Nonetheless, one can note the substantial increase from the 1999 International Labour Office estimate of 13 million workers (Jennings, 1999) to the Communities and Small-Scale Mining estimate of around 35 million in 2005 (CASM, 2005). A more recent estimate from the UN Economic Commission for Africa (2011) suggests that there would have been around 25 million directly employed in informal, artisanal and small-scale mining in 2005, with another 150 to 170 million relying indirectly on these livelihoods. Many of these workers are migrants (ILO, 2016). Half of these jobs are filled by women and around two million children are also involved.

These miners inhabit the margins of the mainstream mining economy. As a consequence, they tend to be associated with the illicit part of the informal economy, and rarely feature in scholarly discourses on mining. They are known by strange names: the wildcat *Garimpeiros* of the Brazilian Amazonia, the *Galampseys* in Ghana, *Barranquilas* in Bolivia, *Ninjas* in Mongolia, and the *Gurandils* (literally, 'those who jump from cliff to cliff') in Indonesia. These names reflect the workers' non-sedentary nature, and the stealth with which they operate. Most states recognise peasants in traditional occupational and demographic categories as belonging to sedentary farming communities. The mobility of such miners—who cannot be easily contained within concession boundaries, and who stealthily extract minerals from claims belonging to larger companies—frustrates national governments. Consequently, they are not included either within mining or labour legislation in these countries. One could say that their very existence remains a myth; a fiction for policymakers, and scholars also tend to pay greater attention to those who mine precious minerals and gems such as gold and diamonds. But the rural migrants toiling in the trenches of the less glamorous stone quarries in India as wage labourers also need to be taken account of. Addressing their absence requires an analytical framework expansive enough to accommodate the considerable social and economic changes that these workers experience.

While the effects of global mining-oriented capital on peasant communities can be explained within traditional Marxist theories, the new and expanding extractive activities of peasants are difficult to frame within a Marxist interpretative framework. A conventional view holds that the peasants will revolt. As Veltmeyer and Petras (2014: 61) write: 'The major protagonists in this struggle are the local peasant farmers and semiproletarianized rural landless workers, who, unlike the traditional proletariat formed under earlier conditions of "primitive accumulation by dispossession", are engaged in a fundamental struggle to preserve their traditional livelihoods and to protect the global commons of land and water on which these livelihoods depend.' However, in Marxist theory,

## 78 K. Lahiri-Dutt

the proletariat is formed by the capitalist development of agriculture, whereby the separation of peasants from their means of production converts them into a class of wage labourers. While participation of the poor in the commoditised economy is explicable in Marxist terms, it fails to account for the extent to which peasants actively determine to engage in mining. Graulau (2001: 98) offers a different perspective, arguing that peasant mining challenges these conventional and oppositional modes of thinking. Indeed, the boundary line between 'survival' and 'livelihood' is exceedingly thin, requiring the use of a flexible and comprehensive analytical framework. Drawing on Escobar (1997), Graulau suggests that rather than being a 'survival strategy', a much-touted model for understanding the responses of the poor to economic oppression, informal mining is a deliberate production strategy to optimise their chances of moving out of dire poverty. The problem, therefore, involves developing a scholarly understanding of constantly mobile, marginal and extremely poor people, and the livelihood choices they make under diverse sets of forces and pressures from market forces.

### How can the peasant mine?

I am using the imprecise and widely debated term 'peasant', primarily to lend historical significance to our contemporary understanding of informal mining practices. Geertz (1961) comments that, conventionally, the term 'peasant' has been associated with the historical, social and economic aspects of life in Europe in the Middle Ages, and confused with the term 'folk'. Shanin (1990: 69) noted that peasants 'are not only an analytical construct . . . but a social group which exists in the collective consciousness and political deed of its members.' One can, therefore, conceive as 'peasants' those engaged in a broad range of subsistence-based or small-scale agriculture in the Global South, including those who own small pieces of land, are tenants on such lands or are sharecroppers or landless agricultural labourers. As peasants, they also occupy particular roles within the development objectives of extractivist states that involve their managed participation in agrarian economies.

Peasants who turn to mining activities are being incorporated into a wide array of mineral extractive occupations that generate cash for their subsistence or the improvement of their wellbeing. I argue that rural people, located on mineral-rich tracts throughout the developed and developing countries of Asia, Africa and South America, are being drawn into the peasant mining economy almost without exception. These 'extractive peasants' use a diverse range of artisanal and small-scale modes of mineral extraction and engage with the market by increasing or decreasing their production, depending on market prices. As a grey zone between the legitimate and the illegal, mineral-based livelihood practices offer incomes and stability to millions of disenfranchised poor, and present us with the opportunity to recognise peasants not just as outcasts of modernity, but as key actors reshaping and redefining contemporary extractive industries.

As a substantial body of evidence put forth by social historians and archaeologists shows, mining and agriculture are not incompatible. Indeed, their work highlights the coexistence of, and similarities between, mining communities and economies, on one hand, and rural peasant societies and economies on the other. The evidence lies largely in three factors: the rural roots of industrial mining labourers, the seasonal complementarities, and the informal and formal systems of mutual exchange such as the tribute system.

## What is driving peasants into mining?

From 'impacts', recent research has turned to the exploration of what might be causing the rural poor to leave traditional forms of subsistence in favour of extractive livelihoods. ASM's relationship with urbanisation in Africa, noted by Bryceson et al. (2014), resonates with the 'rush hypothesis' (Cartier, 2009; Walsh, 2003), which is based on the sudden growth of several 'rush towns' in mineralised regions. Walsh (2003: 292) argues that in Madagascar 'the sapphire trade has offered many the promise, and some the means, of earning previously unattainable sums of money.' Hilson (2010) draws a link to the past in the rush hypothesis, suggesting that the establishment and growth of many such settlements in Sub-Saharan Africa can best be understood when framed by the gold rush that took place in the south-western United States more than 150 years ago.

A different scenario emerged from Jønsson and Bryceson's (2009) detailed analysis of peasants' mobility patterns to newly discovered mining sites, complicating the linearity of history. They suggest that, at the individual level, movements are 'rushed' rather than 'rash', and whereas movement to the first site may be an adventure, movement to subsequent sites is calculated with knowledge of the risks entailed. The question that arises then is: are peasants branching out into a new source of livelihood offering seasonal or temporary income, or is it more accurate to regard this as a shift away from their categorisation as peasants? Received wisdom from peasant studies is that peasants either move out of agriculture in favour of urban jobs, or circulate between better-off rural areas, giving rise to a 'de-agrarianisation versus livelihood diversification' debate in the context of informal mining. Scholars (such as Bryceson, 1996) have speculated that, in response to liberalised markets, rural Africa is experiencing pronounced 'de-agrarianisation', suggesting that the transition out of farming is by no means temporary.

The contention is that agriculture now plays an ancillary role in the livelihoods of rural inhabitants, and that non-farm activities provide the primary source of household disposable income (Bryceson, 2002). In conventional 'de-agrarianised' landscapes, agriculture and mineral extraction play different roles: mining has become a primary source of disposable income; farming is increasingly undertaken to provide household food security; and household finances and other forms of capital now flow between both activities. Jønsson and Bryceson (2009) note that gold digging has become a career in much of rural East Africa, where farming is regarded as a sideline activity, and that for

80    K. Lahiri-Dutt

successful career miners it is best to dissociate from farming. The Structural Adjustment Programme (SAP) and economic liberalisation policies in Africa have led to a plethora of changes in rural productive and marketing infrastructure that have often increased rather than reduced uncertainty, leading to 'multiplex livelihoods' in which, '[i]n addition to proliferating sources of income, the transition encompasses movement away from agriculture towards non-agricultural work, from unpaid towards paid work, and from household-based to more individualised labour activities' (Bryceson, 2002: 2). A complex set of social, political, cultural and economic dynamics are emerging among the critical drivers of informal mining, 'inducing a large-scale search for new, more remunerative activities outside agriculture' (Bryceson, 1999: 173).

Global agricultural production has changed markedly throughout the 1990s, with extensive liberalisation of agricultural markets marginalising subsistence farmers. In less affluent parts of the world, states have privileged urban economies and withdrawn support for agriculture, following a model of development that has been described as 'predatory growth' and has led to the 'internal colonization of the poor' (Walker, 2008: 558). Subsidies on farm inputs were eliminated, export crop taxes were reduced, agriculture was privatised and non-tariff barriers were removed in order to secure loans from the World Bank and the International Monetary Fund (IMF). The withdrawal of state support has placed peasant societies under severe pressure, making farming economically non-viable and eroding its longstanding status as the economic mainstay for rural families. The economic non-viability of agriculture is evidenced by the widespread diversification of rural livelihoods into non-farm activities. As millions of peasants in Asia, Africa and South America move out of the fields, they take up any jobs that are available. Mining as individuals, as families, in groups or as wage-workers constitutes such a livelihood.

At the same time, where economic liberalisation has disrupted rural economies and pauperised smallholders in agriculture, most states have aggressively invited Foreign Direct Investment (FDI)—particularly in large-scale mining—as a means of rapidly securing revenue. To attract foreign mining investments, and under the advice of the World Bank and the IMF, almost all countries have taken steps to reform their mining legislation and regulatory frameworks. Relatively remote regions, portrayed as resource frontiers, are now being drawn into the vortex of industrial change as new mining companies are allowed by states to construct large capital-intensive mining projects. In countries where a harsh environment has exacerbated the detrimental effects on traditional livelihoods, the combined withdrawal of the state and the entry of foreign capital has resulted in near-total retreat from conventional livelihoods to swift adoption of the new, cash-generating labours in mineral extraction. Variations of the story can be found in many corners of the world (for examples see Kamete, 2008, on Zimbabwe and Tripp, 1997, on Tanzania).

Clearly, the factors that are pushing peasants into informal mining are rooted in contemporary—often interlinked and overlapping—economic, social and political changes that were triggered by economic liberalisation. They become

*Peasant mineral resource extractivism* 81

more apparent when seen in the context of globalisation (Akram-Lodhi and Kay, 2009), agrarian transition and peasant mobility (Araghi, 2009), and the incorporation of peasants as wage labourers into informal economies (Breman, 2010). Local contexts, including historical, political, economic and ecological realities, produce unique combinations of factors that drive this unprecedented and widespread shift from agrarian to informal mineral extractive economies. Of these, six can be broadly recognised as significant: the unsustainability and low productivity of agriculture ('agricultural poverty' or the 'push' factor); economic reforms to liberalise land markets and to prioritise FDI ('structural reform'); states' initiatives to earn revenue income from mineral extraction (the 'rentier state'); the equation of mining with development as a rationale for establishing an extractive model that supposedly favours large corporatised operators and local communities (the unproved ideology of 'mining for development'); environmental degradation at the local level, coupled with uncertainties of climate caused by local and global processes ('environmental distress'); and high commodity prices, which add further incentive to earn cash income (the 'pull' factor). Combined, they have compelled peasants to adopt extractive livelihoods in addition to, but more often in lieu of, farming. I will outline two cases from East and South Asian countries that operate on different geographical scales, but represent the diversity of sociopolitical dynamics driving informal mining.

### Nomadic herders digging up the Gobi: Mongolia

Mongolia illuminates how a combination of factors operates to create a spectacular change in livelihoods. Since the liberalisation of its economy in the aftermath of the dissolution of the Soviet Union, Mongolia has established foreign-funded large-scale mining projects producing gold, coal, copper and molybdenum, primarily for the export market. Today the country relies on the mining industry for 30 per cent of its gross domestic product (GDP) and 70 per cent of its total export income. The traditional economy, based on nomadic animal husbandry, now contributes only about 20 per cent of GDP (Dierkes and Khushrushahi, 2006). In 2003, there were at least 100,000 artisanal miners (Grayson et al. 2004). More recently, Buxton (2013: 3) conservatively suggested that numbers could be between 40,000 and 60,000. However, it is useful to remember that this is an estimate focused primarily on gold, thus leaving out workers involved in coal, fluorspar and other industrial commodities, the seasonal miners who switch between mining and other livelihoods, and the gold traders, shopkeepers and restaurant owners involved in the informal mining economy.

As in many countries, modern industrialised mining in Mongolia coexists and shares space with the production and labour processes practiced by ex-nomadic herders. High (2012: 250) argues that 'the Mongolian gold rush is conceived locally' and is 'more than an economic phenomenon of facts and figures.' Frequent conflicts over access to pastureland and water resources

## 82   K. Lahiri-Dutt

occur around large mine sites where mineral extraction has interrupted river regimes, decreasing water availability and quality. At the same time, there has been a rapid increase—within a decade—of informal mining by the nomadic herders, who have been displaced from their traditional occupations (Suzuki, 2013). The push from a rural livelihood into informal mineral extraction has been exacerbated by severe and sudden environmental catastrophes in the form of successive disastrous winters known as *dzuds* (Upton, 2010), as well as the withdrawal of social security systems coincident with the liberalisation of the economy. Although High (2008: 3) refutes the popular notion that ASM is a poverty-driven activity and suggests that artisanal mining is linked to 'Mongolian ideas about patriarchy, generosity and specifically the obligation to share wealth', the need to survive and build a livelihood cannot be ignored as having driven many of the poor in Mongolia to take up informal gold mining to supplement cash-based incomes (see Cane et al., 2015). The Mongolian state is yet to come fully to terms with it, even after a series of legislative efforts to regulate, formalise and control its commodity supply chains.

### Displaced locals creating a moral economy: eastern India

According to the World Coal Association, 71 per cent of India's electricity supplies come from coal-fired power plants, and in a country with over 500 million people without access to electricity, the mining of coal for power generation has assumed great significance. Consequently, coal mining is central in the overall scenario of mining-induced displacement. At the same time, with a full-fledged separate Ministry, coal occupies pride of place in shaping the economic and political milieu of India, dictating its energy future (Lahiri-Dutt, 2014), and continues to enjoy an iconic status as a national symbol, which it assumed after independence, and which led ultimately to its nationalisation in the early 1970s.

Eastern India is one region that witnessed the early advent of coal mining— heralding the emergence of 'modern' industries—during the colonial period (Rothermund and Wadhwa, 1978). Collieries absorbed the local forest-dependent indigenous communities into the labour force (Corbridge, 2004), leading also to urban transformation of the area (Lahiri-Dutt, 2001). As against the colonial period underground mines, large-scale, mechanised open-cut collieries have been established in recent years; some are funded by private entrepreneurs with heavy state, national and World Bank support. These open-cut collieries encroach on forests, grazing/farming land sometimes held as commons (*gair majurwa*) and inalienable land that has been traditionally held by indigenous communities (Lahiri-Dutt et al., 2012). A mining-degraded environment and the physical displacement of forest-dependent communities has seen a significant occupational increase in informal coal mining.

Most of the miners are the dispossessed local poor, who often describe the activity as 'coal collection', reminiscent of gathering wood from forests during the dry season, and who claim a moral right to mine coal from the land that had belonged to them. A 2003 field survey in eastern India conservatively estimated that 2.5 million tonnes of coal was mined outside of that produced by the state-owned Coal India Limited (Lahiri-Dutt and Williams, 2005). A repeat survey in 2012 found that this amount had increased to 3.7 million tonnes (Lahiri-Dutt et al., 2014). Entrepreneurs often carry the coal on bicycles in loads of up to 300 kilograms, earning only marginally more than the minimum daily wage they would have received as wage labourers loading coal into trucks. Whereas the state largely tolerates them, popular media portrays these cycle-pushers as environmental raiders, focusing on the Hobbesian lawlessness, conflicts, chaos and illegality of this livelihood.

The depiction of lawless disorder is not restricted to eastern India, but extends throughout the Global South, where underdevelopment, misery and ethnic violence are considered to drive these workers, and they are portrayed as undeserving opportunists encroaching on the environmental commons— fierce political rebels subverting innocent labour (Wilson, 2013). The recurrent explanation of informal mining as creating the 'deadliest places' in the nation, harbouring 'conflict minerals' (Eichstaedt, 2011), inappropriately invokes notions of the 'resource curse' and 'resource wars' (see VanDeveer, 2013). These simplistic, ahistorical accounts reduce miners to petty criminals, obscure their moral claims over land and its resources, and easily lend themselves to policy recommendations emphasising control and regulation in order to secure revenue for the state.

## Discussion

The two cases above refer to situations at multiple geographical scales, yet the similarities are remarkable: the ongoing transformation from land-based herding, forestry and farming to mineral-based livelihoods. They also present extraordinary diversities: in production processes and labour organisation, in the level of capital accumulation and in market outreach. For example, some coal in eastern India is transported on bullock carts or cycles, while heavy-duty four-wheel vehicles make their own tracks to reach the nooks and crannies of the Mongolian Gobi. This diversity defies the logic of modern industrial labour processes, and contains within it significantly pre-modern modes of production. For example, the family unit in which the wife works with the husband and the child learns a trade by apprenticing with the father in their 'coal collection'; and the casual or itinerant ex-herder swiftly moving from one gold digging site to another. Unlike unionised industrial and factory workers, the absence of proper wages and safe working conditions make those working in informal mines and quarries the poorest, most wretched and most exploited of labourers, engaged in the most insecure and dangerous work in order to survive and build better lives for themselves and their families.

Official data often do not reflect this reality. One difficulty is self-identification. During my fieldwork in the stone and marble quarries of Rajasthan in India, I found that those who had been digging in mines and quarries as wage

84   K. Lahiri-Dutt

labourers for up to 15 years continued to identify as peasants, no matter how peripheral an economic role farming played in their lives. Therefore, instead of asking whether mining is a means of escaping subsistence agriculture, or if it represents a social categorisation outside the class of 'peasant', questions ought to be framed in ways that avoid nomenclature for its own sake, and rather look to continuities and discontinuities among the communities affected by rapid social and economic transformations. This would be possible if experts investigating mineral production were to take into account the continuing peasant traditions in production relations. Similarly, attention needs to be focused on the resource politics of the poor, rather than directed solely at processes occurring on a national scale.

How the empirical data are interpreted also needs consideration. The tendency to criminalise the poor of the Global South has been strongly criticised; in the African context, scholars (such as Mbembe, 2001: 2) have described the 'absolute otherness' that gives rise to negative interpretations that entrap the continent in relations of corruption. Informal mining, envisaged as the illegitimate version of extractive industries, arouses similar negative interpretations. The cases cited here show that grounded and detailed analyses are capable of offering alternatives that can rescue peasants—when they turn to extraction in order to survive—from discourses of criminality. Such a reframed research agenda to explain the unprecedented stampede by peasants to secure mineral-based livelihoods would neither ignore the past nor the contemporary social, political and economic changes sweeping rural areas throughout the world. The extractive peasantry might be crucial to shifting the geographical centre of gravity of the world's extractive industries and redefining mineral production.

## Conclusion

To a significant extent, the perspectives that researchers and policymakers take determine the social and economic structures with which people are confronted. For this reason, the frameworks used to describe peasants, and the concomitant perceptions of their agency under duress and desperation, are crucial. On the one hand, seeing the poor as perpetually trying to survive and barely managing has the effect of limiting them to circumstances that occlude their ingenuity and the differences within their daily contexts, or of depicting their livelihoods as harming or costing others or themselves. The language of survival contributes to an image of the poor as victims who in reality may resort to theft, begging or prostitution, or the reorientation of their consumption patterns, in order to counter unemployment or unaffordable living expenses. On the other hand, past ideals of heroic peasant resistance, widely recognised as the crucial marker of peasant societies, have been crumbling under the oppressive weight of market-oriented economic policy. Yet, the sharp demarcation in theory makes it almost impossible to offer an alternative interpretation of extraction by peasants that incorporates individual agency and market determinism—permitting a view of peasants as neither fully resisting nor succumbing to the fetish of the commodity. We are disciplined to think in binary terms of need or greed, choice or the lack of alternatives, agency or force.

The concept of the extractive peasant offers an alternative to the 'need versus greed' argument central to the concept of environmental sustainability in mining (Ali, 2009), and the various potential interpretations of the moral economy of informal mining. The avoidance of binary options, as suggested by Arnold (2001), allows us to see peasants both as moral agents and as those who take advantage of commodification of resources.

In conclusion, in the contemporary world of heightened resource extractivism, peasants do not encounter the material world as a homogeneous mass, nor do they remain unchanged by it. Rather, peasants redefine themselves in order to be neither the outcasts nor the victims of modernity. In contemporary extractive states, encounters with the material value of minerals and underground resources do not simply undermine peasants and turn them into outcasts of modernity. Paradoxically, they permit peasants to redefine their conception of material and social worlds and their places in them.

However, peasants are not necessarily the free agents envisaged by capitalism (Breman, 2010). Rather, by virtue of their extractivism, peasants in the contemporary world appreciate what has been described as 'three dimensional land' by Bebbington (2013), because they recognise that the yield of mining is many times greater than agriculture. As the state recedes to allow the market to take over, letting commodity prices rise to hitherto uncontemplated levels, the desperate peasants under severe compulsion attempt to turn the tables in their favour in order to scrape at least some benefits from the disruptive changes. In the process, they reconceptualise themselves and the political economy of extractive industries. Through their extractivism, not only do the peasants come to appreciate the three-dimensional value of land, they also challenge seemingly invincible statist (and later, corporatised) rights to mineral resources, and contest the imagined links between corporatised mining and economic, human and social development and poverty reduction in less affluent nations. Through the extraction of resources, peasants engage—albeit not necessarily on their own terms—with the walled-in space of global commodity production and trade, in the process reconceptualising themselves and the political economy of extractive industries.

## References

Akram-Lodhi, H. and Kay, C. (eds) (2009) *Peasants and Globalization: Political Economy, Rural Transformation and the Agrarian Question.* London and New York: Routledge.

Ali, S. (2009) *Treasures of the Earth: Need, Greed, and a Sustainable Future.* New Haven: Yale University Press.

Araghi, F. (2009) 'The invisible hand and the visible foot: peasants, dispossession and globalization', in H. Akram-Lodhi and C. Kay (eds) *Peasants and Globalization: Political Economy, Rural Transformation and the Agrarian Question.* London and New York: Routledge, pp. 111–147.

## 86  K. Lahiri-Dutt

Arnold, T.C. (2001) 'Rethinking moral economy', *American Political Science Review*, 95(1), pp. 85–95.

Bebbington, A. (2013) 'Underground political ecologies: the second Annual Lecture of the Cultural and Political Ecology Specialty Group of the Association of American Geographers', *Geoforum*, 43(6), pp. 1152–1162.

Breman, J. (2010) *Outcast Labour in Asia: Circulation and Informalization of the Workforce at the Bottom of the Economy*. New Delhi: Oxford University Press.

Bridge, G. (2001) 'Resource triumphalism: postindustrial narratives of primary commodity production', *Environment and Planning A*, 33(12), pp. 2149–2173.

Brown, L. (1974) *The Global Politics of Resource Scarcity*, Washington, DC: Global Development Council.

Bryceson, D., Jønsson, J. B., Fisher, E. and Mwaipopo, R. (eds) (2014) *Mining and Social Transformation in Africa: Tracing Mineralizing and Democratizing Trends in Artisanal Production*. London: Routledge Development Studies series.

Bryceson, D.F. (1996) 'Deagrarianization and rural employment in sub-Saharan Africa: a sectoral perspective', *World Development*, 24(10), pp. 97–111.

Bryceson, D.F. (1999) 'African rural labour, income, diversification and livelihood approaches: a long-term development perspective', *Review of African Political Economy*, 80, pp. 171–89.

Bryceson, D.F. (2002) 'Multiplex livelihoods in rural Africa: Recasting the terms and conditions of gainful employment', *The Journal of Modern African Studies*, 40(1), pp. 1–28.

Buxton, A. (2013) *Responding to the Challenges of Artisanal and Small-scale Mining: How Can Knowledge Networks Help?* London: IIED.

Cane, I., Schleger, A., Ali, S., Kemp, D., Mcintyre, N., Mckenna, P., Lechner, A., Dalaibuyan, B., Lahiri-Dutt, K. and Bulovic, N. (2015) *Responsible Mining in Mongolia: Enhancing Positive Engagement*. Brisbane: University of Queensland, Sustainable Minerals Institute.

Cartier, L. (2009) 'Livelihoods and production cycles in the Malagasy artisanal ruby-sapphire trade: a critical examination', *Resources Policy*, 34(1–2), pp. 80–86.

Communities and Small-scale Mining (CASM) (2005) 'Communities and small-scale mining: an integrated review for development planning', Washington, DC: CASM Secretariat, The World Bank.

Corbridge, S. (2004) 'Competing inequalities: The scheduled tribes and resources in Jharkhand', in S. Corbridge, S. Jewitt and S. Kumar (eds) *Jharkhand: Environment, Development and Ethnicity*, New Delhi: Oxford University Press, pp. 175–202. Originally Published in *Journal of Asian Studies*, 59(1).

Dierkes, J. and Khushrushahi, N. (2006) *Mining in Mongolia: Some Recommendations for Long-Term Investment Agreements in the Mongolian Mining Sector*. Vancouver, BC: Institute of Asian Research.

Eichstaedt, P. (2011) *Consuming the Congo: War and Conflict Minerals in the World's Deadliest Place*. Chicago: Lawrence Hill Press.

Escobar, A. (1997) *Encountering Development: The Making and Unmaking of the Third World*. Princeton, NJ: Princeton University Press.

Geertz, C. (1961) 'Studies in peasant life: community and society', *Biennial Review of Anthropology*, 2, pp. 1–41.

Graulau, J. (2001) 'Peasant mining production as a development strategy: the case of women in gold mining in Brazilian Amazon', *European Review of Latin American and Caribbean Studies*, 71, pp. 71–104.

Grayson, R., Delgertsoo, T., Murray, W., Tumenbayar, B., Batbayar, M., Tuul, U., Bayarbat, D. and Erdene-Baatar, C. (2004) 'The people's gold rush in Mongolia: the rise of the ninja phenomenon', *World Placer Journal*, Special Issue, 4, pp. 1–66.

High, M. (2008) 'Wealth and envy in the Mongolian gold mines', *Cambridge Anthropology*, 27(3), pp. 1–18.

High, M. (2012) 'The cultural logic of illegality: living outside the law in the Mongolian gold mines', in J Dierkes (ed.) *Change in Democratic Mongolia: Social Relations, Health, Mobile Pastoralism, and Mining*. London: Brill, pp. 249–270.

Hilson, G. (2010) '"Once a miner, always a miner": poverty and livelihood diversification in Akwatia, Ghana', *Journal of Rural Studies*, 26(3), pp. 296–307.

Hogenboom, B. (2012) 'The new politics of mineral extraction in Latin America', *Journal of Developing Societies*, 28(2), pp. 129–132.

Huber, M. (2014) 'Enforcing scarcity: oil, violence, and the making of the market', *Annals of the Association of American Geographers*, 101(4), pp. 816–826.

International Labour Office (ILO). (2016) *International Migrant Workers in the Mining Sector*. Geneva: ILO Secretariat.

Jennings, N. (1999) *Social and Labour Issues in Small-scale Mines*. Report for Discussion at the Tripartite Meeting on Social and Labour Issues in Small-scale Mines, International Labour Office, Geneva.

Jønsson, J.B. and Bryceson, D.F. (2009) 'Rushing for gold: mobility and small-scale mining in East Africa', *Development and Change*, 40(2), pp. 249–279.

Kamete, A.Y. (2008) 'When livelihoods take a battering ... mapping the "New Gold Rush" in Zimbabwe's Angwa-Pote Basin', *Transformation: Critical Perspectives on Southern Africa*, 65, pp. 36–67.

Lahart, J., Barta, P. and Batson, A. (2008) 'New limits to growth revive Malthusian fears', *The Wall Street Journal*, 24 March, A1.

Lahiri-Dutt, K. (2001) *Mining and Urbanization in the Raniganj Coalbelt*. Calcutta: The World Press.

Lahiri-Dutt, K. and Williams, D.J. (2005) 'The coal cycle: a small part of the illegal coal mining in eastern India', *Resource, Environment and Development*, 2(2), pp. 93–105.

Lahiri-Dutt, K., Krishnan, R. and Ahmad, N. (2012) 'Land acquisition and dispossession: private coal companies in Jharkhand', *Economic and Political Weekly*, XLVII (6), pp. 39–45.

Lahiri-Dutt, K., Alexander, K. and Insouvanh, C. (2014) 'Informal mining in livelihood diversification: mineral dependence and rural communities in Lao PDR', *South East Asia Research*, 22(1), pp. 103–122.

Lahiri-Dutt, K. (ed.) (2014) *The Coal Nation: Histories, Politics and Ecologies of Coal in India*. Aldershot: Ashgate.

Le Billon, P. (2004) 'The geopolitical economy of resource wars', *Geopolitics*, 9(1), pp. 1–28.

Mbembe, A. (2001) *On the Postcolony*. Berkeley: University of California Press.

Rothermund, D. and D.C. Wadhwa. (1978) *Zamindars, Mines, and Peasants: Studies in the History of an Indian Coalfield and its Rural Hinterland*. New Delhi: Manohar.

Shanin, T. (1990) *Defining Peasants: Essays Concerning Rural Societies, Expolary Economies, and Learning from them in the Contemporary World*. Oxford: Blackwell.

Suzuki, Y. (2013) 'Conflict between mining development and nomadism in Mongolia', in N. Yamamura (ed.) *The Mongolian Ecosystem Network: Environmental Issues under Climate and Social Changes*. Tokyo: Ecological Research Monographs, pp. 269–294.

## 88 K. Lahiri-Dutt

Svampa, M. (2011) 'Resource extractivism and alternatives: Latin American perspectives on development'. Paper presented in the meeting of the Permanent Working Group for Alternatives to Development (Grupo Permanente de Trabajo sobre Alternativas al Desarrollo 2011), Quito: Rosa Luxemburg Foundation, available: https://www.tni.org/files/download/beyonddevelopment_resource.pdf [accessed 1 February, 2017].

Tripp, A.M. (1997) *Changing the Rules: The Politics of Liberalization and the Informal Economy in Tanzania.* Berkeley: University of California Press.

United Nations Economic Commission for Africa (UNECA). (2011) *Minerals and Africa's Development: The International Study Group Report on Africa's Mineral Regimes.* Addis Ababa: UNECA.

Upton, C. (2010) 'Introduction: Focus on Mongolia', Special Issue on 'Mongolia: the new politics of safety and identity', *Central Asian Survey*, 29(3), pp. 243–249.

VanDeveer, S. (2013) *Still Digging: Extractive Industries, Resource Curses, and Transnational Governance in the Anthropocene.* New York: The Transatlantic Academy.

Veltmeyer, H. and Petras, J. (2014) *The New Extractivism: A Post-Neoliberal Development Model or Imperialism of the Twenty-First Century?* London: Zed Books.

Walker, K.L.M. (2008) 'Neoliberalism on the ground in rural India: predatory growth, agrarian crisis, internal colonization, and the intensification of class struggle', *Journal of Peasant Studies*, 35(4), pp. 557–620.

Walsh, A. (2003) '"Hot Money" and daring consumption in a Northern Malagasy mining town', *American Ethnologist,* 30(2), pp. 290–305.

Wilson, S.A. (2013) 'Diamond exploitation in Sierra Leone 1930 to 2010: a resource curse?' *Geojournal*, 78(6), pp. 997–1012.

Zimmerman, E.S. (1951) *World Resources and Industries.* New York: Harper & Brothers.

# 6 Whose scarcity, whose security?

Multi-scalar contestation of water
in the Indus Basin

*Douglas Hill*

## Introduction

The use and management of water in South Asia has long been discursively constructed as an issue of scarcity. The range of overlapping and competing stakeholders representing agriculture, industry, sanitation and a variety of other uses necessarily results in contests over how water should be utilised (Adeel and Wirsing, 2017). Moreover, high levels of population growth, issues of water quality, agricultural intensification and economic change have all intensified this contestation (Kugelman and Hathaway, 2009; Laghari, Vanham and Rauch, 2012). Although parts of northern South Asia face these issues to greater and lesser degrees (Hill, 2013), it is arguably in the Indus Basin that this contestation is the most intense and seemingly the most intractable, not least because it involves two countries, which, since gaining independence from Britain, have been mired in long-running and seemingly intractable conflict, namely India and Pakistan. Indeed, the sharing of water between countries, such as between India and Pakistan, has long been imbricated in regional geopolitics (Gilmartin, 2015; Haines, 2016). Just as significantly, the issue of water scarcity and its imbrication with water security is a significant domestic political issue in both countries (Hill, 2008).

While acknowledging that these international and intra-national disputes clearly point to a situation where water scarcity has led to political contestation, I see the need to problematise the seemingly commonsensical reading of how we might understand this particular example of resource scarcity. Like many others in this collection, my reading of water security in the Indus suggests that we need alternative approaches to how we understand the control and allocation of resources than those that prevail in the popular understanding. The long tradition of water resource management in South Asia has followed a supply side dominated, engineering-led understanding of the use of water and this has tended to mean that water sharing is understood in volumetric terms (Akhter, 2017; D'Souza, 2016). This reductionist understanding of water—so that it is confined only to volume per unit of time—has had the effect of confining the debate in ways that impact upon ecosystem services and the livelihoods of many local communities. Key to my critique, then, is the argument that the issue of resource scarcity is inherently concerned with the politics of

90    D. Hill

knowledge and being. The epistemological and ontological closures of orthodox understanding of water security stem from the overwhelming emphasis placed upon a volumetric understanding of water.

In recent years, this volumetric understanding of water has become increasingly securitised, in that the allocation of water at different times of the year to different parts of the basin has become framed by an unhelpful conflation of water scarcity on the one hand, and the propensity towards conflict between nation-states on the other hand (Chellaney, 2011). In this reading, water security is interpreted in a manner more redolent of orthodox international relations ideas of environmental security than a human security centred approach that predominates among donors and civil society (Burgess, Owen and Sinha, 2016). The dominance of a supply-led approach to water also contributes to a lack of transparency around water resource management, since it has become a site for secrecy over data sharing. Indeed, information about how much water is flowing in a river from one point to another at a particular time of year is jealously guarded by different bureaucracies in all countries of South Asia (Ali and Zia, 2017; Surie and Prasai, 2015).

The first part of the chapter analyses water security as it is typically understood in South Asia, asserting why this leads to systemic closures and the implications for livelihoods and ecosystem services. The second part of the chapter considers how this logic is transposed and modified with regard to the geopolitics of water sharing in the Indus Basin. However, we must also keep in mind that all of these other scales of water allocation and scarcity are potentially impacted by what happens at this so-called 'regional scale'. In other words, focusing on the relations between countries and what this means for water scarcity cannot be about privileging the nation-state as unitary or unified in its intents, as is often the case in terms of how hydro politics are analysed (Hill, 2013; 2015). The hydro-geographies prevailing within neighbouring provinces, districts, villages and households do not disappear just because we move analytically to the regional scale. A discussion of resource contestation is therefore necessarily also a discussion of the politics of this rescaling process (Wald and Hill, 2016).

The final part of the chapter considers recent initiatives aimed at broadening understandings of water sharing between India and Pakistan. Many of these initiatives have been promoted by civil society, academia and other non-governmental organisations. While we see some progress in moving towards a broader understanding of the relationship of water to its environs in other basins, in the Indus Basin there is more of a political deadlock, which has meant that these initiatives have not achieved as much as might be thought possible. The chapter concludes by considering how we might move beyond this deadlock and what this case means for broadening our understanding of water security.

## Conceptualising water scarcity and water security in South Asia

There is no doubt that the control and effective use of water is a significant issue for a great number of people living in the Himalayan basins of South

Asia, and that these issues are particularly evident in the Indus Basin. Most basins that originate in the Himalayas are highly populous and are extremely biodiverse. Agriculture is the main use of water in the basins and over time this water has come to be extracted in ever-greater amounts from both surface and groundwater.

Most people in northern South Asia live in sub-basins that are usually classified as water stressed; a technical description that refers to the availability of water per capita (National Research Council, Committee on Population, 2012).[1] Projections of future availability of water per capita in South Asia suggest that this is likely to get considerably worse in the future, such that more and more people will be living in water scarce areas; that is, areas in which there is insufficient water per capita for all necessary uses.

The Indus Basin is an important example of how water scarcity creates and intensifies development challenges for a range of people. Indeed, inhabitants of the Indus Basin face a significant number of challenges related to declining water availability per capita, in terms of both water quality and quantity. This is arguably the most important basin in South Asia with regard to agricultural production, with the Punjab in particular often labelled the breadbasket of India and Pakistan. Agriculture was extended in this basin during the colonial period through the construction of the world's largest contiguous irrigation system (Ali, 2004). Agriculture remains the most important usage of water and the major contributor to the economic base of the basin, as a source of both subsistence food security and rural livelihoods and as an income generating activity (Ahmad, 2012). Many of the most key industries in the Indus are very water intensive, including textiles, sugar and wheat, and their continuing viability—on the Pakistani side in particular—is problematised by the continuing low efficiency of irrigation, technological obsolescence, poor regulatory mechanisms and worsening power shortages (Briscoe and Qamar, 2006).

A changing climate intensifies the vulnerability of people in the Indus to these challenges, creating a cycle of droughts and floods that has already had major impacts on livelihoods and looks likely to increase in the future (Singh et al., 2011). Moreover, while surface and groundwater irrigation have increased enormously in the period since the Green Revolution began, a considerable demise in both quality and quantity of the groundwater resource is now evident (Rodell, Velicogna and Famiglietti, 2009). While there are variations across the Indus Basin, this situation holds true for both India and Pakistan, making the agricultural base, upon which the Punjab's prosperity has been derived, ever more tenuous.

One approach that is often cited as a potential solution to water scarcity is inter-basin transfer; that is, the transfer of water from one basin to another through the building of a lot of infrastructure, such as link canals, storage dams and so on. Such an approach has long had adherents in India, in particular, and in the contemporary period these plans have become tangible through the proposed Inter Linking of Rivers (ILR) scheme (Alley, 2004; Bandyopadhyay and Perveen, 2003; Padma, 2016). Here the logic of water scarcity and the

92   D. Hill

politics of water allocation come into stark relief, since the ILR scheme is premised upon an assessment of which parts of the country are 'water deficit' and which are 'water surplus'. The idea here is that the transfer of water from surplus regions to deficit regions will increase agricultural productivity and will go a considerable way towards 'drought proofing' the country. The realisation of this scheme would have significant environmental impacts and is likely to lead to the disruption of livelihoods and the displacement of those whose villages are in the vicinity of proposed dam sites. It would also exacerbate provincial politics between states over the allocation of water, given that those areas that are in declared water surplus basins are usually in different states from those that are declared water deficit.

It is striking that this debate and the logic under which it proceeds is framed almost entirely in terms of a volumetric understanding of water. As such, very little consideration is given to the broader functioning of these rivers or the many aspects of the human–environment interface. These elisions are both in terms of what happens inside the river but also in terms of the river's role in the functioning of environmental processes and the maintenance of ecosystems.

The ILR scheme has been heavily criticised by social activists and many academics for the fact that it pays very little credence to the environmental impacts of these planned diversions. Many of the regions that are deemed to be water surplus, such as the North-Eastern states that are part of the Brahmaputra and Meghna Basins, are biodiversity hotspots with a significant number of endemic flora and fauna.[2] People living up and down these basins interact with and depend upon both the river and its broader ecosystems for their livelihoods. While agriculture is important here, resources from fisheries and forests are also important. And yet, proponents of river linking rarely account for this diversity or the broader role of water in socio-ecological processes.

## Conceptualising water security within basins

Regardless of whether one believes that inter-basin transfer is practical or desirable, there is little question that such a narrow understanding of water usage and availability—that is, only conveyed as a quantum of flow expressed spatially by basin or sub-basin—limits our capacity to understand who has inadequate access to water and why this is the case. One aspect of this is the significant variations within these basins. For example, those living in the mountainous parts of the Indus Basin continue to rely upon monsoon-variable, rain-fed agriculture and tend to be economically and politically marginalised, whereas in the more prosperous parts of the basin, notably in both parts of (Indian and Pakistani) Punjab, agriculture generates high surplus returns and has provided the opportunity for diversification into non-agricultural industries.

In addition to these regional variations, there are also significant differences between social groups in terms of their control over and access to water. South

Asian societies are more often than not marked by significant inequalities that can typically, but imperfectly, be understood on the basis of social categories such as class, caste, gender and ethnicity. The headline figures on water scarcity cannot capture this complexity unless they are disaggregated on the basis of these social categories. The discursive construction of resource scarcity therefore needs to account more explicitly for the operation of power relations and how these are contested in social, economic and political domains. When we do this, we see that not everyone suffers from water stress in these 'water stressed' basins, and that those that do are likely to be marginalised in other respects as well. Lower caste or class communities are less likely to be able to access water and, when they do, they are more likely to have to enter water markets in order to do so. Women typically have less access to water than men and usually have to spend a considerable part of their working lives accessing it.

While all of these issues ostensibly appear to be mainly questions of limited water supply being outstripped by the multiple demands of a growing population, in reality, at the heart of the challenge of managing water across the Indus is the overcoming of poor governance on both sides of the border (Briscoe and Qamar, 2006; Hill, 2013; Khagram, 2004; Lahiri-Dutt and Wasson, 2008; Mustafa, Akhter and Nasralla, 2013; Roy, 1999). Numerous authors have extensively outlined the systemic failures of the high modernist ambitions of the state, with criticism frequently aimed at the lack of responsiveness from the government with regard to appropriate procedures for the mitigation of social, economic and environmental impacts (Choudhury, 2014; Erlewein, 2013). For example, in assessing governance challenges in Pakistan, Mustafa et al. (2013) argue that there is little evidence that the state intends to shift away from a culture where endemic corruption and little regulatory oversight are normalised. Moreover, there is significant bureaucratic fragmentation with different subjects handled by different departments, as well as numerous bodies of legislation in both India and Pakistan, related to minor and major irrigation, drainage, forestry and environmental protection.

Social, economic and political factors inherently drive who controls water in the Indus and the purpose for which they use it (Mustafa, 2010). One of most notable things about how this water allocation is materially contested in the Indus Basin is that it is mediated through relationships between the state and different social groups. Historically, water resource development in the Indus was extremely state-centric and technocratic in its orientation. While there have been some changes over time, this remains overwhelmingly the case. A range of authors has analysed and documented how the hydraulic state has consistently represented the interests of dominant classes in both India and Pakistan. In the work of Imran Ali (2004), for example, there is a clear demonstration of how the historical trajectory of the canal colonies from the colonial to the post-colonial period in Pakistan has intensified the control of Punjabi landlords, the military and the bureaucracy over

94    *D. Hill*

other social groups. To Ali, the control and distribution of water demonstrates how the state is an instrument of control for these classes and, as such, it is unsurprising that governance issues continue to bedevil the sector.

Thus, while it is certainly the case that Pakistan has a relatively low volume of water available per capita, an environmentally deterministic or neo-Malthusian explanation does not do justice to the institutional context that supports the promotion of the interests of a class of Punjabi large landholders, who themselves have strong connections with the bureaucratic and military apparatus of the Pakistani state (Ali, 2004). In a similar way, the prosperity of Punjabi and Jat farmers is underwritten by the Minimum Support Prices (MSPs) of the Government of India for the purchase of wheat and the highly subsidised electricity (and diesel) that enables the extraction of groundwater (Hill, 2003). An important farmers' movement has developed since the Green Revolution in different parts of India (and Pakistan, in different ways) that has led to widespread concessions for subsidised power, fertiliser, pesticides and, in particular, water. MSPs also continue to encourage the cultivation of water intensive crops, such as cotton, which contribute to the over-utilisation of irrigation, whether it is from canals, rivers or groundwater aquifers.

Thus, we might consider an environmentally deterministic account of intraregional differences between parts of the basin to focus on the relative ease of capturing and utilising water for intensive agriculture in the lower, flatter parts of the Indus Basin compared to the upland parts. In contrast, it is not simply the topography, but also the economic structure and political marginalisation of parts of the Indus, such as Azad Kashmir or Himachal Pradesh, which contribute to the fact that the gains from the development of the Indus Basin are extremely uneven in terms of both spatial distribution and social relations.

## Hydropower in the Indus

Disagreements over the appropriate scale and distribution of hydropower development represent an important factor in controversies over water sharing in the Indus Basin. Hydropower projects for both irrigation and energy have historically been the state's most visible intervention into the geographies of water, particularly in India. While large-scale dams can transfer surface water to areas of greatest demand at times when it is most needed, offer flood protection and be an important source of electricity, too often the gains from their construction in South Asia are not enough to offset the negative impacts that they have generated (D'Souza, 2008; Hill, 2013). Displacement and disruption of livelihoods for people living in the immediate environs of these dams have often been accompanied by impacts on both riverine and riparian ecosystems that have impacted people living downstream.

One of the ways in which we see most clearly that the control of water extends and intensifies pre-existing power relations between different groups within the Indus Basin is that, most often, dams are built in areas where marginalised groups live. Moreover, the building of these projects has significantly disadvantaged these kinds of communities, while creating new revenue streams for other, more powerful, groups. For marginalised peoples, projects that are promoted as being in the 'national interest' lead to the usurpation of their resources, their displacement and, more often than not, their impoverishment. The Tarbela Dam in Pakistan, which was completed in 1974, is a striking example of the failures of the state in this regard. More than 96,000 people from 135 villages were displaced, and despite large cash compensation outlays, many of them have yet to be adequately resettled even to this day (Hill, 2009). Similarly, in India there is a striking predominance of tribal people among those displaced as a consequence of the building of large-scale hydropower projects, despite their comparatively small proportion of the total population of India.

In addition to the state consistently favouring powerful groups within society at the expense of the marginalised, water resources policy also creates disputes between provinces. Indeed, in the Indus Basin, different provinces have long argued with each other over how much water should be utilised by the upper versus the lower riparian territory (Hill, 2008). We can see this most clearly in Pakistan, between Punjab and Sindh provinces, and in numerous examples in India, including between Punjab, Haryana and Rajasthan in the north-west of the country.

The culture around hydropower construction has meant that it has been difficult for other voices and perspectives to penetrate this sphere. In India, civil society has been extremely active in contesting these plans, although they struggle to be able to obtain data on the ecological or livelihood conditions of many rivers in India, particularly in the more remote areas such as Jammu and Kashmir (J&K). In Pakistan, civil society has less capacity to influence decision-making processes and the highly professionalised organisations that are able to participate in conversations about water resources, such as the Islamabad-based Sustainable Development Policy Institute (SDPI), are constrained in the manner in which they can dissent.

Water has also increasingly been securitised and this presents difficulty for those who are attempting to articulate a different vision of what the Indus Basin should be, and how the resources should be utilised. The Hydro Meteorological Data Dissemination Policy, notified in 2013, divides India into three regions, namely the Indus (Region 1), the Ganges, Brahmaputra Meghna (Region 2) and the rest of the country (Region 3). Data is supposed to be readily available for all basins in Region 3, but data about Regions 1 and 2 are subject to a regulatory environment because these data are 'classified' (Government of India, Ministry of Water Resources, 2013: 2).

## Controversies in Indian controlled parts of the Indus

The Chenab sub-basin, which includes the Indian controlled states of J&K and Himachal Pradesh, is one sub-region of the Indus Basin where the expansion of hydropower has been particularly controversial in recent years. The planned expansion of large-scale dams in J&K has attracted criticism for a wide variety of reasons (Hill, 2017). Seismologists suggest that building so many dams in a quake prone zone is hazardous, particularly because a great deal of the Chenab River runs along a fault line. The building of these projects has also been embroiled in Centre-State politics, particularly with regard to the Government of India's treatment of the troubled state of J&K. In that state, there are long-running complaints about the role of the Government of India-owned National Hydroelectric Power Corporation Ltd. (NHPC), which is one of the most significant companies in the entire country in terms of hydropower construction.

One of the objections to the role of the NHPC relates to the proportion of revenue from its hydropower projects given to the state government of J&K, with critics arguing that this should rise to 25 per cent from the current 12 per cent (Shah, 2015). Furthermore, to many people in J&K, the NHPC is directly responsible for the fact that the state continues to suffer significant load-shedding,[3] particularly during the winter, while also having high prices for electricity. Indeed, the state government wants the NHPC to return to state control a number of hydropower projects, including Salal, Uri-I and Dulhasti. Animosities are such that the state government is asserting that it will not give any more projects to the corporation and this is creating difficulties in the People's Democratic Party-Bharatiya Janata Party (PDP-BJP) alliance (Naikoo, 2015).

For its part, the Union Power Ministry rejects the arguments of the J&K government. It asserts that hydropower projects are the responsibility of many different ministries and, as such, the inter-ministerial nature of the projects means that there are too many financial and legal hurdles to return the projects. Further, it argues that the state government gains concessions, including a proportion of the total output as 'free' power, every time a new project begins operating. As such, the most advantageous position for the J&K government to take is to encourage the NHPC to build more dams. Indeed, the Union Power Minister recently asserted that since the Indian Himalayas contains a range of sites in other states, too much agitation from J&K would result in NHPC looking elsewhere.

It is not only in the J&K parts of the Chenab that hydropower construction is controversial. In the adjacent state of Himachal Pradesh, civil society groups have been protesting because a large number of the projects that have been proposed or are under construction have not been following appropriate procedures with regard to gaining clearance and undertaking consultation. They further suggest that, in the building of some of these projects, parts of the Kishtwar High Altitude National Park might be submerged and that environmental mitigation measures (such as fish ladders) have not been put in place and benefit sharing measures (such as adequate compensation for loss of land, or employment) have not been given to local people. Further, many Indian-based civil society groups object to the number of projects proposed or under construction, because no cumulative assessment has been carried out to evaluate their impact. The Union Ministry of Environment and Forests (MoEF) has specifically requested that such cumulative assessments be carried out; but the government of Himachal Pradesh has asked for waivers on environmental clearance, suggesting that cumulative assessments are against the interests of the state. Such a perspective clearly disregards the ecosystem services and the livelihoods of people that are currently living in the Chenab sub-basin and instead prioritises a model of development where large-scale projects can create economic growth and, in doing so, integrate economically poorer areas with wealthier ones, ostensibly for the benefit of both regions. Clearly, though, investment is in itself not enough; there must be a change in the relationship between local people and energy suppliers.

## International contestation of water and the discursive construction of scarcity

Clearly, resource scarcity in countries such as India and Pakistan needs to be understood in terms of the complex interaction between different stakeholders and how the debate is discursively constructed to privilege particular uses and understanding of water. Previous sections have demonstrated that this discursive construction and material contestation elides a whole range of power relations at a variety of scales. This section argues that this contestation takes on added complexity when the dispute over water allocation is between neighbouring countries.

At the whole-of-basin scale, the allocation of water is conditioned by the fact that the Partition of the Indian sub-continent divided the eastern and western rivers between India and Pakistan. The regulatory framework for this division was set out through the 1960 Indus Water Treaty (IWT) and the appointment of the Permanent Indus Commissioners to resolve any disputes or differences that arose between the two countries. While widely regarded as successful (Salman and Uprety, 2002), in recent years there has been debate about whether or not the IWT should be renegotiated (Sinha, 2016). Indeed, at least one influential commentator believes that the Treaty has outlived its usefulness and now is an impediment to both countries cooperating to maximise the possible mutual gains to be had in the Indus (Swain, 2016). Intensifying pressure on the Treaty is the contention over the legality and appropriateness of a range of individual projects in recent years.[4]

Disputes over transboundary water resources have different dimensions on either side of the basin. In India, the harnessing of these rivers is projected to decrease the marginalisation and underdevelopment of marginalised provinces, particularly the troubled J&K province, however, a long-standing collection of civil society groups rejects these claims as not being borne out by the history of dam building both in Kashmir and elsewhere in the country. In Pakistan, many groups use the issue of water sharing with India to create a common enemy,

98    D. Hill

including militant groups such as Jamaat-u-Dawa, who have sought to increase their constituency by continual assertions about India's intention to use water as a strategic weapon. It has been widely noted that the construction of projects in this sub-basin has been controversial because of the perceived impacts that this may have for Pakistan (Briscoe, 2010; Committee on Foreign Relations, 2011). Indeed, Pakistan objects to many projects on the Chenab, including the 1000 MW Pakal Dul, the 120 MW Miyar and the 48 MW Lower Kalnai hydropower projects (Alam, 2015). This continues to be a point of mobilisation, even if the Indus River System Authority (IRSA) itself admits that India is not causing water shortages in Pakistan (*The News International*, 2015).

## Environmental security in the Indus

When thinking through the manner in which the transboundary water resources become securitised in the Indus, it is clear that the terms of the debate about the costs and benefits of hydropower are frequently reduced to a binary representation of 'Indian' interests versus 'Pakistani' interests. The national interest of the nation-state must therefore be defended against the aggressive 'other' who is intent on stealing the 'nation's water'. In this rendering, the national resource of water is easily conflated with other issues of national interest. The portrayal of the Indus as indicative of a neo-Malthusian crisis of environmental security (*a la* Homer-Dixon, 1994; 1999) is reflected in the number of writings in the past few years, which suggest that a water war in the region is a possibility (Chellaney, 2011), although most commentators argue against such a position. A significant recent example of the role of water in the emerging security scenario of South Asia was the fallout after the confrontation at Uri, when Prime Minister Modi declared that 'blood and water cannot flow at the same time', with regard to India's relationship with Pakistan in the Indus Basin.[5] This prompted much speculation about the government's intention to renegotiate or even abandon the IWT, a move that never eventuated. In addition to issues that are clearly largely between India and Pakistan, the securitisation of the Indus Basin has arguably become intensified in the last few years as China has become a larger player in the geopolitics of water in the Indus and elsewhere in South Asia (Hill, 2013; Kondapalli, 2016).

This representation is problematic for a number of reasons. Firstly, by concentrating on the nation-state, the internal dynamics of water use within these countries is not given sufficient emphasis. Indeed, both India and Pakistan have been wasteful in how they have managed the waters and many of their problems are internally generated. To give just one example, canals in Pakistan have fallen in to disrepair, leading to high rates of conveyance loss in transporting water to fields that some estimate accounts for 25–30 per cent of the total (Kahlown and Kemper, 2005). Concentrating on the nation-state as the focus for discussion about the Indus Basin also elides the differential impact of any planned developments between upper and lower riparians within the same country (such as between Punjab and Sindh, for example). Secondly, although most water use in the basin is for agriculture, to confine the debate only to withdrawals for irrigation simplifies the relationship to broader ecosystem services. In so doing, the impacts on biodiversity are not given sufficient consideration. Thirdly, orthodox accounts of water security focus only on the capacity of the sovereign to enforce its territorial integrity against other sovereign states. This limited notion of what constitutes security ignores the issues of human or non-traditional security, which are nevertheless extremely pressing for many people in the Indus Basin.

## Moving beyond the current deadlock in the Indus Basin

We have established thus far that the discursive construction and material contestation of water scarcity in South Asia is implicated in a range of social, political, economic and ecological contestations. Indeed, we have seen that there is nothing natural or commonsensical about the water scarcity that prevails among many people in South Asia. Instead, it is as a consequence of a range of politics at a variety of scales. Development in the basin is all too often exclusionary and serves to inflame tensions between and within Pakistan and India, rather than being a catalyst for joint prosperity. Moreover, it is not only just in terms of human security that a new approach is demanded; the projected cumulative environmental effects of large-scale transformation of the Indus Basin also clearly demand the most serious consideration (Committee on Foreign Relations, 2011).

Clearly, then, in order to increase accountability, transparency and legitimacy of water resource planning in the Indus Basin, there is a need to include a range of other stakeholders and to craft robust and durable institutional arrangements that ensure their participation in the design and implementation of projects. How can such an institutional transformation be achieved in the Indus? One promising trajectory of change may be encouraging dialogue through a range of what Dore (2007) calls multi-stakeholder platforms. There is certainly a central role for Track 1 discussions[6] between the governments of India and Pakistan as is currently occurring as part of the Composite Dialogue.[7] However, beyond these formal bilateral processes, what is needed to build respect and capacity across the basin is a set of processes that encompass think tanks, parliamentarians and civil society. These can contribute to, and be engendered by, the de-securitisation of the politics of water at a range of scales.

Several authors have argued that there are hopeful developments occurring in the Indus and that these suggest new directions in the way water governance is approached (see Adeel and Wirsing 2017; Hill, 2013; 2016). The World Bank has thus far sponsored six rounds of the Abu Dhabi Dialogues under its South Asia Water Initiative (SAWI) and has now expanded to include a knowledge platform. These dialogues are informal and are intended to build

100  D. Hill

a shared basis of understanding (Hanasz, 2017).[8] As well as initiatives driven explicitly by multilateral organisations, there is a bourgeoning corpus of reports that has resulted from dialogues on the Indus,[9] which can serve as an important guide or roadmap to the broader debates about how the Indus could be governed. This roadmap seeks to look beyond the dominance of a supply side hydraulic paradigm that remains the frame of reference of water bureaucracies and to incorporate a number of other factors, such as ecosystem services, adaptive management and capacity building. The roundtables conducted as part of these processes are also important in building links across the Indus, because they can look beyond specific contentious projects.

In a more general sense, multi-track diplomacy initiatives in the Indus Basin are infrequently able to penetrate into government policy and offer significant criticism of government, lessening this potential to an even greater extent. Indeed, in a broader sense, civil society operates in extremely tight spaces with regard to being given 'a seat at the table' in the region, particularly in Pakistan, and there is much greater space given to service delivery than to advocacy groups. As such, many of those groups who are truly trying to challenge the institutional status quo are often excluded from such dialogues. Forging long-standing relationships between groups across the Indo-Pakistan national borders is clearly likely to remain extremely problematic for the foreseeable future.

## Conclusion

It is clear that a significant aspect of how water is discursively and materially constructed is through orthodox ideas of water security and water scarcity. However, as argued throughout this chapter, such conceptions tend to make assumptions about conditions throughout the Indus Basin and posit livelihoods in a way that does not disaggregate for the social geographies of different social groups, as might be understood on the basis of caste, class and gender. The elisions of these discursive constructions have become more pronounced in recent years as water has become increasingly securitised. Again, such an approach gives analytical primacy to the nation-state and the 'national interest' that is taken to be paramount when considering whose water and whose security is involved in the contestation over water.

Any change in the Indus Basin is constrained by a formidable combination of broader political relations, vested interests and a technocratic approach to water resource management that has the effect of discursively delimiting the debate about what can and should be done. As such, the opening of new political spaces around Indus water governance is a long and unenviably difficult process, and there are no guarantees of success in this regard. It is also clear that if water management is to have greater legitimacy among local stakeholders, new approaches must be utilised; but to do so is to challenge a range of power structures that currently exist. For those living in the more economically and politically marginalised parts of the basin, future approaches cannot simply replicate the previous experiences of development in the Indian- and Pakistani-held parts of the Himalayas.

In recent years, a significant counter-discourse has emerged from stakeholders beyond the Indian and Pakistani states, which seeks to imagine Indus Basin-wide management in ways that can augment and ultimately transform existing approaches (Bakshi and Trivedi, 2011; Indus Basin Working Group, 2013; ICPC, n.d). These counter-discourses argue for a move beyond the supply side hydraulic paradigm that remains the dominant frame of reference of water bureaucracies in South Asia. Basin-wide management requires these institutions to consider both upstream and downstream communities and, in doing so, pay equal attention to the watersheds, catchments and headwaters of the Indus Basin (Rasul, 2010; 2014). However, translating these recommendations for enhanced attention to inclusive development, ecosystem services and adaptive management into tangible actions requires capacity building as well as institutional transformation. This process is not simply a mindset shift for policy makers, but is instead an inherently political process that challenges vested interests at a range of scales across the basin.

## Notes

1 Water stress is the ratio of total water withdrawals to available renewable supply in an area. In high-stress areas, 40 per cent or more of the available supply is withdrawn every year. In extremely high-stress areas, that number goes up to 80 per cent or higher. A higher percentage means more water users are competing for limited supplies.
2 This includes both terrestrial species as well as a large number and diversity of aquatic species in the many tributaries.
3 Load-shedding is a term used in many parts of South Asia to describe a situation where electricity is unavailable for certain periods of the day (e.g., eight hours of load-shedding per day). This is used to ration the amount of available power, with the professed aim of making power available when it is needed most.
4 These include the Salal Dam and the Baglihar Hydel Power Project, both on the Chenab, and the Wullar Barrage/Tulbul Navigation Project on the River Jhelum, and the (Pakistani) Neelum-Jhelum and (Indian) Kishanganga projects. On this, see Hill (2013).
5 Uri is a sector of Indian controlled Kashmir. On 18 September 2016 an Indian army base was attacked and 18 Indian soldiers were killed. For its part, the Government of India has asserted that this attack could have been carried out by militants associated with the Pakistan based group Jaish-e-Mohammed (JeM). The Government of Pakistan denies this. See 'Uri attack: initial reports indicate JeM involvement, says military operations chief', *Scroll.in*, 18 September 2016; and 'Blood and water can't flow together, Narendra Modi says on Indus treaty with Pakistan: ANI', *Scroll.in*, 26 September 2016.
6 Track 1 dialogue refers to those discussions that are held between governments. Other tracks, such as Tracks 2 or 3, might include donors, civil society or academia among others. On multi-track water diplomacy, see Islam and Susskind (2012).

102    *D. Hill*

7 The Composite Dialogues began in 1997 as an agreement between the Prime Ministers of India and Pakistan to attempt to discuss a range of issues simultaneously, since it was seen that this might help build confidence between the countries. Perhaps the most important aspect of this peace process was that it meant that India agreed to discuss the issue of Kashmir. On the Composite Dialogue, see Padder (2012).
8 While they include all seven countries involved in Himalayan water sharing, they nevertheless represent an opportunity for stakeholders from Pakistan and India to understand each other's perspectives, with the last iteration (2012) having a focus on transboundary collaboration for floods and disaster management, including in the Indus (International Bank for Reconstruction and Development, 2013).
9 Such dialogues are usually organised jointly between Indian and Pakistani think tanks with collaboration from outside agencies such as the Atlantic Council or Stimson Center. See Ahmad (2012) and Indus Basin Working Group (2013).

## References

Adeel, Z. and Wirsing, R. (eds) (2017) *Imagining Industan: Overcoming water Insecurity in the Indus Basin.* New York: Springer.

Ahmad, S. (2012) 'Water insecurity: a threat for Pakistan and India', Issue Brief. Washington, DC: South Asia Center, Atlantic Council.

Akhter, M. (2017) 'The political ecology of the water scarcity/security nexus in the Indus Basin: decentering per capita water supply', in Z. Adeel and R. Wirsing (eds) *Imagining Industan: Overcoming Water Insecurity in the Indus Basin.* New York: Springer, pp. 21–33.

Alam, I. (2015) 'Pakistan to move ICJ over India's water aggression', *The Nation*, 9 February, available: http://nation.com.pk/national/09-Feb-2015/pakistan-to-move-icj-over-india-s-water-aggression [accessed 29 March 2017].

Ali, I. (2004) 'Historical impact on political economy of Pakistan', *Asian of Journal Management Cases*, 1(2), pp. 129–46.

Ali, S.H. and Zia, A. (2017) 'Transboundary data sharing and resilience scenarios: Harnessing the role of regional organizations for environmental security', in Z. Adeel and R. Wirsing (eds) *Imagining Industan: Overcoming Water Insecurity in the Indus Basin.* New York: Springer, pp. 121–139.

Alley K.D. (2004) 'The making of a river linking plan in India: suppressed science and spheres of expert debate'. *India Review*, 3(3), pp. 210–238.

Bakshi, G. and Trivedi, S. (2011) 'The Indus equation', Mumbai, Strategic Foresight Group, available: http://www.strategicforesight.com/publication_pdf/10345110617.pdf [accessed 29 March 2017].

Bandyopadhyay, J. and Perveen, S. (2003) 'The interlinking of Indian rivers: some questions on the scientific, economic and environmental dimensions of the proposal', Occasional Paper No. 60, SOAS Water Issues Study Group. London, School of Oriental and African Studies/King's College London University of London (June).

Briscoe J. and Qamar, U. (2006) *Pakistan's Water Economy: Running Dry.* Washington, DC: The World Bank and Oxford University Press.

Briscoe, J. (2010) 'Troubled waters: can a bridge be built over the Indus?', *Economic and Political Weekly*, 45(50), pp. 28–32.

## Whose scarcity, whose security? 103

Burgess, P.J., Owen, T. and Sinha, U.K. (2016) 'Human securitization of water? A case study of the Indus Waters Basin', *Cambridge Review of International Affairs*, 29(2), pp. 382–407.

Chellaney, B. (2011) *Water: Asia's New Battleground*. Washington, DC: Georgetown University Press.

Choudhury, N. (2014) 'Environment in an emerging economy: the case of environmental impact assessment follow-up in India', in M. Nüsser (ed.) *Large Dams in Asia: Contested Environments between Technological Hydroscapes and Social Resistance*. Dordrecht: Springer, pp. 101–124.

Committee on Foreign Relations (2011) 'Avoiding water wars: water scarcity and Central Asia's growing Importance for stability in Afghanistan and Pakistan', A Majority Staff Report, One Hundred Twelfth Congress, First Session. Washington, DC: US Government Printing Office.

D'Souza, R. (2008) 'Framing India's hydraulic crisis: the politics of the modern large dam', *Monthly Review*, 60(3), pp. 112–124.

D'Souza, R. (2014) 'Peace is not possible and war is not an option! Should we still be "talking up" nontraditional security?', *Strategic Analysis*, 38(5), pp. 741–748.

D'Souza, R. (2016) 'Pulses against volumes: trans-boundary rivers and pan-Asian connectivity', in S. Ganguly and K. Stoll Farrell (eds) *Heading East: The Dynamics of Security, Trade, and Environment between India and Southeast Asia*. Delhi: Oxford University Press, pp. 240–253.

Dore, J., (2007) 'Multi-stakeholder platforms: unfulfilled potential', in L. Lebel, R. Daniel and Y.S. Koma (eds) *Democratising Water Governance in the Mekong Region*. Chiang Mai: Mekong Press, pp. 197–226.

Erlewein, A. (2013) 'Disappearing rivers—the limits of environmental assessment for hydropower in India', *Environmental Impact Assessment Review*, 43: 135–143

Faiz, A.-u.-H. (2007) *India-Pakistan Dialogue: Bringing the Society*. Colombo, Sri Lanka: Regional Center for Strategic Studies.

Gazdar, H. (2005) 'Baglihar and politics of water: a historical perspective from Pakistan', *Economic and Political Weekly*, 40(9), pp. 813–817.

Gilmartin, D. (2015) *Blood and Water: The Indus Basin in Modern History*. Oakland, CA: University of California Press.

Government of India, Ministry of Water Resources (2013) 'Hydro-meteorological data dissemination policy', available: http://www.cwc.nic.in/main/downloads/hddp2013.pdf [accessed 29 May 2017].

Haines, D (2016) *Rivers Divided: Indus Basin Waters in the Making of India and Pakistan*, London: Hurst & Co.; New York: Oxford University Press.

Hanasz, P. (2018) *Transboundary Water Governance and International Actors in South Asia: The Ganges-Brahmaputra-Meghna Basin*. London: Routledge.

Hill, D.P. (2003) 'Food security, governance and rural development in India under the BJP', *South Asia: Journal of South Asian Studies*, 25(3), pp. 147–164.

Hill, D.P. (2008) 'The regional politics of water sharing: contemporary issues in South Asia', in K. Lahiri-Dutt and R. Wasson (eds) *Water First: Issues and Challenges for Nations and Communities*. New Delhi: Sage, pp. 59–80.

Hill, D.P. (2009) 'Boundaries, scale and power in South Asia', in D. Ghosh, H. Goodall and S. Donald (eds) *Water, Sovereignty, and Borders in Asia and Oceania*. New York: Routledge, pp. 87–103.

## 104   D. Hill

Hill, D.P. (2013) 'Trans-boundary water resources, crisis and uneven development in South Asia', *South Asia: Journal of South Asian Studies*, 32(2), pp. 243–257.

Hill, D.P. (2015) 'Where hawks dwell on water and bankers build power poles: transboundary waters, environmental security and the frontiers of neo-liberalism', *Strategic Analysis*, 39(6), pp. 729–743.

Hill, D. P. (2016) 'Regional integration and its discontents: The case of transboundary water sharing', in K. S. Farrell and S. Ganguly (eds) *Heading East: Security, trade, and Environment between India and Southeast Asia*. Oxford: Oxford University Press, pp. 195–215.

Hill, D.P. (2017) 'The Indus Basin: the potential for basin-wide management between India and Pakistan', in Z. Adeel and R. Wirsing (eds) *Imagining Industan: Overcoming Water Insecurity in the Indus Basin*. New York: Springer, pp. 141–158.

Homer-Dixon, T.F. (1994) 'Environmental scarcities and violent conflict: evidence from cases', *International Security*, 1(5), pp. 5–40.

Homer-Dixon, T.F. (1999) *Environment Scarcity and Violence*. Princeton, NJ: Princeton University Press.

Indus Basin Working Group (2013) 'Connecting the drops: an Indus Basin roadmap for cross-border water research, data sharing and policy coordination', Washington, DC: Stimson, available: https://www.stimson.org/sites/default/files/fileattachments/connecting_the_drops_stimson_1.pdf [accessed 29 March 2017].

International Bank for Reconstruction and Development (2013) *South Asia Water Initiative 2009–2013 Final Report*. Washington, DC: World Bank.

Islam S. and L. Susskind, (2012) *Water Diplomacy: A Negotiated Approach to Managing Complex Water Networks*. Oxford/New York: RFF Press/Routledge.

Jaitly, A. (2009) 'South Asian perspectives on climate change and water policy', in D. Michael and A. Pandya (eds) *Troubled Waters: Climate Change, Hydropolitics, and Transboundary Resources*. Washington, DC: The Henry L. Stimson Center, pp. 17–31.

Kahlown M. A. and W.D. Kemper (2005) 'Reducing water losses from channels using linings: costs and benefits in Pakistan', *Agricultural Water Management*, 74, pp. 57–76.

Khagram, S. (2004) *Dams and Development: Transnational Struggles for Water and Power*. Ithaca: Cornell University Press.

Kondapalli, S. (2016) 'The Indus Basin: The potential for Basin-Wide Management between China and its Himalayan Neighbours India and Pakistan', in Z. Adeel and R.G. Wirsing (eds) *Imagining Industan: Overcoming Water Insecurity in the Indus Basin*. Switzerland: Springer, pp. 159–176.

Kugelman, M. and R.M. Hathaway (eds) (2009) *Running on Empty: Pakistan's Water Crisis*. Washington DC: Woodrow International Centre for Scholars.

Laghari, A., Vanham, N.D. and Rauch, W. (2012) 'The Indus basin in the framework of current and future water resources management', *Hydrology and Earth System Sciences*, 16(4), pp. 1063–1083.

Lahiri-Dutt K. and Wasson, R.J. (eds) (2008) *Water First: Issues and Challenges for Nations and Communities in South Asia*. New Delhi: Sage.

Mustafa, D. (2010) 'Hydropolitics in Pakistan's Indus Basin', Special Report No. 261, United States Institute of Peace, Washington, DC.

Mustafa, D., Akhter, M. and Nasralla, N. (2013) *Understanding Pakistan's Water-Security Nexus*. Washington, DC: United States Institute of Peace.

Naikoo, J. (2015) 'After article 370, NHPC power projects hamper PDP-BJP alliance,' *Early Times*, 7 January, available: http://www.earlytimes.in/m/newsdet.aspx?q=139912 [accessed 29 March 2017].

National Research Council, and Committee on Population (2012) *Himalayan Glaciers: Climate Change, Water Resources, and Water Security*. Washington, DC: National Academies Press.

Padder, S. (2012) 'The composite dialogue between India and Pakistan: structure, process and agency', *Heidelberg Papers in South Asian and Comparative Politics*. Working Paper No. 65, Heidelberg: University of Heidelberg.

Padma, T.V. (2016) 'India's Grand Plan to create world's largest river set to go', *New Scientist*, 28 November, available: https://www.newscientist.com/article/2114431-indias-grand-plan-to-create-worlds-longest-river-set-to-go/ [accessed 29 May 2017].

Rasul G. (2010) 'The role of the Himalayan mountain systems in food security and agricultural sustainability in South Asia', *International Journal of Rural Management*, 6(1), pp. 95–116.

Rasul, G. (2014) 'Food, water and energy security in South Asia: a nexus perspective from the Hindu Kush Himalayan region', *Environmental Science and Policy*, 39, pp. 35–48.

Read, L. and Kuhl, L. (2015) 'Bringing the elephant into the room: integrating risk into interdisciplinary water programmes', *Journal of Contemporary Water Research and Education*, (155), pp. 19–27.

Rodell, M., Velicogna, I. and Famiglietti, J.S. (2009) 'Satellite-based estimates of groundwater depletion in India', *Nature*, 460(7258), pp. 999–1002.

Roy, A. (1999) *The Cost of Living*. London: Flamingo.

Salman S.M.A and Uprety, K. (2002) *Conflicts and Cooperation on South Asia's International Rivers: A Legal Perspective*. London: Kluwer Law International.

Sarwar, B. (2014) 'Pakistan's media wars', *Himal South Asian*, 4 July, available: http://himalmag.com/pakistans-media-wars/ [accessed 29 March 2017].

Scroll.in (2016) 'Blood and water can't flow together, Narendra Modi says on Indus treaty with Pakistan: ANI', *Scroll.in*, 26 September 2016 (updated 3 January 2017), available: https://scroll.in/latest/817544/blood-and-water-cant-flow-together-narendra-modi-says-on-indus-treaty-with-pakistan-ani [accessed 29 May 2017].

Scroll.in (2016) 'Uri attack: Initial reports indicate JeM involvement, says military operations chief', Scroll.in, 18 September, available: https://scroll.in/latest/816848/uri-attack-initial-reports-indicate-jem-involvement-says-military-operations-chief [accessed 29 May 2017].

Shah, U. (2015) 'Time to call return of power projects from NHPC', *Kashmir Monitor*, 4 March, available: http://www.kashmirmonitor.in/Details/80381/time-to-call-return-of-power-projects-from-nhpc [accessed 29 May 2017].

Singh, S.P., Bassignana-Khadka, I., Karky, B.S. and Sharma, E. (2011) *Climate Change in the Hindu Kush-Himalayas: The State of Current Knowledge*. Kathmandu: ICIMOD.

Sinha, U.K. (2016) *Riverine Neighbourhood: Hydropolitics in South Asia*. Delhi: Pentagon Press.

Surie, M. and Prasai, S. (2015) 'Strengthening transparency and access to information on transboundary rivers in South Asia', The Asia Foundation, New Delhi.

Swain, A. (2016) 'Review the Indus Waters Treaty, not for revenge but for development and peace', Scroll.in, 30 September, available: https://scroll.in/article/817641/review-the-indus-waters-treaty-not-for-revenge-but-for-development-and-peace [accessed 29 May 2017].

The News International (2015) 'India not causing water shortage in Pakistan: Irsa', *The News International*, 12 July, available: https://www.thenews.com.pk/print/13570-india-not-causing-water-shortage-in-pakistan-irsa [accessed 29 March 2017].

Wald, N. and Hill, D.P. (2016) '"Rescaling" alternative food systems: from food security to food sovereignty', *Agriculture and Human Values*, 33(1), pp. 203–213.

# 7 Protecting our global ocean heritage

## Unprecedented threats will require bold interventions

*Todd L. Capson*

## Introduction

Over the coming century, marine organisms will be confronted with a suite of environmental conditions that have no analogue in human history. The effects of overexploitation, habitat degradation and other impacts on marine ecosystems stand to be amplified by changes in ocean temperature and chemistry. Just as the threats to the world's oceans are unprecedented, successfully addressing them will require an unprecedented degree of political will, transparency, cooperation and boldness. In 2014, US Secretary of State John Kerry initiated the Our Oceans initiative with a focus on some of the key ocean issues of our time: fisheries, marine protected areas (MPAs) and climate-related impacts on the oceans, each of which I will address in this chapter.

It is instructive to place the issues discussed in this chapter in the context of resource scarcity. Extractive activities such as fisheries are not only depleting fish stocks of global importance but are also restructuring key ecosystems. This has led to a scarcity of resources that affects not only humans but other species that depend upon those resources. A classic example of the impacts of capture fisheries on other species in an ecosystem regards the decline in the Alaska Steller sea lion and commercial fisheries (Hennen, 2006). The walleye pollock is the largest fishery by weight in the United States and one of the largest in the world—fishermen landed almost three billion pounds in 2011 with a dockside value of just under $375 million (National Marine Fisheries Service, 2013). At the same time, the Steller sea lion population in Alaska declined by more than 80 per cent between 1970–2000, prompting the species to be listed as 'threatened' under the Endangered Species Act (ESA) (National Research Council, 2003). In November 2000, an ESA consultation prepared by the National Marine Fisheries Service concluded that the Alaska groundfish fishery posed a threat to the recovery of the Steller sea lion and imposed more restrictive measures on its management. While the exact nature of the relationship between the captures of groundfish and the decline in Steller sea lion populations remains controversial, positive correlations exist between several metrics of historical fishing activity and the population decline (Hennen, 2006).

108  *T. L. Capson*

As described below, recent studies indicate that many well-assessed fisheries in developed countries are moving towards sustainability, which suggests that scarcity is not a significant problem for the fish stocks involved. The situation is different, however, in the developing world where fish populations are on a continuing trajectory of decline with repercussions for local and national economies and food security (Pikitch, 2012; Costello et al., 2012). Despite this trend, there are examples of well-managed fish stocks in Latin America and in the Western and Central Pacific Ocean, including fisheries that have been certified by the Marine Stewardship Council (see, for example, Orensanz and Seijo, 2013; Marine Stewardship Council, 2016a; 2016b).

Also addressed in this chapter, and relevant to the issue of scarcity, are MPAs, which are indisputably the flagship tool for protecting both ecosystems and biodiversity by limiting direct human impacts (Mouillot et al., 2015). The importance of MPAs in protecting biodiversity is reflected in the targets that were established during the tenth meeting of the Conference of the Parties of the Convention for Biological Diversity in October 2010, one of which explicitly addresses the expansion of both marine and terrestrial protected areas. The scarcity of both marine and terrestrial resources in Panama is reflected in my efforts to establish a protected area in the country's Tropical Eastern Pacific, as I describe in this chapter.

Understanding how climate change is likely to alter the fisheries revenues of maritime countries is a crucial next step towards the development of effective socioeconomic policy and food sustainability strategies to mitigate and adapt to climate change (Lam et al., 2016). Recent studies reveal that climate change is already having an impact on fisheries, in particular, warmer ocean temperatures are driving marine species towards cooler, deeper waters and this, in turn, has affected global fisheries catches (Cheung et al., 2013). Developing countries that are dependent on fisheries for food and livelihoods are likely to be the hardest hit. I address in this chapter the closely related issue of ocean acidification. Regions that are particularly vulnerable to ocean acidification include the cold waters of the North and South Poles, which naturally absorb more carbon dioxide ($CO_2$) from the atmosphere than warmer waters do, and areas with upwelling currents that bring more acidic waters to the surface. Given that both types of regions contain globally important fisheries, rising $CO_2$ levels will lead to a scarcity of species that are the target of commercially important fisheries, such as the walleye pollock, and those that depend upon them, such as the Steller sea lion.

## Fisheries: between sustainability and depletion

The debate on the sustainability of fisheries has moved to a global level over the past 20 years as fisheries have become recognised as a major driver of ecological and evolutionary change in the world's oceans (Worm and Branch, 2012). The global demand for seafood is increasing, driven in part

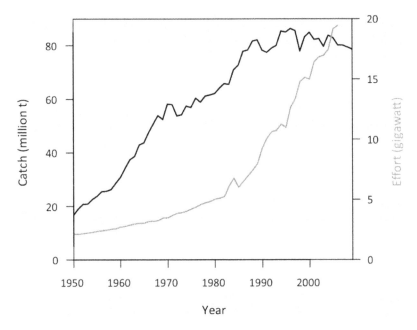

*Figure 7.1* Increases in global catches (dark line, reported tonnage to FAO) and fishing effort (light line, total engine power in gigawatts [109 watts] expended per year)

Source: Adapted from Worm and Branch (2012) (used with permission from the authors

by a growing population and rising incomes in countries such as China and India (Béné et al., 2015). The UN Food and Agriculture Organization (FAO) estimates that there is no room for expansion of 90 per cent of monitored fish stocks as they are either fully exploited or overexploited (FAO, 2016a). A study by Pauly and Zeller (2016) reports that even these statistics are conservative as they understate the size of the global seafood catch by about 30 per cent. In particular, fishers caught an estimated 109 million metric tons (mt) of fish in 2010, well above the 77 million mt reported by the FAO. An analysis of global catch data by Worm and Branch (2012) showed that catches peaked during the mid-1990s and have since declined despite an *increase* in fishing effort over the same time period (Figure 7.1).

While many marine species have declined in abundance and are regionally and/or functionally extinct, there are still only a few well-documented examples of global marine extinctions in recent centuries (Harnik et al., 2012). Consequently, meaningful rehabilitation of affected marine animal populations remains within the reach of marine resource managers (McCauley et al., 2015).

# 110   T. L. Capson

## Assessed stocks stabilise, others decline

Recent reports suggest that many well-assessed fisheries in developed countries are moving towards sustainability while previously unassessed fish populations are on a continuing trajectory of decline (Pikitch, 2012; Costello et al., 2012). These poorly understood fisheries, which represent about 80 per cent of the world's fish catch, are in much worse shape than the relatively well-studied fisheries upon which previous reviews of global fish stocks have relied. A key problem in global fisheries is that much of the world's catch, and a large fraction of its biodiversity, resides in regions that urgently require increased food production and employment, but that have little capacity for scientific assessment and management controls (Worm and Branch, 2012). Africa, Asia and Latin America harbour most of the marine fish species richness and are hotspots of marine biodiversity, but have lower capacity for scientific assessment of fish stocks and management controls than other regions. Good fisheries management does not require perfect science if precautionary measures are taken. Tools for the assessment of fish stocks have been developed to meet the requirements of fisheries management where information on fish populations is either lacking or highly uncertain, making these tools particularly useful in resource-poor settings (Pilling et al., 2008). Among the assessed fish stocks are the target species of regional fisheries management organisations (RFMOs). Any country's commercial fishing fleets that wish to fish in regions of the high seas managed by an RFMO must abide by the conservation and management measures of the organisation (Cullis-Suzuki and Pauly, 2010). There are five tuna RFMOs, one of which—the Western and Central Pacific Fisheries Commission (WCPFC)—is discussed by Jollands and Fisher (this volume, Chapter 11). As I will discuss below, tuna RFMOs have significant impacts on non-target species.

## The role of aquaculture in reducing pressures on wild fisheries

Between 1987 and 1997, global production of farmed fish and shellfish more than doubled in weight and value (Naylor et al., 2000). Aquaculture now provides half of all fish for human consumption (FAO, 2016b). Many people believe that such growth may relieve pressure on ocean fisheries, but the opposite is true for some types of aquaculture, and the conversion of habitats, pollution, disease and diversion of forage fish from poor communities threaten its sustainability (Smith et al., 2010).

## Bycatch: implications for marine ecosystems and food security

Fish is a critical source of protein in the developing world (UN General Assembly, 2011). There are at least 30 countries in which fisheries contribute more than one-third of total animal protein supply, 22 of which are low-income food-deficit countries (LIFDCs) (FAO, 2014). Despite the critical importance of fish to diets in the developing world, limited attention has been given to

*Protecting our global ocean heritage* 111

fish as a key element in food security and nutrition strategies in development discussions and interventions at national levels and beyond (Béné et al., 2015). Going forward, it will be increasingly important to take advantage of all accessible sources of seafood. One such source is 'bycatch', which is the catch that is not the main objective of a fishing fleet and consists of: (i) retained catch of non-targeted, but commercially valuable species; (ii) discarded catch, whether the reason for non-retention is economic or regulatory; and (iii) unobserved mortalities (Gilman, 2011). Eighty per cent of global bycatch comes from industrial fishing fleets, generating an estimated *7.3 billion kg annually* of highly nutritious seafood, much of which is wasted (Béné et al., 2015; Smith et al., 2010). Retaining bycatch for human consumption also means that a ship's hold will fill up faster, reducing total capture of both target and non-target species, and has the benefit of driving fisheries towards selective fishing gears and the avoidance of areas and times with high bycatch (Chan et al., 2014).

There are also important ecological considerations associated with bycatch. Minimising or eliminating bycatch is necessary to maintaining marine biodiversity, ecosystem structure, processes and services, including sustainable fishery resources. Bycatch in purse seine and pelagic longline tuna fisheries— the two primary gear types for catching tunas—is a primary mortality source of some populations of seabirds, sea turtles, marine mammals and sharks (Gilman, 2011). There has been substantial progress in identifying gear technology solutions to seabird, sea turtle and dolphin bycatch, and, with sufficient investment, gear technology solutions are probably feasible for the remaining bycatch problems. Most binding conservation and management measures of tuna RFMOs fall short of gear technology best practice for minimising bycatch. The lack of quantifiable performance standards for reducing bycatch, inadequate observer coverage for all but large Pacific Ocean purse seiners in the Inter-American Tropical Tuna Commission (IATTC) and the WCPFC, and incomplete data collection on bycatch captures, hinder the ability to assess the efficacy of RFMO conservation and management measures and vessel crew's compliance with those measures (Gilman, 2011).

### Illegal, unreported and unregulated (IUU) fishing

IUU fishing is prevalent worldwide (Agnew et al., 2009) and has been identified as one of the greatest threats to marine ecosystems by the UN General Assembly (Österblom and Bodin, 2012). Estimates of total IUU catches globally range from 11 to 26 million tons annually, and the monetary value of IUU catch ranges from US$10 to $23.5 billion. Developing countries are particularly vulnerable to IUU fishing due to their limited governance and enforcement capacity over their fish stocks (Agnew et al., 2009). IUU fishing has generated significant attention recently, as evidenced in encounters with illegal vessels on the high seas (Urbina, 2015) and the capture and destruction of vessels fishing within the exclusive economic zone of Indonesia (Bever, 2016). In many other instances, IUU has been largely overlooked, particularly

## 112    T. L. Capson

where it is unreported and unregulated. For example, small-scale fisheries that cumulatively include about 90 per cent of the world's fishers are ubiquitous in the world's coastal waters but generally operate without controls or records (Vincent and Harris, 2014; Worm and Branch, 2012). Most of these 100 million or so fishers depend on the ocean for livelihoods and exploit marine resources persistently and intensely. Such relentless pressure has led to fisheries collapse and the serial depletion of species (Vincent and Harris, 2014).

### Addressing IUU fishing

A range of tools, international agreements and management practices have been implemented to address IUU fishing, several of which are presented below. The sections in this chapter entitled *Marine protected areas* and *Optimal management regimes for rebuilding global fisheries*, discuss two additional means of addressing IUU fishing.

#### UN Port State Measures Agreement

Twenty-nine countries and the European Union (EU) have become parties to the 2009 FAO Agreement on Port State Measures to Prevent, Deter and Eliminate IUU Fishing (FAO, 2016a). The agreement officially entered into force on 5 June 2016, making it the world's first ever binding international accord specifically targeting IUU fishing to become international law. The treaty requires that parties designate specific ports for use by foreign vessels, making monitoring and control far easier. Those vessels must request permission to enter ports ahead of time, provide local authorities with information on the fish they have on board and allow inspection of their log book, licences, fishing gear and actual cargo, among other requirements. The Agreement calls on countries to deny entry or inspect vessels that have been involved in IUU fishing and to take necessary action, including the sharing of information regionally and globally about any vessels discovered to be involved in IUU fishing.

#### Technology platforms to detect and deter IUU fishing

Global Fishing Watch is the product of a technology partnership between SkyTruth, Oceana and Google that is designed to show all of the trackable fishing activity in the ocean (Global Fishing Watch, 2016). This interactive web tool is being built to enable anyone to visualise the global fishing fleet in space and time. A global feed of vessel locations is extracted from Automatic Identification System (AIS), tracking data that is collected by satellite and revealing the movement of vessels. Another recent technology used to combat IUU fishing is electronic monitoring, which automatically collects high-resolution data on when and where each boat is fishing, the type of activity in which a

Protecting our global ocean heritage   113

vessel is engaged and the composition of catch, bycatch and discards (WCPFC, 2013). Electronic monitoring has the advantage of being deployable on a wide range of vessels, including smaller ones where personal accommodations are limited and on vessels that spend long periods at sea.

*Cooperation between levels of government and capacity for enforcement*

Enhanced cooperation between communities and local managers, provincial governments and national governments, working on different scales to regulate and enforce fisheries laws, could have a major impact on IUU fishing (Vincent and Harris, 2014). In countries that lack the capacity for effective fisheries management and enforcement, government engagement must be accompanied by serious investments in technical capacity and governance skills in order for government agencies to work at their full potential (Costello et al., 2016).

*Public and scientific engagement*

The political will to effectively conserve marine species and spaces will only emerge when public opinion insists on action for ocean protection. Market-based incentives for the purchase of sustainable seafood provide a means to involve consumers and fishers in making choices that foster sustainable fishing (Vincent and Harris, 2014). The community of conservation professionals, from both academia and non-governmental organisations (NGOs), must do a much better job at communicating a compelling and comprehensive vision of the threats to ocean health, including IUU fishing, that transcends traditional disciplinary and societal boundaries and the immediate needs of their institutions (Noss et al., 2011).

*EU rules to combat IUU fishing*

The EU works to close the loopholes that allow illegal operators to profit from their activities including an EU Regulation to prevent, deter and eliminate IUU fishing that entered into force on 1 January 2010. Among the regulation's provisions include: (i) only marine fisheries products validated as legal by the competent flag state or exporting state can be imported to, or exported from, the EU; (ii) the publication of an IUU vessel list that is updated regularly and based on IUU vessels identified by RFMOs; and (iii) the potential blacklisting of states that turn a blind eye to illegal fishing activities (European Commission, 2016). In one case, the European Commission put Thailand on formal notice for not taking sufficient measures in the international fight against IUU fishing by issuing a warning (yellow card) that it needed to improve its poorly regulated seafood industry or face 'red card' bans on exports to the EU market (European Commission, 2015).

## 114 T. L. Capson

*Elimination of bottom trawl fisheries and improving data collection for capture of non-target species in tuna RFMOs*

Of all indiscriminate fisheries, bottom trawling is the most catastrophic for both species and habitats. It also contributes substantially to IUU take, mainly through bycatch (Vincent and Harris, 2014). The incomplete data collection on bycatch captures in tuna RFMOs also contributes to large gaps in our understanding of the scope and magnitude of the captures of non-target species.

### Shark conservation

Efforts to conserve shark populations provide an example of the need to address marine conservation efforts on multiple fronts, including fisheries. Despite their evolutionary success, many species of chondrichthyans, which include sharks and their relatives, are increasingly threatened with extinction as a result of their low reproductive rates in the face of human activities, primarily overfishing (Camhi et al., 2009). Quantifying the extent of sharks' decline, the risk of species extinction and the consequences for marine ecosystems has been challenging and controversial, mostly due to data limitations. In the most comprehensive study to date of shark mortality, Worm et al. (2013) considered all sources of mortality, from direct fishing, finning and discard mortality, and concluded that sharks are being harvested at an unsustainable rate (approximately 100 million sharks per year for the period 2000 through 2010, which is highly likely an underestimate of shark mortality). Though many estimates and approximations went into calculating these figures, one message is clear: *sharks are being harvested at an unsustainable rate and global shark mortality needs to be reduced drastically in order to rebuild depleted populations and restore marine ecosystems with functional top predators.* Another key finding is that, despite increased public awareness and advocacy, the authors did not detect a significant decrease in shark fin consumption over the period 2000–2010, suggesting that the publicity associated with finning and the regulations that resulted do not appear to have reduced the volume of fins traded in global or regional markets (Worm et al., 2013).

There are a growing number of studies that address the ecological consequences of declines in shark populations and suggest that wider community rearrangements often follow declines in shark populations (Ferretti et al., 2010; Worm et al., 2013). Large sharks can exert strong control on the large long-lived marine animals that they prey upon. In a study on the cascading effects of the loss of 11 apex predatory sharks from a US coastal ocean, whose populations fell between 87 and 97 per cent over a 35-year period, the populations of other elasmobranchs (rays, skates and small sharks) that they consumed exploded, resulting in the loss of a century-long scallop fishery (Myers et al., 2007).

### Shark captures on the high seas

Shark captures in large-scale purse seiners provide a window into shark mortality on the high seas. Figure 7.2 reveals the difference between captures of the

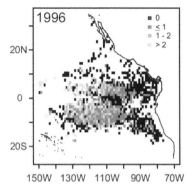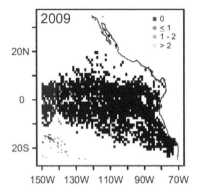

*Figure 7.2* Oceanic whitetip shark in the Eastern Pacific Ocean. Average oceanic whitetip capture per floating object set in 1996 (left) and 2009 (right).
Source: Guillermo Compeán, IATTC (used with permission from the author)

oceanic whitetip shark (*Carcharhinus longimanus*) in tuna purse seine vessels of the IATTC in 1996 (left panel) and 2009 (right panel) in the Eastern Pacific Ocean. The extent to which the difference in the numbers of sharks captured in 1996 and 2009 reflects oceanic whitetip sharks captured in purse seine fisheries, is a reflection of shark mortality caused primarily by other fisheries (e.g. longline) or is some combination of the two is not clear. What is clear, however, is that, in 2009, there were far fewer oceanic whitetip sharks left to be captured than in 1996. The authors of a recent report by the IATTC that drew upon this data wrote, 'The signal in this case is impossible to miss—the species has practically disappeared from the fishing grounds' (Hall and Roman 2013: p. 149). The same report indicates that the situation with the oceanic whitetip in the Western and Central Pacific Ocean is comparable where the current levels of catch per unit effort are compatible with a drop of 80–95 per cent from the population levels in the late 1990s. This catastrophic loss of sharks on the high seas has received little attention by the marine conservation community.

*Policies relevant to high seas shark captures*

The UN Fish Stocks Agreement (UNFSA) is the primary international instrument for encouraging countries to undertake the cooperation essential to manage shared fish stocks (Pew Charitable Trusts, 2016). The UNFSA includes provisions for precautionary fisheries management (i.e. to take conservative measures when information is uncertain, unreliable or inadequate) to minimise bycatch and impacts on associated and dependent species including sharks, seabirds and turtles (Gilman, 2011), among other important provisions. The UNFSA has become the point of departure for negotiations to establish new RFMOs, including the WCPFC, while others, including the IATTC, have revised their charters to incorporate UNFSA provisions (Balton

116 *T. L. Capson*

and Koehler, 2006). In addition, many states, both parties and non-parties to the UNFSA, have begun to incorporate its provisions into their domestic laws and regulations. While the 'UNFSA sparked a concerted effort to implement an "ecosystem approach to fisheries management"', namely, focusing on the ecosystem in which the target species (tuna, in this case) is captured, in practice, implementing such an approach requires considerable scientific research, which is difficult and costly for nations with even the most sophisticated fisheries management systems (Balton and Koehler, 2006: p. 8).

*Progress in international shark conservation*

A positive development in the field of international shark conservation came in 2013 with the addition of the oceanic whitetip shark, scalloped hammerhead shark (*Sphyrna lewini*), great hammerhead shark (*Sphyrna mokarran*), smooth hammerhead shark (*Sphyrna zygaena*), porbeagle shark (*Lamna nasus*) and manta rays (Manta spp.) to Appendix II of the Convention on International Trade in Endangered Species of Wild Fauna and Flora (CITES). These listings mean that, for the first time, trade in shark species of great commercial value will require verification of the sustainability and legality of that trade, which cannot be incompatible with the species' survival (CITES, 2014). A major challenge to the implementation of the CITES convention will be to ensure that developing country signatories have the necessary capacity to implement their treaty obligations. Market-based mechanisms are another potential means of addressing shark conservation that are largely unexplored (Gilman, 2011). The Eastern Tropical Pacific tuna-dolphin issue provides a market-based model that could be relevant to shark conservation. In this case, concerns about high dolphin mortality in tuna purse seine fisheries and publicity generated by NGOs drove the IATTC to begin a dolphin conservation programme in 1979 known as the Agreement on the International Dolphin Conservation Program (AIDCP). Between 1986 and 1998 dolphin mortality in Eastern Tropical Pacific tuna fisheries declined by 98 per cent (Hall et al., 2000).

### Optimal management regimes for rebuilding global fisheries

Of all the problems that beset marine species, excessive exploitation may be the most egregious; but it may also be one of the more tractable (Vincent and Harris, 2014). Costello et al. (2016) evaluated 4713 fisheries worldwide, representing 78 per cent of global reported fish catch, in order to estimate the status, trends and benefits of alternative approaches to recovering depleted fisheries. They found that effective fisheries reforms span a range of approaches, from scientifically informed harvest policies to institutional reforms that restructure incentives that align profits with conservation. While their business-as-usual scenario projects the continued collapse for many of the world's fisheries, their results also showed that common sense reforms to fishery management would dramatically improve overall fish abundance while increasing food security and profits.

*Protecting our global ocean heritage*   117

They also found that some of the greatest economic improvements in fisheries may come from improving institutions for fisheries managements rather than improving the status of fished stocks (Costello et al., 2016).

## Marine protected areas (MPAs)

The scientific literature makes increasingly clear the positive impacts of MPAs in terms of the greater size and number of fish within the area, including predators such as sharks, and that the biomass of targeted fish species can increase outside MPAs without disadvantaging fishers (Kerwath et al., 2013; Edgar et al., 2014; Caselle et al., 2015). Large and strategically placed reserves with their full component of trophic levels and greater genetic and species diversity are likely to be more resilient to some environmental changes and could be important tools in climate adaptation (Lubchenco and Grorud-Colvert, 2015).

The parties to the Convention on Biological Diversity (CBD) established the Aichi Biodiversity Target 11, which includes the objective to put 17 per cent of terrestrial and 10 per cent of marine regions under protected area status by 2020. This has contributed to nearly 10 million $km^2$ of new MPAs, a growth of approximately 360 per cent in a decade (Klein et al., 2015). Some examples include the Easter Island Marine Park and Nazca-Desventuradas Marine Park in Chile announced in 2015; the four-fold expansion of the Papahānaumokuākea Marine National Monument off the coast of Hawaii, creating the world's largest MPA (2016); Kiribati's ban on commercial fishing in its Phoenix Island Protected Area (2015); the United Kingdom's Pitcairn Islands Marine Reserve (2015); New Zealand's Kermadec Ocean Sanctuary (Lubchenco and Grorud-Colvert, 2015); and the 1.57 million $km^2$ MPA that protects the Ross Sea that was established by the Commission for the Conservation of Antarctic Marine Living Resources (CCAMLR), which will come into force in December 2017 (CCAMLR, 2017).

Despite the recent growth in MPAs, a number of studies point out significant shortcomings in their capacity to protect marine biodiversity. A recent study assessed the overlap of global MPAs with the ranges of 17,348 marine species (fishes, mammals, invertebrates), and found that more than 97 per cent of species have less than 10 per cent of their ranges represented in stricter conservation classes (other classes permit most human activities, including mining and fishing) (Klein et al., 2015). Similarly, when all categories of MPA protection are considered together, from lightly to strongly protected, only 1.6 per cent of the world's oceans fit the latter category (Lubchenco and Grorud-Colvert, 2015). Another study showed that less than 6 per cent of scleractinian coral species and 22 per cent of labrid fish species reach the minimum protection target of 10 per cent of their geographic ranges within MPAs (Klein et al., 2015). The requirements for effective MPAs are well known, as is our understanding of the performance metrics necessary to assess their effectiveness, meaning that reaching Aichi Target 11 has the potential to generate genuine benefits for marine biodiversity (Watson et al., 2016).

## 118  *T. L. Capson*

### Case study: protection of the Coiba National Park

Located off the southwest coast of Panama in the Gulf of Chiriquí and comprising an area of 2700 km², the Coiba National Park includes an insular area of 535 km², a marine area of 2165 km² and an adjacent buffer zone of 1600 km² of ocean (UNESCO, 2016a). The park is located within the Tropical Eastern Pacific (TEP), a unique tropical marine region, one of the most isolated regions in the world's oceans, which has probably the highest rate of endemism of any equivalent region in the world (Robertson and Allen, 2015). Due to a combination of geographic and oceanographic factors no other continental shore marine park could do as much for marine conservation in the entire TEP as the Coiba National Park and its buffer zone (ANAM, 2005). With an area of 503 km², Coiba Island is the largest tropical island on the continental shore of the Pacific coast of the Americas. Located at the centre of the Coiba National Park, Coiba Island retains 85 per cent of its original primary forest due to its designation as a penal colony in 1919, where the prisoners and the guards assigned to protect them served as a deterrent to exploitation of the park's resources.

The President of Panama passed an Executive Decree in 2003 that would have permitted logging, hunting, fishing and the destruction of cultural artefacts within the park, among other destructive activities. In response, I launched a campaign to save the Coiba National Park that changed its image from that of a forbidding penal colony to valued national treasure, resulting in legislation for the park's protection, and its inscription to the UNESCO list of World Heritage Sites; the only national park in Panama to achieve this recognition for its natural character. The campaign that I organised, with input from colleagues in Panama, emphasised four themes: (i) how the park could benefit local fishermen, citing studies that showed how the size and numbers of commercially important species would increase if fishing intensity within the park's boundaries is sufficiently low; (ii) the potential of the park's ecosystems for scientific research including the discovery of chemical compounds with activity against disease; (iii) the potential of low impact activities to generate revenue, for example, scuba diving; and (iv) that the park represented unique natural patrimony for its own sake and for future generations. The campaign to protect the Coiba National Park provides insight into the argument about protecting nature for its own sake (referred to as 'traditional' or 'old' conservation), or saving nature to help ourselves (known as 'new conservation'). As described by Tallis and Lubchenco (2014), infighting in the conservation community about new versus old conservation is stalling progress to protect the planet. In the campaign for the park's protection, I adopted the approaches of both 'new' and 'old' conservation, stressing both the economic benefits to be gained from the park's protection as well as the park's importance as unique natural patrimony.

The President abandoned the Executive Decree and legislation was adopted for the protection of the Coiba National Park in July of 2004, the first law of its kind for the Republic of Panama (ANAM, 2005). Starting in November of 2002, I worked closely with the National Authority of the

Environment (known by the acronym 'ANAM') to have the Coiba National Park inscribed into UNESCO's list of approximately 160 World Heritage Sites. In July of 2005, the park was formally designated as such (UNESCO, 2016a). The addition of the park to the list of World Heritage Sites was an intensely political process in which the Government of Colombia played a key role. The following year, Colombia added the Malpelo Fauna and Flora Sanctuary, located some 300 miles off the west coast of Colombia and also within the TEP, to the list (UNESCO, 2016b). The importance having the Coiba National Park declared a World Heritage Site became evident in August of 2008 when the head of Panama's Legislative Assembly allowed for a change in the law that would have permitted tuna fishing by purse seine vessels within the boundaries of the park. Panama-based environmental organisations vigorously opposed the change in the legislation and notified UNESCO of the potential threat to the Coiba National Park. In April of 2009, the ban on purse seine fisheries in the park was reinstated. The international scrutiny from UNESCO likely had an impact on this outcome.

## Climate change impacts on the oceans

In the coming decades and centuries, three independent factors linked to anthropogenic $CO_2$ emissions—ocean acidification, ocean deoxygenation and rising temperatures—will affect the ocean's biogeochemical cycles and ecosystems in ways that we are only beginning to fathom (Gruber, 2011). Approximately one-quarter of the $CO_2$ released into the atmosphere is absorbed by the oceans, causing measurable declines in surface ocean pH and carbonate ion concentration (Albright et al., 2016). This process, referred to as 'ocean acidification', represents a major threat to marine ecosystems, in particular marine calcifiers that build their shells or skeletons out of calcium carbonate, such as tropical corals, echinoderms, molluscs and small marine snails called pteropods. The literature on the biological and ecological impacts of ocean acidification on marine organisms and ecosystems is rapidly growing (Kroeker et al., 2013).

Albright et al. (2016) measured the response of a coral reef community in the Great Barrier Reef to ocean chemistry conditions that were characteristic of the pre-industrial era and showed that, all other things being equal, net coral reef calcification would have been around 7 per cent higher than at present, suggesting that ocean acidification may already be diminishing coral reef growth. Shelled molluscs comprise some of the most lucrative and sustainable fisheries in the United States (Ekstrom et al., 2015). Ocean acidification has already cost the oyster industry in the US Pacific Northwest nearly US$110 million, and directly or indirectly jeopardised about 3200 jobs (Ekstrom et al., 2015). In another study, researchers from the US National Oceanic and Atmospheric Administration (NOAA) showed that large portions of the shelf waters along the coasts of Washington and Oregon are corrosive to pteropods, an important prey group for ecologically and economically important species, including fishes, birds and whales (Bednaršek et al., 2014).

120   *T. L. Capson*

### There is no known geological precedence for current rates of ocean acidification

A survey of the geologic record for evidence of ocean acidification over the past 300 million years found that the current rate of ocean acidification is faster than at any time during this vast period. The most comparable was 56 million years ago, the Palaeocene-Eocene Thermal Maximum, which was characterised by a decline in ocean pH of between 0.25 and 0.45 units. However, current acidification is occurring at almost ten times this rate, meaning that we are embarking on an uncharted course in the Earth's history. Historically, sustained periods of acidification and $CO_2$ increase have led to the collapse of coral reefs and, in one instance, to the extinction of 96 per cent of marine life (Hönisch et al., 2012; The Earth Institute at Columbia University, 2012). Once these changes occur it takes centuries for the oceans to recover (Gruber, 2011).

### Local and regional factors that contribute to ocean acidification

Globally, the phenomenon of ocean acidification is driven by anthropogenic $CO_2$ emissions, but in the coastal areas where the effects of ocean acidification may be most significant for human communities, local drivers can strongly influence coastal acidification (Strong et al., 2014). Coastal ecosystems are impacted by a multitude of these drivers, including impacts from watershed processes, nutrient inputs from agricultural fertiliser, sewage, atmospheric deposition and changes in ecosystem structure and metabolism, many of which can be positively impacted by policy and management interventions. As the scientific understanding and monitoring of the dynamics of coastal acidification continue to advance, coastal resource and fisheries managers will be able to make increasingly informed decisions about mitigation and adaptation strategies in the socio-ecological systems in which they operate (Strong et al., 2014).

### Addressing ocean acidification on international, national and state-wide levels

Despite the ocean's critical roles in regulating climate and providing food security and livelihoods for millions of people, international climate negotiations have only minimally considered impacts of rising $CO_2$ levels on the oceans (Gattuso et al., 2015). In light of the 21st session of the Conference of the Parties (COP21) to the UN Framework Convention on Climate Change (UNFCCC) held in December 2015, recent publications have addressed the impacts of $CO_2$ emission scenarios for ocean and society. Gattuso et al. (2015) report that several key marine and coastal ecosystems will face high risks of impact well before 2100, even under the most stringent $CO_2$ emission scenario adopted by the Intergovernmental Panel on Climate Change (IPCC), Representative Concentration Pathway (RCP2.6). Small island developing states have argued for several years that a temperature increase of 1.5°C above

*Protecting our global ocean heritage*    121

pre-industrial levels, rather than 2°C, should be the UNFCCC target, which contributed to the COP21 goal of holding the global mean atmospheric temperature rise by the end of this century to 2°C (Magnan et al., 2016).

As part of the COP21 process, 185 countries, representing 94 per cent of current global greenhouse gas emissions and 97 per cent of the world's population, submitted their emissions pledges mostly with a time horizon of 2030. Based on those projections, a median global temperature increase by 2100 of between 2.7°C and 3.5°C was estimated. Even the most optimistic assessment of 2.7°C by 2100, '*profoundly and negatively affects the ocean and the services it provides to the world population*' (Magnan et al., 2016, emphasis added), meaning that the 185 countries that committed to a reduction in $CO_2$ emissions by 2030 'must consider the imperative for faster and deeper decarbonization post-2030' (Magnan et al., 2016). It is noteworthy that only 1.5 hours were dedicated to oceans-related issues during COP21, which consisted of 12 days of talks. Ironically, the 1.5-hour session 'highlight(ed) the dynamics and concrete action of civil society stakeholders committed to raising the issue of oceans as a solution for climate change' (UNFCCC, 2016, p. 12). A good start towards 'raising the issue' of the impact of $CO_2$ on the oceans would be for the UNFCCC to devote more resources to the issue, and more time to oceans-related issues at COP22.

### Actions by the United States

In the United States, the Federal Ocean Acidification Research and Monitoring (FOARAM) Act of 2009 was passed in Congress and signed into law by President Obama. Among other actions designed to spur federal agency collaboration and research on the challenges of ocean acidification, the passage of the FOARAM Act created an Interagency Working Group on ocean acidification, which published the Strategic Plan for Federal Research and Monitoring of Ocean Acidification in 2014. NOAA created the Ocean Acidification Program, which is organised around six core issues: monitoring carbonate chemistry changes, measuring biological impacts, assessing socioeconomic impacts, managing and coordinating ocean acidification data, coordinating education and outreach, and engaging directly in the process of developing adaptation strategies.

### State-wide actions in the Unites States

A seminal event in driving ocean acidification policy and research in the Unites States was the near collapse of oyster hatcheries in Oregon and Washington where researchers showed a clear link between increased $CO_2$ levels in seawater and the mortality of oyster larvae (Barton et al., 2015). In response, Washington State established the Blue Ribbon Panel on Ocean Acidification in 2012, whose recommendations led to legislation that funded a centre for ocean acidification research at the University of Washington and formed

## 122    T. L. Capson

the Washington Marine Resources Advisory Council in the Office of the Governor (Strong et al., 2014). Funding procured from the federal government was crucial for the establishment of monitoring stations in Oregon and Washington, which provided the ability to observe carbonate chemistry data in real-time and allowed shellfish growers to take adaptive measures, enabling them to restore most of their original production of oyster larvae (Barton et al., 2015). Following the lead of Washington, the states of Maine and Maryland convened ocean acidification panels, which have produced actionable recommendations to protect their fishing and aquaculture industries that are tailored to local conditions and needs. The states of Massachusetts and Rhode Island are following similar courses of action.

A key player in resolving the ocean acidification issue in the Oregon oyster hatchery mentioned above was Alan Barton of the Whisky Creek Shellfish Hatchery. In addressing representatives from industry, government and academia during a 2013 workshop in New Zealand on ocean acidification impacts on shellfish aquaculture Barton told participants: 'The only way we're going to stop acidification is to get out in front on this issue—nobody else is going to do it, and we're the guys who will first go out of business. So I encourage you to get on board with this issue, convince yourself first, and get out there and convince other people before it's too late' (Capson and Guinotte, 2014: p. 3).

### Summary

The scientific literature makes clear that piecemeal, business-as-usual interventions will be inadequate to confront the threats to ocean health including an unprecedented combination of overexploitation of resources, marine pollution, ocean acidification, deoxygenation and ocean warming (Harnik et al., 2012; Gruber, 2011; Rands et al., 2010). The IPCC stated that due to the nature of the threats to marine and terrestrial ecosystems, 'The resilience of many [marine and terrestrial] ecosystems is likely to be exceeded this century' (IPCC, 2007). While this is an estimate, society would be ill advised to try and prove this estimate incorrect.

Decades of research and experience in the field provide a wealth of experience that can be drawn upon in order to protect marine biodiversity in a diversity of settings. Effective conservation will require bold, well-informed and common-sense approaches that include political will that is driven by an informed public, inclusivity, funding and good science (Fisher et al., 2013; Noss et al., 2011; Rands et al., 2010; Watson et al., 2016). The need for an informed public highlights the essential role of scientists in informing the public and policy. Bold approaches by conservation professionals will be necessary in order to counteract the 'pro-growth norms of global society (that) foster timidity among conservation professionals, steering them toward conformity with the global economic agenda and away from acknowledging what is ultimately needed to sustain life on Earth' (Noss et al., 2011). This is particularly true of many large NGOs that focus on conservation trends that are often

*Protecting our global ocean heritage* 123

driven by an institution's need to secure donations and focus on politically palatable measures (Redford et al., 2013; Pressey, 2014). Other NGOs take a bolder tack; for example, the tracking for 110 days and across 10,000 nautical miles of a fugitive fishing ship considered the world's most notorious international poacher, by the NGO Sea Shepherd. The ship was ultimately scuttled by its own crew (Urbina, 2015).

Cooperation among conservation professionals from academia and NGOs and between disciplines will be key in order for practitioners to respond to complex ecological, social and political uncertainties and challenges (Beever et al., 2014). Cooperation across disciplines will also help conservation professionals do a better job in communicating a compelling, convincing and honest vision across traditional disciplinary and societal boundaries. The messages must be based on the best available science and expert opinion and geared towards the protection of nature and not secondary to economic or political considerations (Noss et al., 2011). Anything less will fail to provide policy makers with either a thorough understanding of what is at stake, or the arguments they will need in order to defend their positions.

## References

Agnew, D.J., Pearce, J., Pramod, G., Peatman, T., Watson, R., Beddington, J.R. and Pitcher, T.J. (2009) 'Estimating the worldwide extent of illegal fishing', *PLoS ONE*, 4(2): e4570. doi:10.1371/journal.pone.0004570

Albright, R., Caldeira, L., Hosfelt, J., Kwiatkowski, L., Maclaren, J.K., Mason, B.M., Nebuchina, Y., Ninokawa, A., Pongratz, J., Ricke, K.L., Rivlin, T., Schneider, K., Sesboüé, M., Shamberger, K., Silverman, J., Wolfe, K., Zhu, K., Caldeira, K. (2016) 'Reversal of ocean acidification enhances net coral reef calcification', *Nature*, 531, pp. 362–365.

ANAM (National Authority of the Environment) (2005) 'Proposal for the inscription of the Coiba National Park in the list of World Heritage Sites of UNESCO', National Authority of the Environment, Republic of Panama (15 July), available: http://whc.unesco.org/en/list/1138 [accessed 20 July 2016].

Balton, D.A. and Koehler, H.R. (2006) 'Reviewing the United Nations fish stocks treaty', *Sustainable Development Law & Policy*, 7, pp. 5–9.

Barton, A., Waldbusser G.G., Feely, R.A., Weisberg, S.B., Newton, J.A., Hales, B., Cudd, S., Eudeline, B., Langdon, C.J., Jefferds, I., King, T., Suhrbier, A. and McLaughlin, K. (2015) 'Impacts of coastal acidification on the Pacific northwest shellfish industry and adaptation strategies implemented in response', *Oceanography*, 28, pp. 146–159.

Bednaršek, N., Tarling, G.A., Bakker, D.C.E., Fielding, S. and Feely, R.A. (2014) 'Dissolution dominating calcification process in polar pteropods close to the point of aragonite undersaturation', *PLoS ONE*, 9: e109183. doi:10.1371/journal.pone.0109183

Beever, E.A., Mattsson, B.J., Germino, M.J., Van Der Burg, M.P., Bradford, J.B. and Brunson, M.W. (2014) 'Successes and challenges from formation to implementation of eleven broad-extent conservation programs', *Conservation Biology*, 28, pp. 302–314.

124  *T. L. Capson*

Béné, C., Barange, M., Subasinghe, R., Pinstrup-Andersen, P., Merino, G., Gro-Ingunn, H. and Williams, M. (2015) 'Feeding 9 billion by 2050—putting fish back on the menu', *Food Security,* 7, pp. 261–274.

Bever, L. (2016) 'Indonesia's harsh response to illegal fishing: blowing up ships', *Washington Post,* 15 March, available: https://www.washingtonpost.com/news/speaking-of-science/wp/2016/03/15/indonesias-harsh-response-to-illegal-fishing-blowing-up-ships [accessed 12 September 2016].

Conservation of Antarctic Marine Living Resources (CCAMLR) (2017) 'CCAMLR to create world's largest Marine Protected Area', modified 24 February 2017, available: www.ccamlr.org/en/news/2016/ccamlr-create-worlds-largest-marine-protected-area [accessed 16 March 2017].

Capson, T.L. and Guinotte, J. (2014). 'Future proofing New Zealand's shellfish aquaculture: monitoring and adaptation to ocean acidification', Ministry for Primary Industries, Wellington, pp. 1–48.

Caselle, J.E., Rassweiler, A., Hamilton, S.L. and Warner, R.R. (2015) 'Recovery trajectories of kelp forest animals are rapid yet spatially variable across a network of temperate marine protected areas', *Scientific Reports,* 5(14102), pp. 1–14.

Camhi, M.D., Valenti, S.V., Fordham, S.V., Fowler, S.L. and Gibson, C. (2009) 'The conservation status of pelagic sharks and rays: Report of the IUCN Shark Specialist Group Pelagic Shark Red List workshop', IUCN Species Survival Commission Shark Specialist Group, Newbury, UK, pp. 1–78.

Chan, V., Clarke, R., and Squires, D. (2014) 'Full retention in tuna fisheries: benefits, costs and unintended consequences', *Marine Policy,* 45, pp. 213–221.

Cheung W.W.L., Watson, R., and Pauly D. 2013. 'Signature of ocean warming in global fisheries catch', *Nature,* 419, pp. 365–369.

CITES (2014) 'Stronger protection for five shark species and all manta rays', available: https://cites.org/eng/shark_ray_listings_come_into_effect.php [accessed 19 July 2016].

Costello, C., Ovando, D., Hilborn, R., Gaines, S.D., Deschenes, O. and Lester, S.E. (2012) 'Status and solutions for the world's unassessed fisheries', *Science,* 338, pp. 517–520.

Costello, C., Ovandoa, D., Clavellea, T., Strauss, C.K., Hilborn, R., Melnychukc, M.C., Branch, T.A., Gaines, S.D., Szuwalski, C.S., Cabrala, R.B., Raderb, D.N. and Leland, A. (2016) 'Global fishery prospects under contrasting management regimes', in *Proceedings of the National Academy of the Sciences USA,* 113, pp. 5125–5129.

Cullis-Suzuki, S. and Pauly, D. (2010) 'Failing the high seas: a global evaluation of regional fisheries management organizations', *Marine Policy,* 34, pp. 1036–1042.

Edgar, G.J., Stuart-Smith, R.D., Willis, T.J., Kininmonth, S., Baker, S.C., Banks, S., Barrett, N.S., Becerro, M.A., Bernard, A.T., Berkhout, J., Buxton, C.D., Campbell, S.J., Cooper, A.T., Davey, M., Edgar, S.C., Försterra, G., Galván, D.E., Irigoyen, A.J., Kushner, D.J., Moura, R., Parnell, P.E., Shears, N.T., Soler, G., Strain, E.MA. and Thomson, R.J. (2014) 'Global conservation outcomes depend on marine protected areas with five key features', *Nature,* 506(7487), pp. 216–220.

Ekstrom, J.A., Suatoni, L., Cooley, S.R., Pendleton, L.H., Waldbusser, G.G., Cinner, J.E., Ritter, J., Langdon, C., Van Hooidonk, R., Gledhill, D., Wellman, K., Beck, M.W., Brander, L.M., Rittschof, D., Doherty, C., Edwards, P.E.T. and Portela, R. (2015) 'Vulnerability and adaptation of US shellfisheries to ocean acidification', *Nature Climate Change,* 5, pp. 207–214.

European Commission (2016) 'Illegal fishing (IUU). The EU Rules to combat illegal, unreported and unregulated fishing', 11 June, available: http://ec.europa.eu/fisheries/cfp/illegal_fishing/index_en.htm [accessed 12 September 2016].

European Commission 92015) 'EU acts on illegal fishing: yellow card issued to Thailand while South Korea & Philippines are cleared', European Commission press release, available: http://europa.eu/rapid/press-release_IP-15-4806_en.htm [accessed 12 September, 2016].

Food and Agriculture Organization of the United Nations (FAO) (2014) 'High level panel of experts on food security and nutrition', Report on Sustainable Fisheries and Aquaculture for Food Security and Nutrition, available: www.fao.org/cfs/cfs-hlpe [accessed 12 September 2016].

Food and Agriculture Organization of the United Nations (FAO) (2016a) 'Ground-breaking illegal fishing accord soon to enter into force', 16 May, available: www.fao.org/news/story/en/item/414494/icode/ [accessed 12 September 2016].

Food and Agriculture Organization of the United Nations (FAO) (2016b) 'The state of world fisheries and aquaculture 2016—contributing to food security and nutrition for all', FAO, Rome, available: http://www.fao.org/3/a-i5555e.pdf [accessed May 2017].

Ferretti, F., Worm, B., Britten, G.L., Heithaus, M.R. and Lotze, H.K. (2010) 'Patterns and ecosystem consequences of shark declines in the ocean', *Ecology Letters,* 13, pp. 1055–1071.

Fisher, B., Balmford, A., Ferraro, P.J., Glew, L., Mascia, M., Naidoo, R. and Ricketts, T.H. (2013) 'Moving Rio forward and avoiding 10 more years with little evidence for effective conservation policy', *Conservation Biology*, 28, pp. 880–882.

Gattuso, J-P., Magnan, A., Billé, R., Cheung, W.W., Howes, E.L., Joos, F., Allemand, D., Bopp, L., Cooley, S.R., Eakin, C.M. and Hoegh-Guldberg, O., Kelly, R.P., Pörtner, H.-O., Rogers, A.D., Baxter, J.M., Laffoley, D., Osborn, D., Rankovic, A., Rochette, J., Sumaila, U.R., Treyer, S. and Turley, T. (2015) 'Contrasting futures for ocean and society from different $CO_2$ emissions scenarios', *Science,* 349(6243), pp. 45–56.

Gilman, E.L. (2011) 'Bycatch governance and best practice mitigation technology in global tuna fisheries', *Marine Policy*, 35, pp. 590–609.

Global Fishing Watch (2016) 'Partners', available: http://globalfishingwatch.org/partners [accessed: 20 July 2016].

Gruber, N. (2011) 'Warming up, turning sour, losing breath: Ocean biogeochemistry under global change', *Philosophical Transactions of the Royal Society A,* 369, 1980–1996.

Hall, M.A., Alverson, D.L. and Metuzals, K.I. (2000) 'By-catch: Problems and solutions', *Marine Pollution Bulletin*, 41, pp. 204–219.

Hall, M. and Roman M. (2013) 'Bycatch and non-tuna catch in the tropical tuna purse seine fisheries of the world', FAO Fisheries and Aquaculture Technical Paper No. 568, Inter-American Tropical Tuna Commission, La Jolla.

Harnik, P.G., Lotze, H.K., Anderson, S.C., Finkel, Z.V., Finnegan, S., Lindberg, D.R., Liow, L.H., Lockwood, R., McClain, C.R., McGuire, J.L., O'Dea, A., Pandolfi, J.M., Simpson, C. and Tittensor, D.P. (2012) 'Extinctions in ancient and modern seas', *Trends in Ecology and Evolution,* 27, pp. 608–617.

Hennen, D. 2006. 'Associations between the Alaska Steller sea lion decline and commercial fisheries', *Ecological Applications*, 16, pp. 704–717.

126   *T. L. Capson*

Hönisch, B., Ridgwell, A., Schmidt, D.N., Thomas, E., Gibbs, S.J., Sluijs, A., Zeebe, R., Kump, L., Martindale, R.C., Greene, S.E. and Kiessling, W., Ries· J., Zachos, J.C., Royer, D.L., Barker, S., Marchitto Jr., T. M., Moyer, R., Pelejero· C., Ziveri, P., Foster, G.L. and Williams, B. (2012) 'The geological record of ocean acidification', *Science,* 335, pp. 1058–1063.

Inter-Governmental Panel on Climate Change (IPCC) (2007) 'Climate change 2007: synthesis report', available: www.ipcc.ch/publications_and_data/ar4/syr/en/mains3-3-1.html [accessed 12 September 2016].

Kerwath, S.E., Winker, H., Götz, A. and Attwood, C.G. (2013) 'Marine protected area improves yield without disadvantaging fishers', *Nature Communications,* 4, pp. 1–6.

Klein, C.J., Brown, C.J., Halpern, B.S., Segan, D.B., McGowan, J., Beger, M. and Watson J.E.M. (2015) 'Shortfalls in the global protected area network at representing marine biodiversity', *Scientific Reports,* 5, pp. 1–7.

Kroeker, K.J., Kordas, R.L., Crim, R., Hendriks, I.E., Ramajo, L., Singh, G.S., Duarte, C.M. and Gattuso J-P. (2013) 'Impacts of ocean acidification on marine organisms: quantifying sensitivities and interaction with warming', *Global Change Biology,* 19, pp. 1884–1896.

Lam V.W.Y., Cheung W.W.L., Reygondeau G. and Sumaila, U.R. (2016) 'Projected change in global fisheries revenues under climate change', *Scientific Reports,* 6, pp. 1–8.

Lubchenco, J. and Grorud-Colvert, K. (2015) 'Making waves: The science and politics of ocean protection mature science reveals opportunities for policy progress', *Science,* 350(6259), pp. 382–383.

Magnan, A.K., Colombier, M., Billé, R., Joos, F., Hoegh-Guldberg, O., Pörtner, H.-O., Waisman H., Spencer, T. and Gattuso, J-P. (2016) 'Implications of the Paris Agreement for the ocean', *Nature Climate Change,* 6(8), pp.732–735.

Marine Stewardship Council (2016a) 'PNA Western and Central Pacific skipjack and yellowfin, unassociated/non FAD set, tuna purse seine', available: https://fisheries.msc.org/en/fisheries/pna-western-and-central-pacific-skipjack-and-yellowfin-unassociated-non-fad-set-tuna-purse-seine [accessed 20 October 2016].

Marine Stewardship Council (2016b) 'Fiji albacore tuna longline', available: https://fisheries.msc.org/en/fisheries/fiji-albacore-tuna-longline [accessed 20 October 2016].

McCauley, D.J., Pinsky, M.L., Palumbi, S.R., Estes, J.A., Joyce, F.H. and Warner, R.R. (2015) 'Marine defaunation: Animal loss in the global ocean', *Science,* 347(6219), pp. 247–255.

Mouillot, D., Parravicini, V., Bellwood, D.R., Leprieur, F., Huang, D., Cowman, P.F., Albouy, C., Hughes, T.P., Thuiller, W. and Guilhaumon, F. (2015) 'Global marine protected areas do not secure the evolutionary history of tropical corals and fishes', *Nature Communications,* 7, pp. 1–8.

Myers, R.A., Baum, J.K., Shepherd, T.D., Powers, S.P. and Peterson, C.H. (2007) 'Cascading effects of the loss of apex predatory sharks from a coastal ocean', *Science,* 315(5820), pp. 1846–1850.

National Marine Fisheries Service. (2013) 'Keeping an eye on pollock', available: http://www.nmfs.noaa.gov/podcasts/2013/05/eye_on_pollock.html#.WAkFV5OLQ_V [accessed 20 October 2016].

National Research Council. (2003) *The Decline of the Steller Sea Lion in Alaskan Waters: Untangling Food Webs and Fishing Nets.* Washington, DC: The National Academies Press.

Naylor, R.L., Goldburg, R.J., Primavera, J.H., Kautsky, N., Beveridge, M.C.M., Clay, J., Folke, C., Lubchenco, J., Mooney, H. and Troell, M. (2000) 'Effect of aquaculture on world fish supplies', *Nature*, 405(6790), pp. 1017–1024.

Noss, R.F., Dobson, A.P., Baldwin, R., Beier, P., Davis, C.R., Dellasala, D.A., Francis, J., Locke, H., Nowak, K., Lopez, R., Reining, C., Trombulak, S.C. and Tabor, G. (2011) 'Bolder thinking for conservation', *Conservation Biology*, 26, pp. 1–4.

Orensanz, J.M. and Seijo, J.C. (2013) 'Rights-based management in Latin American fisheries', Technical Paper No. 582, FAO, Rome.

Österblom, H. and Bodin, Ö. (2012) 'Global cooperation among diverse organizations to reduce illegal fishing in the southern ocean', *Conservation Biology*, 26, pp. 638–648.

Pauly, D. and Zeller, D. (2016) 'Catch reconstructions reveal that global marine fisheries catches are higher than reported and declining', *Nature Communications*, 7, pp. 1–9.

Pew Charitable Trusts. (2016) 'Global progress toward implementing the United Nations fish stocks agreement', available: www.pewtrusts.org/en/research-and-analysis/reports/2016/05/global-progress-toward-implementing-the-united-nations-fish-stocks-agreement [accessed 20 July 2016].

Pilling, G.M., Apostolaki, P., Failler, P., Floros, C., Large, P.A., Morales-Nin, B., Reglero, P., Stergiou, K.I. and Tsikliras, A.C. (2008) 'Assessment and management of data-poor fisheries', in A. Payne, J. Cotter and T. Potter (eds) *Advances in Fisheries Science: 50 Years on from Beverton and Holt*. New Jersey: Blackwell Publishing, pp. 280–305.

Pikitch, E.K. (2012) 'The risks of overfishing', *Science*, 338, pp. 474–475.

Pressey, B. (2014) 'Maximize returns on conservation', *Nature*, 515(7525), pp. 28–29.

Rands, M.R.W., Adams, W.M., Bennun, L., Butchart, S.H.M., Clements, A., Coomes, D., Entwistle, A., Hodge, I., Kapos, V., Scharlemann, J.P.W., Sutherland, W.J., and Vira, B. (2010) 'Biodiversity conservation: challenges beyond 2010', *Science*, 329, 1298–1303.

Redford, K.H., Padoch, C., and Sunderland, T. (2013) 'Fads, funding, and forgetting in three decades of conservation', *Conservation Biology*, 27(3), pp. 437–438.

Robertson, D.R., and Allen, G.R. (2015) 'Shorefishes of the Tropical Eastern Pacific: online information system. Version 2.0', Smithsonian Tropical Research Institute, Balboa, Panama, available: http://biogeodb.stri.si.edu/sftep/en/pages [accessed: 12 September 2016].

Smith, M.D., Roheim, C.A., Crowder, L.B., Halpern, B.S., Turnipseed, M., Anderson, J.L., Asche, F., Bourillón, L., Guttormsen, A.G., Khan, A. and Liguori, L.A., McNevin, A., O'Connor, M.I., Squires, D., Tyedmers, P., Brownstein, C., Carden, K., Klinger, D.H., Sagarin, R. and Selkoe, K.A. (2010) 'Sustainability and global seafood', *Science*, 327, 784–786.

Strong, A.L., Kroeker, K.J., Teneva, L.T., Mease, L.A. and Kelly, R.P. (2014) 'Ocean acidification 2.0: managing our changing coastal ocean chemistry', *Biosciences*, doi: 10.1093/biosci/biu072.

Tallis, H. and Lubchenco, J. (2014) 'Working together: a call for inclusive conservation', *Nature*, 515(7525), pp. 27–28.

The Earth Institute at Columbia University (2012) 'Ocean acidification rate may be unprecedented, study says', The Earth Institute, Columbia University, available: http://www.earth.columbia.edu/articles/view/2951 [accessed 12 September 2016].

## 128 T. L. Capson

UN General Assembly (2011) 'General Assembly adopts resolution aimed at ensuring sustainability of world's fisheries, as it holds annual debate on UN regime protecting seas, oceans', available: https://www.un.org/press/en/2011/ga11185.doc.htm [accessed 12 September 2016].

UNESCO (2016a) 'Coiba National Park and its special zone of marine protection', available: http://whc.unesco.org/en/list/1138 [accessed 12 September 2016].

UNESCO (2016b) 'Malpelo fauna and flora sanctuary', available: http://whc.unesco.org/en/list/1216 [accessed 12 September 2016].

Urbina, I. (2015) 'A renegade trawler, hunted for 10,000 miles by vigilantes', *The New York Times*, 28 July, available: http://www.nytimes.com/2015/07/28/world/a-renegade-trawler-hunted-for-10000-miles-by-vigilantes.html [accessed 12 September 2016].

UNFCCC (2016) 'Lima–Paris action agenda', Programme, CoP21 Agenda, PART III: increasing the resilience of oceans to climate change, pp. 12–13.

Vincent, A.C.J. and Harris J.M. (2014) 'Boundless no more', *Science*, 346(6208), pp. 420–421.

Watson J.E.M., Darling, E.S., Venter, O., Maron, M., Walston, J., Possingham, H.P., Dudley, N., Hockings, M., Barnes, M. and Brooks, T.M. (2016) 'Bolder science needed now for protected areas, *Conservation Biology*, 30, pp. 243–248.

Western and Central Pacific Fisheries Commission (WCPFC). (2013) 'Potential for e-reporting and e-monitoring in the Western and Central Pacific tuna fisheries', available: https://www.wcpfc.int/node/5586 [accessed 12 September 2016].

Worm, B. and Branch, T.A. 2012 'The future of fish', *Trends in Ecology and Evolution*, 27(11), pp. 594–599.

Worm, B., Davis, B., Kettemer, L., Ward-Paige, C.A., Chapman, D., Heithaus, M.R., Kessel, S.T. and Gruber, S.H. (2013) 'Global catches, exploitation rates, and rebuilding options for sharks', *Marine Policy*, 40, pp. 194–204.

# Part III

# Building resilience through resource cooperation

# 8 Food sovereignty and the politics of food scarcity

*Alana Mann*

## Introduction

As this chapter is written, 16 million people in Somalia, Kenya, Ethiopia and South Sudan are desperately in need of food, water and medical treatment. In South Sudan alone, one million are on the brink of famine. Economic and social collapse, driven by constant conflict, is leading to large-scale displacement, disease and destitution in what might be the largest humanitarian crisis since the creation of the United Nations. Given this situation it is clear that hunger, 'the world's greatest solvable problem' (World Food Program, 2012), appears no closer to being solved. Nor is the evidence from non-conflict zones convincing. Housing stress, low incomes, disability and poor access to transport are among the complex factors that contribute to alarming rates of food insecurity even in comparatively wealthy economies including the European Union, North America and Australia. Yet, paradoxically, obesity has eclipsed hunger as the most widespread global health problem.

It is in its dialectical pairing with abundance that the relational and socially constructed nature of scarcity in food politics emerges. This chapter discusses how peoples' movements are using the concept of food sovereignty to contest the naturalisation of scarcity in discourses about hunger. By unveiling the webs of power and social relations that govern access to and control over productive resources, advocates of food sovereignty draw attention to the politics of allocation and attendant policies that are legitimised by predominant framings of scarcity. In decoupling hunger from food production, food sovereignty reveals scarcity to be socially-mediated and the result of socio-political processes.

The very fact that scarcity is prone to naturalisation in discourses related to food and agriculture demands a political ecology approach (Peet et al., 2011) that recognises food systems as complex networks through which productive resources flow and are governed by issues of allocation, access and entitlement. Drawing attention to how scarcity is constructed discursively reveals it to be a floating signifier, relative to temporal, spatial and cultural contexts, but also as a technical device that defines the neoliberal economics that dictate resource allocation.

## 132   A. Mann

The unsustainability of an industrial food system that relies on supply solutions generating overproduction belies the myth that free trade will feed the world. Episodes of crisis, including the food price hikes of 2007–2008, are generating resistance against the increasing power and reach of transnational corporations, exploitation of labour and the encroachment of regulations in both public and private spheres. Supporters of food sovereignty reject the notion of food as a commodity, adopting a rights-based approach that asserts the right to food is indivisible from other human rights including gender and racial equality. Demanding inclusive political spaces and pluralistic notions of sovereignty to facilitate transnational cooperation in the management of food and agricultural systems they are also driving new forms of collaboration (Schiavoni, 2015).

## The emergence of food sovereignty as a mobilising frame

Food has long been recognised as a political weapon, and the discursive production of scarcity is key to this. Scarcity relies on an imbalance of systems and establishes the basis of the free market. In shifting to new opportunities, capital itself creates and manipulates scarcities. Terms such as 'food violence' (Eakin et al., 2010) draw attention to the structural inequalities that lead to hunger, obesity and diseases of malnutrition, and their disproportionate impact on populations subject to chronic economic marginalisation, social exclusion and discrimination. Critical food scholars, civil society organisations and peoples' movements argue for more democratic governance of food systems that accommodates 'alternative perspectives on food and its value to society' and addresses 'the differential power and political interests associated with different perspectives on food values' (Eakin et al., 2010: 263).

Framing scarcity as an inherent characteristic of productive resources such as soil, water and seeds naturalises it, and effectively sidesteps issues of social justice that run counter to the interests of elites. Linking hunger with wider socio-political and institutional processes, advocates of food sovereignty draw attention to power relations and unequal property rights. They call on governments to support radical transformations to domestic food systems held hostage to an unjust trade regime and the interests of multinational corporations.

Ordinary people, many of whom are the most affected by hunger, are actively promoting the rights-based concept of food sovereignty in local, regional and international policy circles. Through grassroots mobilisations and engagement in global forums, peoples' movements are engineering a paradigm shift that exposes the flaws in traditional approaches to addressing hunger. Coalitions of small-scale farmers in the Global North and South are especially active in progressively articulating this new vision of food production and consumption. Over the past 20 years many of these groups have joined La Via Campesina ('the peasant way'), the world's largest social movement with over 160 member organisations mobilising in more than 70 countries. The members of La Via Campesina collectively project food sovereignty beyond farmers' interests towards a democratic political project embracing themes of diversity, inclusivity and social justice.

*Food sovereignty and scarcity*  133

The goal of food sovereignty demands a dynamic shift in state–society relations and terms of engagement (Schiavoni, 2015). Food sovereignty emerged out of the reduced power of the state in domestic food systems and seeks to reclaim some of this power. It also valorises local control of food production and consumption informed and legitimised by the participation of eaters and growers.

In its purest interpretation, the concept of food sovereignty is a proposal for radical social transformation that aspires to democratise food systems. In the current context, food sovereignty is perhaps more accurately described as 'a set of reactions to neoliberal globalisation and the industrial food system that is presented as an alternative approach predicated on the dispersal of power' (Andrèe et al., 2014: 11). The concept has served as a compelling master frame for the mobilisation of La Via Campesina as a transnational coalition (Mann, 2014), which is creating collaborative spaces and ways of working that enable people with diverse social, economic and cultural backgrounds to come together to recognise scarcity as a social construction and demand that governments address issues of access and distribution.

The emergence of this coalition was triggered by the creation of the World Trade Organization (WTO) in 1993, which coincided with the establishment of the North American Free Trade agreement (NAFTA). For small farmers, the globalisation of the trade regime would subject them to the full impacts of neoliberalism's structural violence, 'the unprecedented concentrations of wealth and power and the rapid destruction of life-ways and livelihoods, ecosystems and species' (Reitan, 2007: 16). Countering this, food sovereignty grants people, through their elected government representatives, control over their food security policies, including the right to impose protective tariffs against the dumping of subsidised exports, and the support and promotion of local markets. It also puts the onus on governments to respect, protect and fulfil the rights of citizens to food and the productive resources to produce it, including land, forests, fisheries, water and seeds.

La Via Campesina characterised the reaction of the WTO, World Bank and G8 governments to the crippling escalation of food prices in 2007–2008 as disastrous, claiming the policies they called for, including further trade liberalisation and a second Green Revolution in Africa, are at the root of a decades-long food crisis. The movement remains highly critical of internationally sourced food aid, financed largely by the World Bank's Global Agriculture and Food Security Programme, a multilateral trust fund set up by the United States, Canada, Spain and the Bill and Melinda Gates Foundation (Holt-Giménez and Shattuck, 2011). Coupled with a series of industry–non-governmental organization (NGO) and public–private partnerships (PPPs), the programme represents a continuation of what Philip McMichael (2005) calls the 'development project', which assumes that agriculture is the main source of economic growth, and therefore increasing productivity is the solution to poverty, and scarcity. Also referred to as the 'productionist paradigm' (Lang and Heasman, 2016), this approach is committed to raising output, intensification of farming, mass processing, mass marketing, homogeneity of product, monocultures and a reliance on chemical and pharmaceutical solutions.

134   *A. Mann*

Advocates of food sovereignty argue that the neoliberal model of production is based on the principle of overproduction by the 'grain-livestock complex' in the temperate world (Weis, 2007: 86–87). The United States, specifically, has achieved 'tremendous productivity gains, exported surpluses, industrial innovations and the rise of its agro-TNCs [transnational corporations]' (ibid.), resulting in extreme concentration of production and insurmountable inequality among producers. As a result, farmers throughout the Global North are trapped in a 'cost-price squeeze', while distorted competition from cheap exports has ruined largely unsubsidised farmer livelihoods in the Global South, exacerbating the detrimental effects of the shift from domestic food crops to export-bound cash crops. The rhetoric of scarcity is hollow; excess production is in fact the problem (Guthman, 2011).

La Via Campesina promotes an alternative system based on small producers using sustainable and local resources in production for domestic consumption. In this model peasant and farmer-based sustainable production methods have to be 'supported and strengthened' (La Via Campesina, 2008). Smallholder farmers' engagement in pluriactivity—involvement in activities unrelated to agriculture—is one of the many ways in which land is improved. Pluriactivity is a form of risk management, in that the impact of the failure of a single crop and the longer-term negative environmental impacts of farming are reduced and biodiversity maintained. Miguel Altieri and Victor Manuel Toledo (2011) argue that not only are small-scale, pluriactive farms more productive and resource-conserving than large monocultural set-ups; they represent a sanctuary of agrobiodiversity free of GMOs, are more resilient to climate change and create carbon stores. Through practising agroecology, 'the application of ecological concepts and principles to the design and management of sustainable agricultural ecosystems', small-scale farmers can, according to Altieri and Toledo, lay the foundation of an 'epistemological, technical and social revolution . . . from below' (2011: 587; see also Ploeg, 2008).

## Agroecology as farming, and framing

While scarcity is not 'natural' in the sense that it is naturalised in the discourse of the market, it is a 'concrete period of dearth' (Mehta, 2011: 382) felt acutely by a rural population when a productive resource, such as water, is limited. In response farmers adapt. On a daily basis they apply strategies rooted in local knowledge systems and practices that deal with seasonality and uncertainty in weather conditions. These highly differential coping mechanisms are designed to respond to the lived experience of scarcity, or coping with the 'regularly irregular', such as rainfall (Mehta, 2011: 379).

The instrumental and economic rationality embedded in industrial food production has led to a reliance on 'expert' discourses or 'monocultures of knowledge' according to Boaventura de Sousa Santos (in Martinez-Torres and Rosset, 2014). Conspicuously absent from these discourses are local and traditional knowledges of those that have been historically excluded from land management and policy-making, such as indigenous peoples. La Via Campesina redresses these absences through *diàlogo de saberes*—dialogue among different knowledges and ways of knowing. This practice is 'key to the durability of the LVC [La Via Campesina] constellation . . . as organisations take mutual inspiration from the experiences and visions of others' (Martìnez-Torres and Rosset, 2014: 980). Accordingly, agroecology is not only a farming method, but also a framing device that has emerged from, and incorporates, social movement dialogues.

For opponents of the industrial food system agroecology represents a solution to declining local economies and rural unemployment. As an alternative to a production model that relies on fertilisers, seeds and herbicides as well as high levels of regulation and certification, agroecology is affordable and sustainable. Its methods are knowledge- rather than input-intensive, and it aims to 'improve links between the land and consumption', reduce waste and risk, and empower producers (Lang and Heasman, 2016). La Via Campesina declared at a regional meeting on agroecology and peasant seeds in Thailand in 2002 that:

> Agroecology is giving a new meaning to the struggle for agrarian reform to empower the people. The landless farmers who fought to reclaim back their land, and those who received land through land reform programs in Brazil and Zimbabwe, are implementing agroecology as a tool to defend and sustain their farming, not only for their families but to provide healthier food for the community. Therefore, land reform, together with agroecology, has become the contribution of peasant and family farmers to give better and healthier food to our societies.
>
> (Surin Declaration, 2012)

The agroecological paradigm recognises that 'food embodies social, cultural and ecological values over and above its material value' (McMichael, 2008: 49) and demands a revitalised politics of 'agrarian citizenship' (Wittman, 2009) within which conventional terms such as sovereignty and rights need redefinition. For La Via Campesina, the question is fundamentally social—who should provide food, and how? Whose livelihoods should be protected?

## The path to food security

Food security and food sovereignty are complementary rather than oppositional concepts. The latter frames food security in terms of rights, in which food is a basic human right that can only be realised in a system where food sovereignty is guaranteed (Rosset, 2006). As a legal concept, the right to food arguably has more force than the concept of food security, being indivisible from other economic, social and cultural rights. It embraces worker and labour rights within the food system and is linked to rights to water, land and access to other productive resources, such as seeds. According to Jean Ziegler, the first UN Special Rapporteur for the Right to Food:

The right to food includes all the elements of food security—including availability, accessibility and utilisation of food—but it also goes beyond the concept of food security because it emphasises accountability. A rights-based approach focuses attention on the fact that making progress to reduce hunger is a legal obligation, not just a preference or choice.

(Ziegler et al., 2011: 7)

The rift between the food security discourse of the neoliberal model, on the one hand, and that of food sovereignty, on the other, can be traced to modern theories of economic development and the socially constructed notion of scarcity. Food sovereignty is premised on 'justice between all economic actors' achieved by agricultural trade based on 'relationships of equality, cooperation and fair exchange' (La Via Campesina, 2009: 61). In contrast, the relationship between the industrial or corporate food regime and the project of global development, represented by the WTO's (failed) Doha Development Round, has redefined and institutionalised food security as an 'internationally managed market relation' (McMichael, 2004: 57).

The idea of food sovereignty as a foil to the notion of food security exposes questions around the 'how' of the food system—its social control. As Raj Patel explains, 'as far as the terms of food security go, it is entirely possible for people to be food secure in prison or under a dictatorship' (2009: 665). Advocates of food sovereignty challenge glaring absences in the social construction of food security, asking 'who produces what, how it is produced and where it is produced' (Martinez-Torres and Rosset, 2014: 983).

Tactically reclaiming the role of the state in managing markets, La Via Campesina members challenge democratic, enabling states to act in the spirit of the movement's food sovereignty framework by reversing the priority given to exports and guaranteeing food security for citizens before engaging in responsible trade that does not damage the prospects of profit for farmers in the domestic markets of either trade partner. This position was validated a decade ago by La Via Campesina on the grounds that:

The first problem for farmers is a lack of access to their own local market because the prices are too low for their products and the import dumping they are confronted with. The access to international markets affects only 10 per cent of the world production, which is being controlled by transnational companies and biggest agro-industrial companies. The example of the tropical products (coffee, bananas) is illustrating this clearly.

(La Via Campesina, 2006)

This goes to the heart of what is 'sovereign' in food sovereignty. Food sovereignty promotes the role of the state as guarantor of rights, but recognises the *sovereignty of people* as the originators of claims. Claiming the need for strong, enabling states that can regain power over markets, food sovereignty may aim to 'widen policy spaces for the nation state in international regimes such as

*Food sovereignty and scarcity*   137

the trade regime' (Windfuhr and Jonsèn, 2005: 29), but the direction comes from the people. Within this framework, it is the responsibility of national governments to manage their trade relationships in a manner that protects food producers against dumping and unfair competition, thereby protecting the rights of people within a democratic framework.

Food sovereignty policies incorporate claims for the defence of cultural difference and territories. These claims challenge base inequalities and demand protection from activities that threaten the organic links between producers and consumers. They go beyond the primacy of individual property rights to a model of land reform based on the special nature of agriculture and its multifunctionality, and are focused on preserving landscapes, protecting livelihoods and valuing rural traditions (Rosset, 2006). Therefore, reform embraces the comprehensive revision of agricultural systems to favour the production and marketing of small farm produce. According to La Via Campesina, the external constraints imposed by international trade agreements not only lessen economic prospects, but also threaten the livelihoods, identities and cultures of individuals and communities that are inextricably tied to the land. The movement argues that the global trade regime lacks the capacity to go beyond class-based notions of political representation to a model that protects against the negative impacts of the market and also protects the environment. Food sovereignty does the latter by 'encompassing the role of civil society and of democratic communication while also acknowledging ecological limits' in recognition that 'an increasingly unsupportable model of food production is ruining soil quality, depleting water supplies and contributing to climate change' (Wittman, 2009: 808).

La Via Campesina's definition of food sovereignty simultaneously invokes the power of the state to provide protection and challenges its subordination to the market. It demands that the state provide social support and implement land reform, but also pushes the concept of food sovereignty beyond borders into transnational political arenas to pressure governments and educate publics regarding widespread injustices perpetuated by the architects of free trade areas (FTAs) and economic partnership agreements (EPAs). It emphasises that the solution to the global food crisis does not lie in market-led agrarian reform (MLAR), which has led to the dispossession and migration of a significant proportion of rural peasants, a point stressed at the Fifth World Social Forum (WSF) on Migrations held in November 2012 in Manila. Carlos Marentes, director of the US Border Agricultural Workers Project (a La Via Campesina member), describes the affinity between peasants and migrants:

> In reality, many migrants are peasants who have been displaced by the capitalist system and forced to migrate ... eight out of ten agricultural workers in the US are Mexican migrants—poor peasants that cannot survive on their own land and are forced to cross the border to look for work.
>
> (La Via Campesina, 2012)

138   *A. Mann*

Accordingly, La Via Campesina claims the neoliberal agribusiness offensive has recruited not only productive resources, but also people themselves. The pressure to resist a 'race to the bottom' whereby peasant farmers become a source of cheap labour for plantation owners and export-processing zones (EPZs), such as those in countries from Mexico to Sri Lanka, has driven the movement to engage in global advocacy that integrates social, environmental, economic and cultural concerns with demands for access to land, over which conflicts are escalating.

## 'New scarcities': land and water

Land and water scarcity have been presented as a growing threat to food security (FAO, 2011). A political ecology analysis of the trend of land-grabbing (which essentially also entails water- grabbing) again reveals the power and social relations that govern access to and control over these vital productive resources. The food price crisis of 2008 triggered a wave of large-scale land acquisitions that signal major changes in agricultural production, land use and labour relations. In 2011 the High Level Panel of Experts on Food Security and Nutrition (2011) reported that land-grabbing is damaging to the food security, income, livelihood and environment of those most vulnerable to hunger and malnutrition. In fewer than 25 per cent of recorded cases has the practice resulted in tangible agricultural output (HLPE, 2011: 9; see also Lawther, 2015). A lack of transparency and limited consultation with local communities characterise most deals, particularly where corrupt governments are involved. Local people without formal tenure are rarely consulted and do not give prior consent, sometimes resulting in violent evictions and human rights violations. Efforts to create a code of conduct for investors in the form of the Principles for Responsible Agricultural Investments (RAI) have been described as a corporate 'extreme makeover' designed to make TNCs appear responsive and sensitive to the needs of communities and the environment, particularly in developing countries (Borras and Franco, 2012: 35; see also FIAN International, 2010).

Access to land is fundamental to the right to food and, accordingly, food sovereignty. This is especially true for women, who are frequently denied tenure on the basis of their non–recognition as food producers or agricultural workers (Ziegler et al., 2011: 25). Advocates of food sovereignty argue that while market-assisted land reform has failed spectacularly in countries such as Guatemala (ibid.: 334), genuinely redistributive land reform is good economics and effective social policy, as it creates employment and can reverse outmigration from rural areas. It is also productive. The inverse relationship between farm size and output is particularly striking in the Global South, where many smaller farms have been discovered to be two to ten times more productive than larger ones (Rosset, 1999; see also Ziegler et al., 2011).

While calling for protection from global multilateral institutions against market forces in the form of 'food sovereignty rights', La Via Campesina calls

Food sovereignty and scarcity   139

on people, through the enabling state, to determine the content of those rights. These include access to land and choices regarding what to plant and what to trade, thereby 'asserting substantive reformulation of sovereignty through context-specific rights, situated in particular, historical subjectivities' (McMichael, 2008: 52). The rights of women, for example, are central to the food sovereignty framework, which recognises them as 'agents and actors and not merely consumers', emphasising 'social reproduction and social development as central components of rural development and rural employment' (Spieldoch, 2007: 12). As the producers of 60–80 per cent of food in developing countries, and as primary carers in most societies, women are affected more than men by food insecurity. Considering the intergenerational consequences of maternal and child malnutrition, discrimination against women as food producers is not only a violation of human rights but has consequences for society at large. Women's access to land, extension services and finance or credit must be improved if their role as small-scale food producers is to be protected.

Drawing connections between the structural violence of economic and political systems, the feminisation of agriculture and domestic oppression, 'food sovereignty is about ending violence against women' (Vivas, 2012). This gendered perspective of food sovereignty is one very important example of how the concept calls into question the neoliberal project as a whole on behalf of billions of rural poor. Far from aiming to reconstruct a nostalgic rural utopia, food sovereignty is about 'countering the catastrophic and ecological effects of the neoliberal assault on the agrarian foundations of society' (McMichael, 2014: 338).

## Cooperation from catastrophe

La Via Campesina's genesis provides evidence that collective action and cooperation can emerge from catastrophe (Solnit, 2004). There is growing recognition that addressing the imbalances in our food systems demands new approaches on all levels of governance. Former Special Rapporteur for the Right to Food, Olivier De Schutter, claims that 'there is certainly a new interest in food issues in the North due to the public health impacts attributed to the way food systems have developed and their effects on the environment, the inadequate attention given to nutrition, and the disappearance of small-scale and family farms in the region' (De Schutter, 2014: 17). During his tenure, De Schutter also drew attention to the impacts of changes in supply chains as significant for food producers. Global, vertically-integrated value chains comprise firms that engage directly with producers, cooperatives or local buyers that manage primary commodities such as cacao, in the case of chocolate. The development of these chains, which involve a number of countries at a time, has been enabled by reduced government intervention in agriculture markets, the deregulation of financial services and commodity futures market and the expansion of hybrid trade and investment agreements, of which NAFTA is the prototype (Burnett and Murphy, 2013). De Schutter claims:

140  *A. Mann*

> Food systems are undergoing deep transformations ... the increase in direct [foreign] investment is part of a larger transformation of the global supply chain in the agri-food sector. Commodity buyers (wholesalers) are larger and more concentrated than previously and they seek to respond to the requirements of their food industry clients by increased vertical coordination, tightening their controls over suppliers ... this [processing] sector is increasingly globalized and dominated by large transnational companies.
>
> (De Schutter, 2009: 4–5)

He argues for corrections to the imbalances of power in the food system where the relationships between actors are based 'solely on their relative bargaining strength' and believes that participation in agro-export networks should not be mandatory for farmers who wish to produce crops for local markets. Improvement of communication and transport infrastructure is essential in levelling the playing field for smallholders, while other instruments such as 'farmers' cooperatives, marketing arrangements, and public procurement' should be considered by states as a means to strengthen rural economies (De Schutter, 2009: 11). In this respect, he accords with the food sovereignty framework, which is not opposed to trade per se, but recognises that 'the current trade system is based on the reality that current international trade practices and trade rules are not working in favour of smallholder farmers' (Windfurh and Jonsén, 2005: 32). For members of La Via Campesina, trade is acceptable when prioritised below satisfying the needs of citizens and where domestic production cannot meet needs.

> Food sovereignty emphasises ecologically appropriate production, distribution and consumption, social-economic justice and local food systems as ways to tackle hunger and poverty and guarantee sustainable food security for all peoples. It advocates trade and investment that serve the collective aspirations of society.
>
> (Nyéléni, 2013)

Proposed policies that operate within a food sovereignty framework include a revised Common Agriculture and Food Policy (CAFP) that 'relocalises agricultural production close to where consumers live', put forward by the Coordination Europèenne Via Campesina. This model would rely on the European Union to regulate production, markets and distribution, and 'to take all the actors in the food chain into consideration' (La Via Campesina, 2010). More radical options include the development of trade groupings such as that proposed for sustainable cocoa to protect members of the Economic Community of West African States (ECOWAS) against cheap imports (Koning and Jogeneel, 2006).

Over the past decade the International Planning Committee on Food Sovereignty (IPC) has facilitated the participation of La Via Campesina and its allies in international governance after decades of marginalisation in discussions

*Food sovereignty and scarcity* 141

over world food security. In late 2009, the 127 UN member states agreed that the Committee on World Food Security (CFS) would become the primary global forum focused on food security and nutrition, with a difference; civil society organisations would become official participants on the Committee. Established in the 1970s in response to an earlier food crisis, the original CFS was largely ineffective in meeting its mandate to review and follow up food production and security issues, and was poorly supported by member states in terms of commitment and funding (Shaw, 2007).

The reformed CFS is promoted as a new space for engagement, a multi-stakeholder forum committed to eliminating hunger following three guiding principles: *inclusivity*, to ensure that voices of all relevant stakeholders are heard in the policy debates on food, agriculture and nutrition; *strong linkages to the field*, to ensure the work of the CFS is based on the reality on the ground; and *flexibility*, in the face of a changing external environment and the needs of countries (CFS, 2012: 9). Unlike the case in previous UN platforms, civil society actors will be recognised as meaningful political agents representing their own interests in the CFS mission to develop a global strategic framework on ending hunger. An autonomous international food security and nutrition civil society mechanism (CSM) facilitates the participation of organisations from countries that regularly experience food insecurity, many of which are members of La Via Campesina. In the reformed CFS, states remain the principal actors in voting and decision-making, but they will also be held accountable for addressing food insecurity.

The challenges for the CFS in creating a model for genuinely legitimate, inclusive and transparent global governance include balancing participation and representation, bringing about consensus while being sensitive to diversity, building trust, overcoming language barriers and engineering efficiency. The new platform has been described as an opportunity for state and non-state actors to 'challenge the logic of embedded neoliberalism' (Duncan and Barling, 2012: 158). Yet, whether it is legitimate, or even possible, for the UN to influence trade, is doubtful. As attractive as the idea is of considering trade alongside social, cultural and economic rights such as the right to food, the FAO has no mandate. Thus, the question remains—what institutions and mechanisms are needed to empower smallholders as economic actors and to value diverse modes of production?

The shared vision of agroecology and the systematic dissemination of agroecological farming practices through the *campesino-a-campesino* (farmer to farmer) methodology, is an increasingly significant 'socially activating tool' in consolidating and mobilising the food sovereignty project (Martìnez-Torres, 2014: 994). Over 40 peasant agroecology training schools now operate in the Americas, Africa, Asia and Europe. In 2014, the International Year of Family Farming, a series of FAO multi-stakeholder meetings in Latin America, Africa and Asia determined that agroecology should become an integral part of sub-national, national and regional agricultural policies and that governments should be encouraged and supported to mainstream agroecological approaches

142    *A. Mann*

to food production in their research and development programmes. Pilot projects, marketing strategies, educational programmes and monitoring systems are planned to alleviate the move to industrialised food production that continues to threaten local and indigenous communities in the regions. While this wider, formalised engagement with the agroecology concept is welcome, La Via Campesina is equally wary of the co-option of the concept by elites including the World Bank who have enabled corporate actors to successfully enter, and dominate, niche organic markets (Martìnez-Torres, 2014).

The new institutional frameworks needed to navigate the competing sovereignties must engage civil society actors in governance on multi-scalar levels and also address the urban–rural divide. Venezuela's urban *comunas* provide a working example of *corresponsabilidad*, which is defined as 'a means of bridging the formation of popular power and the existence (and gradual redistribution) of established state power' (Schiavoni, 2015: 477). In a nation where 90 per cent of the population is urbanised, this model is rebuilding rural–urban relationships through direct marketing channels and also reframing food sovereignty in terms of eaters' relationship to food and the processes of food production, distribution and consumption. Schiavoni (2015: 476) refers to the *comunas* as 'a demonstration of internal sovereignty in that, through joining together and organizing themselves into a comuna, the communal councils and communities that run them are demonstrating their intent to function as a sovereign unit'. As such, *corresponsisbilidad* is an example of the 'interactive governance' (Hospes, 2014: 125) that can drive the development of new forms of dialogue between state and civil society actors collaborating on food and agriculture policy.

## Conclusion

This chapter has addressed how food sovereignty exposes food scarcity as a socio-political construct that legitimises further intensification of production at the expense of people and environments. The food industry itself is a major contributor to overproduction, food insecurity and environmental degradation. Food sovereignty offers an alternative view of food as a natural resource. It resists simplistic linkages between population growth, climate change, conflict and resource scarcity, and reminds us that technological solutions are not neutral.

A political economy analysis exposes the ideology and forms of governance that normalise scarcity. Awareness of the representation of scarcity in hegemonic discourses that dominate global debates on food and agriculture reveals the machinations and contradictions of sovereign power. Food sovereignty challenges us to rethink where, and with whom, that sovereignty lies.

Critics of food sovereignty contest significant 'boundary issues' (Bernstein, 2014). How can states assert sovereignty in a globalised trade regime and reconcile this with local communities' desires to manage local food systems? How can 'both the state and units lying within it be sovereign with respect to food at the same time . . . are all communities to be equally sovereign with respect to food, rural and urban alike?' (Schiavoni, 2015: 468). Importantly, how are inequalities in food production capacities, within and between countries, to be resolved? These issues must be tackled if the epistemic community of food sovereignty is to advance its political project. A promising first step lies in refusing to allow the socially constructed notion of scarcity to remain the dominant frame for policy debate.

## References

Altieri, M. A., and Toledo, V.M. (2011) 'The agroecological revolution in Latin America: rescuing nature, ensuring food sovereignty and empowering peasants', *The Journal of Peasant Studies*, 38(3), pp. 587–612.

Andrèe, P., Aryes, J., Bosia, M. and Massicotte, M. (2014) *Food Sovereignty and Globalization*. Toronto: University of Toronto Press.

Bernstein, H. (2014) 'Food sovereignty via the "peasant way": a sceptical view', *The Journal of Peasant Studies*, 41 (6), pp. 1031–1063.

Borras, S. and Franco, J. (2012) 'Land grabbing and trajectories of agrarian change: a preliminary analysis', *Journal of Agrarian Change*, 12(1), pp. 34–59.

Burnett, K. and Murphy, S. (2013) 'What place in international trade for food sovereignty?' Paper presented to International Conference on 'Food Sovereignty: A Critical Dialogue', Yale University, 14–15 September.

CFS (2012) *The Committee on World Food Security: A Guide for Civil Society*. http:// www.eurovia.org/IMG/pdf/CFS_Booklet_PageByPage_Final.pdf.

De Schutter, O. (2014) 'The right to food guidelines, food systems democratization and food sovereignty', *Right to Food and Nutrition Watch*, FIAN.

De Schutter, O. (2009) 'Report of the Special Rapporteur on the right to food: Agribusiness and the right to food', 22 December, available: http://www.srfood. org/index.php/en/component/content/article/1-latest-news/641-agribusiness-and-the-right-to-food [accessed 8 February 2017].

Duncan, J. and Barling, D. (2012) 'Renewal through participation in global food security governance: implementing the international food security and nutrition civil society mechanism to the Committee on World Food Security', *International Journal of Sociology of Agriculture and Food*, 19(2), pp. 143–161.

Eakin, H., Bohle, H.G., Izac, A.M., Reenberg, A., Gregory, P. and Pereira L. (2010) 'Food, violence and human rights', in J. Ingram, P. Ericksen and D. Liverman (eds) *Food Security and Global Environmental Change*. London: Earthscan, pp. 245–271.

FAO (2011) 'Scarcity and degradation of land and water: Growing threat to good security', available: http://www.fao.org/news/story/en/item/95153/icode/ [accessed January 2016].

FIAN International (2010) 'Why we oppose the principles for Responsible Agricultural Investment (RAI)', available: http://www.viacampesina.org/en/images/stories/ pdf/whyweopposerai.pdf [accessed 23 December 2016].

Guthman, J. (2011) 'Excess consumption or over-production: US farm policy, global warming and the bizarre attribution of obesity', in R. Peet, P. Robbins and M.J. Watts (eds) *Global Political Ecology*. Abingdon: Routledge, pp. 51–66.

High Level Panel of Experts on Food Security and Nutrition (2011) *Land Tenure and International Investments in Agriculture*. Rome: Committee on World Food Security, available: http://www.fao.org/fileadmin/user_upload/hlpe/hlpe_documents/HLPE-Land-tenure-and-international-investments-in-agriculture-2011.pdf [accessed 11 May 2017].

## 144 A. Mann

Holt-Gimènez, E. and Shattuck, A. (2011) 'Food crises, food regimes and food movements: rumblings of reform or tides of transformation?', *The Journal of Peasant Studies*, 38(1), pp. 109–144.

Hospes, O. (2014) 'Food sovereignty: the debate, the deadlock, and a suggested detour', *Agriculture and Human Values*, 31, pp. 119–130.

Koning, N. and Jongeneel, R. (2006) 'Food sovereignty and export crops: could ECOWAS create an OPEC for sustainable cocoa?' Forum on Food Sovereignty, ROPPA.

Lang, T. and Heasman, M. (2016) *Food Wars: The Global Battle for Mouths, Minds and Markets* (second edition). London: Routledge.

Lawther, I. (2015) 'Land grabbing: new actors in a longstanding process', *Canadian Food Studies*, 2(2), pp. 250–255.

La Via Campesina. (2012) 'Peasants and migrants are building an International unity for the full rights of all migrants', available: http://viacampesina.org/en/index.php/mainissues-mainmenu-27/migrations-and-rural-workers-mainmenu-41/1345-peasants-and-migrants-are-building-an-international-unity-for-the-full-rights-of-all-migrants [accessed 24 December 2013].

La Via Campesina (2010) 'Towards a common agriculture and food policy 2013 within a food sovereignty framework', available: http://www.eurovia.org/spip.php?article274&lang=fr [accessed May 2016].

La Via Campesina (2009) *La Via Campesina Policy Documents: 5th Conference*, available: http://viacampesina.org/downloads/pdf/policydocuments/POLICY DOCUMENTS-EN-FINAL.pdf [accessed 20 September 2016].

La Via Campesina (2008) 'Via Campesina proposal to solve food crisis: strengthening peasant and farmer-based food production', available: http://www.foodfirst.org/en/node/2109 [accessed 20 September 2016].

La Via Campesina (2006) 'Food sovereignty', available: http://viacampesina.org/en/index.php/main-issues-mainmenu-27/food-sovereignty-and-trade-mainmenu-38/33-food-sovereignty [accessed 20 September 2016].

Mann, A. (2014) *Global Activism in Food Politics: Power Shift*. Basingstoke: Palgrave Macmillan.

Martìnez-Torres, M. and Rosset, P. (2014) 'Diàlogo de seberes in La Via Campesina: Food sovereignty and agroecology', *The Journal of Peasant Studies*, 41(6), pp. 979–997.

McMichael, P. (2014) 'Conclusion: the food sovereignty lens', in P. Andrèe, J. Aryes, M. Bosia and M. Massicotte (eds) *Food Sovereignty and Globalization*. Toronto: University of Toronto Press.

McMichael, P. (2008) 'Peasants make their own history, but not just as they please', *Journal of Agrarian Change*, 8(2–3), pp. 205–228.

McMichael, P. (2005) 'Global development and the corporate food regime', in F.H. Buttel and P. McMichael (eds) *New Directions in the Sociology of Global Development (Research in Rural Sociology and Development, Volume 11)*. Bingley, UK: Emerald Publishing Group Limited, pp. 265–299.

McMichael, P. (2004) 'Global development and the corporate food regime', Paper presented at Symposium on New Directions in the Sociology of Global Development, XI World Congress of Rural Sociology, Trondheim, 25–30 July, available: http://www.iatp.org/files/451_2_37834.pdf [accessed 24 December 2013].

Mehta, L. (2011) 'The social construction of scarcity: The case of water in western India', in R. Peet, P. Robbins and M.J. Watts (eds.) *Global Political Ecology*. Abingdon: Routledge, pp. 371–386.

Nyéléni (2013) 'Editorial: food sovereignty', available: http://www.nyeleni.org/DOWNLOADS/newsletters/Nyeleni_Newsletter_Num_13_EN.pdf [accessed 10 September 2014].

Patel, R. (2009) 'What does food sovereignty look like?', *The Journal of Peasant Studies*, 36(3), pp. 663–706.

Peet, R., Robbins, P. and Watts, M.J. (eds) (2011) *Global Political Ecology*. Abingdon: Routledge.

Ploeg, J. D. van der (2008) *The New Peasantries: Struggles for Autonomy and Sustainability in an Era of Empire and Globalisation*. London: Earthscan.

Reitan, R. (2007) *Global Activism*. New York: Routledge.

Rosset, P. (2006) 'Moving forward: Agrarian reform as part of food sovereignty', in P. Rosset, R. Patel and M. Courville (eds) *Promised Land: Competing Visions of Agricultural Reform*. Oakland, CA: Food First Books, pp. 301–322.

Rosset, P. (1999) 'The multiple functions and benefits of small farm agriculture', Policy Brief 4. The Institute for Food and Development Policy, available: https://foodfirst.org/wp-content/uploads/2013/12/PB4-The-Multiple-Functions-and-Benefits-of-Small-Farm-Agriculture_Rosset.pdf [accessed 11 May 2017].

Schiavoni, C.M. (2015) 'Competing sovereignties, contested processes: Insights from the Venezuelan food sovereignty experiment', *Globalizations*, 12(4), pp. 466–480.

Shaw, D.J. (2007) *World Food Security: A History Since 1945*. New York: Palgrave Macmillan.

Solnit, R. (2004) *Hope in the Dark: Untold Histories, Wild Possibilities*. Chicago: Haymarket Books.

Spieldoch, A. (2007) 'A row to hoe: the gender impact of trade liberalization on our food system', IATP Reports. Bonn, Germany: Friedrich-Ebert-Stiftung (FES), available: https://www.files.ethz.ch/isn/47736/2007-01-01_RowToHoe_EN.pdf [accessed 24 December 2013].

Surin Declaration (2012) 'First global encounter on agroecology and peasant seeds', available: https://viacampesina.org/en/index.php/main-issues-mainmenu-27/sustainable-peasants-agriculture-mainmenu-42/1334-surin-declaration-first-global-encounter-on-agroecology-and-peasant-seeds [accessed 10 September 2014].

Vivas, E. (2012) 'La Via Campesina: food sovereignty and the global feminist struggle', available http://www.pambazuka.org/en/category/features/85137 [accessed 11 May 2017].

Weis, T. (2007) *The Global Food Economy: The Battle for the Future of Farming*. London: Zed Books.

Windfuhr, M. and Jonsèn, J. (2005) *Food Sovereignty: Towards Democracy in Localised Food Systems*. Rugby: Food First Information and Action Network.

Wittman, H. (2009) 'Reworking the metabolic rift: La Via Campesina, agrarian citizenship, and food sovereignty', *The Journal of Peasant Studies*, 36(4), pp. 805–826.

World Food Program (2012) 'Hunger: the world's greatest solvable problem', available http://www.wfp.org/stories/hunger-worlds-greatest-solvable-problem [accessed 24 December 2013].

Ziegler, J., Golay, C., Mahon, C. and Way, S. (2011) *The Fight for the Right to Food: Lessons Learned*. Basingstoke: Palgrave Macmillan.

# 9 Rare earth diplomacy
## Mitigating conflict over technology minerals

*Elliot Brennan*

## Introduction

The minerals that combine to help make our technology are crucial building blocks for our modern world. These 'technology minerals'[1] are key in our everyday lives and are not only used in cell phones and automobiles but are also critical in aiding their functionality through fibre optic cables and the make-up of complex communication systems. Far from just being essential for everyday civilian uses, these minerals are also key components in many defence technologies. It is not, therefore, surprising that governments are eager to secure the supply chains of these technology minerals. Indeed, one could say that ensuring the continued and unimpeded access to such resources for use by private and public companies is an essential part of prudent and good governance. Without free market access to such minerals entire manufacturing sectors could grind to a halt, the manufacture and maintenance of key defence equipment might be interrupted or development of vital communication infrastructure could become severely impaired.

Of these minerals, some of the most crucial comprise the *lanthanides*, found on the periodic table between numbers 57 and 71, as well as *yttrium* at number 39. Together these elements are known as rare earth elements (REEs).

While many countries have significant deposits of REEs they do not necessarily have the viable mining, processing or refining capacities that make their industrialisation possible. There are numerous impediments to the creation of such industry, including the impact on the environment, significant operating costs and the dearth of mining companies willing to take a bet on commodities susceptible to the significant price volatility of REEs.

As new 'disruptive technologies'[2] come online, supply chains will be forced to transform, as will the refining and processing of such ores to make different grades of minerals for new end-users. In this fluid environment of technological change, supply chains will undergo constant pressure to adapt to meet new requirements. In the foreseeable future, supply chain shocks for technology minerals are increasingly likely.

The nature of availability and supply of REEs also makes them important features of international diplomacy. Economic competition has spilt over into the political realm, including the emergence in 2010 of a coercive diplomacy. Similar to the intimidation present in the nineteenth and twentieth century use of gunboat diplomacy, that which emerged is a coercive diplomacy for the modern, globalised era. This 'rare earth diplomacy' sought to pressure Japan and other manufacturing states in Asia, which are reliant on REEs, to relocate operations closer to the source of supply.

Recent disputes over REEs offer a cautionary tale as to how conflict over technology minerals can occur and may result in international conflicts. New and disruptive technologies force the emergence of new markets for critical minerals and, as a result, supersede current supply chains or create new ones. The contest for a stable supply of rare earth elements offers lessons in the resolution of disputes, which may be crucial to mitigating future resource conflict. This chapter explores recent conflicts over REEs and how, as a result, both the private sector and governments around the world have relearned the crucial importance of supply chain vulnerability in the face of new disruptive technologies. The discussion is divided into two sections. The first looks at the history of REEs and the origins of the disputes from the 1980s to late 2010. The second section explores how governments and the private sector have acted to address the global supply chain vulnerabilities inherent in the production and use of REEs.

## A prelude to conflict: REEs from the 1980s to 2010

### On scarcity

As discussed in greater detail later in this chapter, despite their name, REEs are not rare; instead they are difficult to find in large, economically viable and minable concentrations. Indeed, the processing of the mined ore to the final rare earth metal is capital and labour intensive, often requiring a thousand processing steps from mining to end use. The misconception of REEs being 'rare' is due to this misnomer itself. However, the contemporary understanding of scarcity is also misleading. Drivers of scarcity are often economic, and thus inherently social, rather than reflecting the absolute finiteness of the resource itself. Indeed, contemporary debates apportion blame for scarcity onto nature not humanity (Rayner, 2010). This is disingenuous and ignores the power of cultural change and other innovations that can shape allocation or even alter the fundamental dynamics of supply and demand.

The traditional understanding of scarcity observes the earth as a closed system writing-off the possible impacts of effective recycling regimes and improved efficiency. Similarly, in the race for new supply, extra-terrestrial and non-traditional supply of minerals (such as deep-sea resources) are increasingly seen as feasible sources of extraction. Indeed, the very idea of scarcity needs to be challenged (Mehta, 2010). Putting aside the obvious concerns of wanton consumption and over exploitation, the scarcity narrative often overlooks alternative models of consumption—alternative

148   *E. Brennan*

allocation or consumption models such as recycling of 'scarce' commodities. These emerge not from economic drivers but rather the evolution of socio-political discourse in our ever-changing societies. That scarcity, as it is commonly perceived, is socially generated and is overlooked in favour of countable tonnes and megatonnes and other misleading notions of recoverable and non-recoverable quantities. These in themselves provide a simplistic and hyperbolic understanding of scarcity. The evolution of socio-political discourse combined with on-going innovations means that what is 'scarce' one day, may be abundant (in terms of demand) the next. This is certainly true in the recent history of rare earth elements.

A more nuanced approach to the idea of scarcity is needed when observing REEs. Not least because the evolving nature of demand, in line with technological change, for different REEs means they vary in their 'scarcity' or perceived 'finiteness' (Xenos, 2010). Perception of REE scarcity is due to insufficient supply rather than the known reserves. This is further a result of unequal dispersion and unequal control over the global supply chain, as discussed later in this chapter. By a similar token, many of the technological products that contain REEs have become 'status products'; while not essential items for survival they are current sociological markers of status and wealth. As such, perceived scarcity of REEs differs from the perceived scarcity of other more vital life-supporting elements described in this volume—water, food and even the elements that support modern-day food production such as phosphorous. Thus, in the context of this book, the perceived scarcity of REEs (despite their character as essential building blocks of our modern technological world) should be viewed differently in that REEs are to some extent more adaptable and susceptible to change.

Regardless, the inequalities in the supply chain of REEs renders them to some extent scarce in the political and security realm. This in itself is an important consideration, for securing a stable supply of technological minerals, such as REEs, often leads to these minerals being described as 'scarce' for the purposes of strategic debates and foreign policy agendas. In other words, scarcity narratives around some minerals are simply perpetuated to justify interventions to secure the stable supply of technology minerals for domestic use.

### What are REEs?

REEs are a group of 17 elements on the periodic table. These elements are crucial in most high-tech products from advanced military technology to clean energies, automobiles and cell phones. The early use of REEs in televisions and computer monitors allowed for colour television sets and computer displays. *Europium,* which glows red under ultra violet (UV) light, is used in bank notes to allow the detection of forgeries and in thin super-conducting alloys. Fibre optic cables employ *erbium* as a key enhancer of optical properties. Permanent magnets, now crucial components in most high-tech goods, include alloys containing *neodymium, samarium, gadolinium, dysprosium* or *praseodymium.*

*Table 9.1* Selected applications for REEs

| | |
|---|---|
| **Electronics** | Lasers, fibre optics, display phosphors, medical imaging phosphors |
| **Magnets** | Motors, disk drives, power generation, microphones and speakers, MRI, car parts, communication systems |
| **Metal Alloys** | Cast iron, aluminium, magnesium, steel |
| **Catalysts** | Petroleum refining, catalytic converters, diesel additives, chemical processing |
| **Ceramics** | Colourants, sensors |
| **Glass** | Optical and UV glass, polishing compounds |
| **Others** | Fertiliser, water treatment, fluorescent lighting |

Source: author

The inclusion of these REEs is credited in the miniaturisation of e-goods. The use in fluorescent lamps of *yttrium, lanthanum* and *cerium*, among others, has enabled significant energy cuts through more efficient lighting. Similarly, the rise of green technologies such as wind turbines is unthinkable without REEs.

REEs can be divided into the heavier (HREE) elements and the more abundant lighter (LREE) elements, a distinction that relates to their atomic weights. LREEs comprise *cerium, europium, gadolinium, lanthanum, neodymium, praseodymium, promethium* and *scandium*. HREEs comprise, *dysprosium, erbium, holmium, lutetium, terbium, thulium, ytterbium* and *yttrium*. The LREEs are often found in bastnaesite deposits, while the HREEs are found in monazite deposits. Together, these constitute the majority of deposits found in China and North America. Also contained in monazite deposits are *thorium* and sometimes *uranium*, and, as a result, a small amount of radioactive waste is produced during the process of mining and refining. The prevalence of the different REEs varies greatly. For example, there is an abundance of *cerium* in many bastnaesite deposits and the market is well supplied. Conversely, the criticality of other REEs, particularly less abundant HREEs, such as *dysprosium*, remains a concern for end-users. Currently, *cerium* and *lanthanum* are the least valued REEs, while *neodymium* and *praseodymium*, the 'magnet metals', are two of the most highly valued. A 2010 US Department of Energy criticality matrix notes the importance of different REEs in the medium-term (2010–2025) development of green technologies (see Figure 9.1). This example of criticality demonstrates a common supply constraint for industry.

The ability of the People's Republic of China (hereafter China) to bear both the large capital investments needed for mining REEs and what one could call its higher 'social pain threshold' for the negative environmental and social impacts of their mining, has meant that the lion's share of HREEs is produced in China. The importance of REEs, particularly HREEs, in high-tech products makes them increasingly deemed to be in the national interest and has seen HREEs stockpiled by numerous governments in recent years. At the heart of the concern surrounding REEs is the global supply chain. The supply chain is heavily balanced in China's favour, which produces approximately

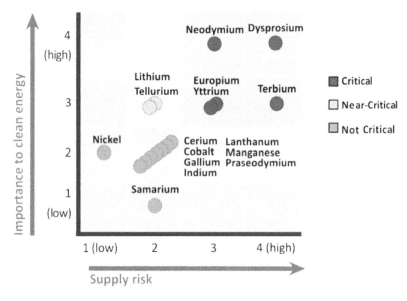

*Figure 9.1* Criticality matrix for green technology substrates
Source: US Department of Energy (2010)

90 per cent of global supply.[3] China's monopoly over production runs in tandem with the country being the biggest manufacturer of rare earth containing e-goods. However, despite China's production monopoly, it holds less than half of proven global reserves of rare earths. Estimates of China's reserves differ but range between 23 per cent and 42 per cent of global reserves (Information Office of the Chinese State Council, 2012; US Geological Society, 2015).

*Table 9.2* Global production and known reserves

| Country | Mine Production (metric tons) 2013 | 2014 | Reserves (metric tons) |
|---|---|---|---|
| US | 5,500 | 7,000 | 1,800,000 |
| Australia | 2,000 | 2,500 | 3,200,000 |
| Brazil | 330 | – | 22,000,000 |
| China | 95,000 | 95,000 | 55,000,000 |
| India | 2,900 | 3,000 | 3,100,000 |
| Malaysia | 180 | 200 | 30,000 |
| Russia | 2,500 | 2,500 | inc. in 'other countries' total |
| Thailand | 800 | 1,100 | N/A |
| Vietnam | 220 | 200 | inc. in 'other countries' total |
| Other countries | N/A | N/A | 41,000,000 |
| **World Total** | **110,000** | **110,000** | **130,000,000** |

Source: USGS, Mineral Commodity Summaries, January 2015; compiled by author

As noted, despite their name, REEs are not rare. They are, however, difficult to find in large, economically viable and minable concentrations and, furthermore, processing is costly in terms of financial and human resources. China's low labour costs, state-owned mining firms and centralised governance system, which can 'manage' the environmental cost, allows Beijing to operate mines at commercially viable levels. Nonetheless, this 'rare earth' misnomer hints at the potential conflict that surrounds the supply of the critical minerals.

A key problem with the production and processing of REEs is the industry's large environmental footprint.[4] Surface and ground water pollution, excessive exploitation leading to landslides, clogged rivers and environmental emergencies are some of the potential environmental problems associated with mining operations (Information Office of the Chinese State Council, 2012). While these issues are better monitored in Europe, Australia and North America, traditionally under tighter regulatory frameworks, the concerns remain the same and the monitoring of mining operations is costly. Environmental safety concerns were largely responsible for the initial closure of the Mountain Pass rare earth mine in the US. Similarly, a US$100 million clean-up was required at Mitsubishi's REE refinery in Malaysia. The environmental costs of China's REE mining were estimated to be approximately US$6 billion in 2012 (Els, 2012). Publicly, and in conversations between the author and Chinese diplomats, Beijing has increasingly expressed its concerns over the industry's environmental footprint (Information Office of the Chinese State Council, 2012).[5] In recent years, China has shut down mines, particularly around Beijing and other population centres, due in part to the negative effects on air quality.

REEs, like some other critical minerals, differ from ordinary commodities. The processing and production of REEs is more complex than the mining of other ores, such as iron ore. Typically, once commodities are mined they are then directly delivered to an end-user. For rare earth ore, once it is mined from a mineral deposit it must then be separated into individual rare earth oxides before the oxides can be refined into metals. The metals are then processed into rare earth alloys and manufactured into components used in a variety of e-goods, products and technologies. For commodities like iron ore it is often the logistics that are the crux of the operation, for REEs it is the processing.

### *Historical background to the strategic importance of REEs*

China's rare earth resources can be likened in importance to the Middle East's oil. They have immense strategic significance and we must certainly deal with rare earth issues with care, unleashing the advantages they bring.
Attributed to Deng Xiaoping (in Morrison and Tang, 2012: 1)

At the beginning of the technology boom in the 1980s, the US, propelled by the military-industrial complex of the Cold War, held the keys to much of the innovation leading the burgeoning global technology revolution. The US was the leading rare earth producer and, supported by a booming middle class,

152 *E. Brennan*

was also the largest manufacturer of rare earth containing e-goods. Beijing, through the remarkable foresight of Deng Xiaoping who likened China's REE resources to the Middle East's oil, had its eye fixed on developing China's rare earth and manufacturing industries.

In the 1980s, Magnequench, a leading US tech firm that was a crucial manufacturer for the US Department of Defense's Joint Direct Attack Munition Project, pioneered the manufacture of high-powered neodymium-iron-boron (NdFeB) magnets—vital to computer systems and used in advanced weaponry—for its then parent company, General Motors (GM). GM's restructuring in the early 1990s resulted in the sale of Magnequench. The consortium of companies that purchased the high-tech firm included two Chinese state-owned metals firms: San Huan New Materials and the China National Nonferrous Metals Import and Export Company. Both firms were run by a son-in-law of Deng Xiaoping. After the purchase, the chairman of the San Huan company took over as chairman of Magnequench. Shortly thereafter, the company's NdFeB magnet production line was duplicated in China. The transfer of the critical rare earth technology by Chinese state-owned firms was complete in 2001 when, on the day of the expiration of the terms of the agreement that stipulated Magnequench operations must stay in the US, the work force was made redundant and the equipment shipped to Tainjin China (Tkacik, 2008). As China's rare earth mining industry emerged in the late 1990s and early 2000s, the industry collapsed in the US. By 2002, the Mountain Pass rare earth mine in California was closed.

The strategy for China's takeover of the rare earth industry was perfectly executed and met with little resistance from the federal government or the relevant regulatory body, the Committee on Foreign Investment, in the US. At the time, still at the beginning of the technology revolution, rare earths were not given their due credit as a critical strategic resource. This, combined with the significant environmental backlash toward the mining of REEs in the US, meant there was little resistance to the downscaling of REE mining. In the coming years, as China came to control a near monopoly share of the global supply chain of rare earths, many in the US came to see the retreat from REE industry as a grave error.

China's own ambitions in the REE industry did not stop with the takeover of Magnequench, nor did it with the collapse of the mine at Mountain Pass or Beijing's near total monopoly of REE production. In 2009 a similar bid by a Chinese state-owned enterprise (SOE) was lodged to buy a majority stake in the company running Australia's largest rare earth mine at Mount Weld, in Western Australia. Perhaps having learnt from the Magnequench experience, the bid was rejected by Australian authorities. China Nonferrous Metal Mining Company (CNMC) had attempted to purchase a 51.66 per cent stake of Lynas Rare Earths. In a decision now seen as one of the most significant ever by Australia's Foreign Investment Review Board (FIRB), the Board requested that the ownership bid be reduced to below 50 per cent. The minutes of the FIRB meeting recorded that: 'We have concluded that they would not be able to exclude the possibility that Lynas' production could be controlled to the detriment of non-Chinese end-users' (Keenan, 2011). The Board deemed that this would have been 'inconsistent with the government's policy of maintaining Australia's position as a reliable supplier to all our trading partners and hence potentially contrary to national interest' (Keenan, 2011). The state-owned CNMC subsequently withdrew its bid. Beijing's aggressive acquisition strategy then gave way to a more coercive use of its REE dominance and ultimately witnessed a tipping point in how states viewed REEs.

### The tipping point: conflict between China and Japan

In September 2010, China halted exports of REEs to Japan. The move followed a diplomatic incident—a dispute over the arrest of a Chinese fishing boat captain after a collision with a Japanese coast guard vessel. Chinese exports of REEs to Japan dropped from 2300 to 400 metric tonnes between September and November 2010 (Morrison and Tang, 2012). Japan's high-tech manufacturing sector, reliant on Chinese REEs, was crippled. All of Japan's major firms were hit including Nissan, Toyota, Sony, Mitsubishi, Nissan, Honda and Hitachi.

The move drew wide criticism and was seen as 'economic intimidation' and an 'informal embargo' (Mazza et al., 2013). Despite the quick release of the detained fishing boat captain by Tokyo, the REE export ban from China to Japan was not lifted and the dispute dragged on for months. The export reductions forced high-tech and manufacturing firms, both from Japan and elsewhere, to relocate to China or buy rare earth metals on the black market to guarantee access to REE supply. After several months, with the export ban creating an inevitable REEs price increase that initiated a boom in illicit sale and smuggling of rare earth metals by disobliging Chinese suppliers willing to flout the export restrictions, the embargo finally ended.

### Global supply chain concerns

The 2010 dispute between China and Japan was of major concern to manufacturing countries that relied on China for REE supply. It also caught Washington off-guard. In the early 2000s, the US relied entirely on imports of REEs. Between 2006 and 2009, 92 per cent of the US' rare earth compounds and metals came from China (Mazza et al., 2013). By 2013, that number had fallen to 75 per cent (USGS, 2015). It is a figure that may fall even further, but without significant new production outside of China the supply chain remains heavily in China's favour.

REEs are part of a fragmented supply chain outside of China, with some locations having downstream but not upstream components of the REE value chain and others the inverse. As such, in order to reduce dependence on supply from China, mining alone is not sufficient. Instead, the full value chain—both upstream and downstream—must be developed. Despite concerns following

154  *E. Brennan*

the 2010 Japanese embargo, much of the REEs mined outside of China still needed to be shipped to China for processing or manufacturing.

Today, China's 'heavy handed mercantilist' approach to rare earths (An, 2015) is largely driven by Beijing's 'Go Global' policy, which aims to extend internationalisation of domestic firms and invest in the acquisition of strategic resources. Beijing is concerned for its own resource security to support its development. These concerns were expressed in China's twelfth Five-Year Plan (2011–2015), which anticipated a growing middle class, rapid urbanisation and growing consumption, including a significant push for renewable energies. With growing domestic demand predicted in coming years, REE exports from China are likely to continue in a downward direction.

## Addressing vulnerabilities: REEs after 2010

The study of conflict in recent years has evolved to have a more nuanced view of conflict (Brunk, 2012). Certainly, the impacts of high-intensity, long-lasting and deadly conflict are undeniably negative. Low-intensity and short-lived conflict aligns more closely with a positive interpretation of conflict, where the hostilities or disputes stimulate creative thinking, innovation and a more rapid change than would have likely occurred had the status quo persisted. The latter view can be observed in the global reaction to REE supply chain concerns since the 2010 tipping point that saw the dispute emerge between China and Japan.

Resource security and relevant disputes, frequently driven by supply chain imbalances, often promote new investment in research, exploration and technology innovation. For example, over the past half a century, high global energy prices have been the catalyst for the development of new and often cleaner energies, such as nuclear, wind, solar and, most recently, shale gas. Conflict over energy resources is also promoting an efficiency revolution where new technology is aimed at minimising wastage across the energy grid. China's assertive approach to its REEs has promoted a similar pattern of change. Technology innovation, new REE exploration (often unconventional) and processing efficiency, in the form of recycling regimes, have all emerged in recent years. Most importantly, it has provoked new strategic thinking at a governmental level on resource and supply chain security.

More specifically, the pathways out of the crisis of 2010, and the more general supply chain vulnerability, have led to an increase in production of REEs to diversify the points of supply, stockpiling of critical minerals, research and development toward substitution of REEs, new recycling regimes, and exploration of frontier deposits through deep-sea mining. Together these approaches have begun to whittle away a few percentage points of China's monopoly on the global supply chain of REEs. These changes have given governments and the manufacturing industry more of a buffer, albeit still wafer-thin, to insulate from sudden supply shocks. Most importantly, the debate that has occurred since 2010 has vastly improved the visibility of the global REE supply chain.

This identification and recognition of the problem has been the crucial first step to finding viable, long-term solutions. Importantly, the conflict allowed governments to address supply chain vulnerabilities and build resilience into a volatile and vulnerable supply chain that was necessary for adaptation toward a more balanced model.

### World Trade Organization (WTO) resolution

The most unified step following China's export cuts was to challenge Beijing in the rules-based system that governs global trade. In March 2012, Japan, the US and the EU joined together in an unprecedented demonstration of unity and launched a dispute settlement case against China at the WTO. The case revolved around the interpretation of China's invoking of 'General Exceptions' under Article XX(b), on resource conservation and environmental protection, as well as Article XX(g) on conserving an exhaustible natural resource. On 26 March 2014, the WTO ruled against Beijing. The panel in the dispute settlement case (DS431) found that: '[T]he overall effect of the foreign and domestic restrictions is to encourage domestic extraction and secure preferential use of those materials by Chinese manufacturers' (WTO, 2014). It continued to note that the restrictions were 'designed to provide Chinese industries that produce downstream goods with protected access to the subject materials' and that the intent of the restrictions was to 'control the international market for a natural resource' (WTO, 2014).

Despite the result, the arbitration process itself was long and costly. Exploiting long drawn out legal processes, whether it be over protectionism in the WTO or over territorial disputes as seen in the Permanent Court of Arbitration in The Hague, has been shown to work in Beijing's favour in the past. During such processes, Beijing has made important gains in market position (Wu, 2014) with little sanction from governing bodies. As such, even though successful, the arbitration mechanism alone was not a panacea to addressing the global supply chain problem.

### Stockpiling

Following the 2010 embargo particular emphasis was placed on creating strategic stockpiles of REEs by various governments. After much debate, in January 2013 the US Department of Defense recommended the stockpiling of US$120.43 million of HREEs (Humphries, 2013). At the same time, the US Department of Energy created the Critical Materials Institute, to act as an 'innovation hub for critical materials' for academics, industry partners and national laboratories. In September 2015, the US Defense Logistics Agency, part of the Department of Defense responsible for stockpiling, signed a contract with Texas Rare Earth Resources, a US exploration company focused on HREEs, to supply ultra-high purity rare earths (Texas Rare Earth Resources Corp., 2015). The contract is indicative of the more proactive government response to

156 *E. Brennan*

aid the domestic development of the REE sector in the US, as well as to rein-force strategic stockpiles. Worryingly, however, this announcement only came after the bankruptcy of the US' largest rare earth company, Molycorp.

Tokyo set out its need to stockpile REEs in a 2009 report from the Ministry of Economy, Trade and Industry titled 'Strategy for Ensuring Stable Supplies of Rare Metals'. Understandably, the importance of this stockpiling increased after 2010 and has been carried out by Japan Oil, Gas and Metals National Corporation (JOGMEC) under the Rare Metals Stockpiling Program. Much of the detail of Japan's stockpiling program remains undisclosed, but it is likely built on a similar programme, established in 1983 following the 1970s oil crisis, which aims to stockpile goods and resources equivalent to 42 days of standard consumption.

China also began stockpiling for what may be seen as a different purpose. China's stockpiles, managed by the State Bureau of Material Reserves and according to some estimates involving approximately 100,000 tonnes, have allowed Beijing greater control over global REE prices (An, 2015). The State Bureau of Material Reserves continued to expand these stockpiles in 2014 (USGS, 2015).

### Efficiency: new recycling regimes

There has been a renewed push to establish an industry that can manage the recycling of REEs and other critical materials already in circulation in an economy. For example, the European Association of Electrical and Electronic Waste Take Back Systems, or WEEE Forum, has grown to become the largest organisation of its kind in the recycling of e-waste. The US and Japan have also explored REE recycling programmes and to varying degrees these have been initiated. Amongst the programmes, the US Critical Materials Institute, along with scientists from the Korea Institute of Industrial Technology, are research-ing improvements for the recycling of REEs.

Globally, however, there remains very limited recycling of REEs due to the significant costs associated in the recovery of rare earth metals in e-waste. In 2011, REE recycling was estimated to account for around 1 per cent of sup-ply (Ali, 2014). The recovery of metals in the products is complicated by 'the dispersed nature of the rare earth compounds which are intricately embedded into the products' (Haque et al., 2014: 626).

While recycling alone is unlikely to meet demand for new REEs, the inte-gration of recycling costs in the pricing of consumer goods would support greater sustainability of the resource. Similarly, the mandatory or incentivised collection of e-waste and an effective trade-in regime would further support the necessary move away from a linear 'take–make–dispose' economy model toward a more integrated 'circular economy' model. Toward this end, the EU Parliament passed a law in 2012 forbidding the dumping of electronic scrap. The law will compel EU member states to collect tons of e-waste—an important first step in the recycling process.

Indeed, an increase in recycling is the next logical step to secure critical materials and free-up global supply chain problems, particularly in developed economies. If mass-scale recycling is established it may prove more cost effective than the capital- and labour-intensive recovery and processing of rare earth ores.

### Research and development (R&D): technological advances

The uncertainty in the market that the 2010 China–Japan dispute brought to the fore shocked the industry into action. Manufacturers in Japan began, where possible, to reduce the amount of REEs in their products and boost investment for research into REE substitution. Such substitution is two part; material substitution and functional or technical substitution. The former relies on the substitution of the REE in the product with another element, while the latter relies on the advancement of entirely new technologies to supersede the function of the REE-containing products.

The Japanese government has invested heavily in REE substitution research. The New Energy and Industrial Technology Development Organization poured US$81 million into a REE reduction and substitution research program. Similarly, the Rare Metal Substitute Materials Development Project, which ran for eight years, had an estimated annual budget of US$66 million (An, 2015). The National Institute for Materials Science conducts similar research and controls equally impressive annual budgets. An example of a successful REE substitute can be found in Toshiba's 2012 development of a dysprosium-free permanent magnet that employs samarium (a less-critical REE) and cobalt. Despite research, substitutes to date are largely less effective than their REE-containing components.

As well as REE substitution R&D, there have also been considerable advances in processing and mining, where new techniques are allowing REEs to be more easily separated from other ores. These advances have enabled new frontiers to emerge in exploration and recovery.

### Exploration: new frontiers

The 2010 crisis that exposed the REE supply chain vulnerabilities saw the opening of a host of new exploration and production frontiers and the injection of new capital into frontier projects. India, a long-time producer of REEs through its Indian Rare Earths Limited, has increased production from monazite sands with a view toward increased processing to reduce imports from China. Investments from Japan have also supported REE production ventures in Vietnam, India and Malaysia amongst others. Central Asia and several countries in Africa and Latin America have also emerged as new sources of onshore production.

Similarly, there has been renewed interest and significant investment into offshore mining. In 2013 Japan confirmed the discovery of a deposit with a high concentration of HREEs. The catch is that the deposit is 5700m below

158   *E. Brennan*

sea level. Japan's discovery exemplified a wider trend in the hunt for new resources. Nowhere has this been more prominent than in the Pacific Islands.

REEs can be found between 800m and 2500m in the cobalt-rich manganese crusts below the ocean floor in the South Pacific Islands. Much deeper deposits (below 4000m) are also indicated in the Indian Ocean. At the time of writing, over 300 exploration licences for deep seabed minerals had been granted in Pacific Island countries, including Tonga, Fiji, the Solomon Islands and Vanuatu, as well as dozens more in the Indian and Pacific oceans.

The Papua New Guinean (PNG) government has been the first to undertake the venture to tap this new source of potential supply. The first ever deep-sea mining project is being led in a joint venture with Canadian Company, Nautilus Minerals. The Solwara 1 project in the Bismark Sea, some 50km off the coast of PNG, will mine the hydrothermal sea floor vents at a depth of 1500m. The technique for mining hydrothermal vents on the ocean floor, which one commentator explains is similar to 'cutting grass' (Begley, 2010), will use remotely operated vehicles to harvest hydrothermal vents rich in high-grade copper, gold, silver and zinc deposits. The ore will then be pumped to a platform on the surface for processing. Amongst these high-grade ores are significant concentrations of REEs.

As well as these ventures in the Pacific Islands, there are others in deeper international waters involving India and China. Since 2001, the International Seabed Authority (ISA)[6] has issued 26 contracts for exploration of deep-sea minerals in the Indian, Pacific and Atlantic Oceans. The body is drafting environmental management guidelines and exploitation regulations due to be implemented by 2016. Still, some commentators are concerned that the ISA will not have 'sufficient teeth' to monitor compliance of companies engaged in deep-sea mining regulations (Maurin, 2013). Environmental concerns also loom large (Wedding et al., 2015). Commentary in an article in *Science* on deep-sea mining noted that: 'today's low rates of marine extinction may be the prelude to a major extinction pulse, similar to that observed on land during the industrial revolution, as the footprint of human ocean use widens' (McCauley et al., 2015). Yet despite these concerns, the demand for a new supply of REEs and other high-grade ores seems certain to outstrip environmental concerns, particularly given that operations are far more remote and mine sites near-impossible to picket.

The prospect of access to abundant high-grade deposits of REEs and other minerals has attracted significant interest from resource hungry countries. In 2012, India's Minister for Earth Sciences, Ashwani Kumar, noted the strategic importance of such mining when he commented that 'countries like China have taken to deep-sea mining with a strategic purpose' (Mukherji and Wright, 2012). In recent years, India has poured money into exploration activities, including the purchase of a US$135 million deep-sea exploration vessel, staffed with a multidisciplinary team of scientists. The race for deep-sea minerals has begun. If successful it could be a game-changer for the REE supply chain, as well as for other technology minerals.

## REEs as an instrument for transitions in Myanmar, Afghanistan and North Korea

Concern over the REE global supply chain has also given impetus for engagement in new frontiers where conflict and military governments dominate. North Korea, Myanmar and Afghanistan all have significant and largely untapped mineral wealth. In East Asia, North Korea's reportedly large rare earth deposits offer a new carrot for diplomacy. The prospect of new mining joint ventures in resource rich Myanmar, which could improve competition and diversify the sector away from Chinese dominance, was one of the key reasons for Myanmar's transition from military junta to democracy. Similarly, as Afghanistan attempts to stabilise after a decade and a half of war, the country's mineral wealth is an important source of income to aid in its transition from a war-torn country to a developing nation. While these troubled but resource rich countries offer potential for significant new sources of rare earth ores, they carry obvious high degrees of risk.

While interest in these untapped resources is significant, none captures the imagination of the rare earth hungry world more than North Korea. In 2011, the late Kim Jong Il channelled Deng Xiaoping saying that North Korea's rare earth and mineral resources were 'a precious natural resource that is urgently needed for the country's wealth, prosperity and development, it must thoroughly utilize them without wasting even a lump of ore' (Korean Central Broadcasting Station, 2011).

In May and June 2014, Pyongyang shipped US$1.8 million in REEs to China (Kang, 2014). The export was significant, more so for the dramatic increase than the simple volume. The exports were a sizeable increase on the first shipments of rare earth ores to China in January 2013, which totalled a mere US$24,700. Many analysts saw the increase as proof of earlier assertions that North Korea could be a new hub for the highly sought-after ores. This development, along with what is believed to be trillions of dollars' worth of mineral deposits, could aid the emergence of a new era in North Korea relations in East Asia—and a more cooperative, rather than coercive, type of rare earth diplomacy.

While reports of the Jongju super deposit remain contentious, it would be the largest deposit of its kind with an estimated 216 tonnes of total rare earths oxides—of which at least 2 per cent are HREEs (SRE Minerals, 2015)—and other minerals. The geology of much of North Korea's deposits is reported to be easier to mine than in other countries, and while there remain questions about the exact size of these deposits and the obvious difficulties of operating in North Korea, the prospects offer possible leverage in future negotiations with Pyongyang.

A more promising and immediate source of REEs is in Myanmar. Rare earths are known to exist across the area known by geologists as the Eastern Highlands in eastern Myanmar. Much of the area in which rare earths may occur is held by ethnic armed groups and as a result has not been extensively surveyed. In 2014, significant exports of tin ore from Wa State in eastern Shan State in Myanmar to China were described as a 'black swan' event that impacted on tin prices in the global markets (Gardiner et al., 2015). A similar prospect may await REEs from south-eastern Myanmar. As well as REEs, Myanmar's untapped resources promise other technology minerals including antimony, platinum group of metals and tungsten. Only after resource sharing agreements and lasting peace can be achieved between the Tatmadaw (the Myanmar armed forces) and ethnic armed groups will deposits of REEs in the country be fully surveyed (Brennan, 2013). In the meantime, they risk becoming conflict minerals much like the now infamous jade and rubies in Myanmar's restive north.

In a world that is increasingly reliant on high-tech manufacturing—and therefore REEs—improving the overall stability of the global supply chain of REEs is a key concern for economies the world over. The untapped technology minerals, such as rare earths, that lie beneath the feet of military-run governments can be powerful incentives to open up to new foreign investment and transition to more democratic forms of government.

However, such political 'openings' are fraught with difficulties. Russia demonstrates an example of a political opening that was heavily supported by allowing greater access for the sale of the country's resources. The rise of Vladimir Putin to control Russia's key resources demonstrates that such openings, supported by resource wealth, can quickly turn back into resource-controlling oligarchies. Similar problems have also been witnessed in Myanmar's political transition (Brennan, 2013). Regardless of where minerals or mining is centred, the wealth generated is more often than not centred in individuals rather than sovereign wealth funds. Such a cooperative-type of rare earth diplomacy should have, as a central tenet, a moral underpinning that prohibits the purchase of conflict minerals and demands transparency, such as is required by the Extractives Industries Transparency Initiative.

## Conclusion

The history of disputes over the REE global supply chain offers a cautionary tale for other technology minerals. Governments must be cognisant of how new disruptive technologies can create international disputes. They must employ numerous tools to avert conflict and provide sufficient capital and incentives to boost research, as well as innovation to allow policy options and pathways out of such conflicts. Greater emphasis of the strategic importance of technology minerals and their supply chains is needed in academic research, along with greater awareness to build them into foreign policy.

Employing an array of tools to address such supply chain problems—R&D, international arbitration, new exploration, strategic stockpiles and recycling regimes—is the best approach for governments to tackle future problems. There is a need for an International Agreement for Global Minerals. Yet, such a binding agreement remains unlikely and instead, industry self-regulation that is founded on international treaty obligations is the most probable way forward for the foreseeable future. As such, regional regulatory frameworks, like those implemented by the European Parliament in 2015 for a mandatory monitoring system for minerals from conflict regions, will have more success in establishing global standards.

Diplomatic crises over access to technology minerals will continue in the future. In order to minimise the fallout from such incidents, and the potential for an escalation to conflict, numerous avenues for arbitration are needed. However, the most influential component to secure the global supply chain will remain the ability of technology to adapt and innovate to new conflicts and issues as they arise. That said, technological advances will also create new and, at least to some extent, unpredictable dynamics of supply and demand. Technology is not static and its constant evolution will continue to create new trends in supply and demand. Monopolies can quickly emerge and can, just as quickly, become insignificant. The response of governments and industry to rare earth supply chain vulnerability should be looked at as a case study for future shocks and conflict over the supply of technology minerals.

## Notes

1 Technology minerals include REEs, antimony, platinum group of metals (PGM), tungsten, indium, gallium, magnesium, germanium, graphite and beryllium.
2 'Disruptive technology' can be defined as a technology, often a new innovation, that significantly alters the status quo. A disruptive technology may change the supply chain or general business operation. For example, the discovery and exploitation of oil acted to overhaul other energy sources such as the use of oil from whale blubber, in effect ending the whaling industry.
3 As of May 2014, production of REEs in China occurred in Fujian, Guangdong, Guangxi, Hunan, Inner Mongolia, Jiangxi, Shangling and Sichuan provinces.
4 Despite the large environmental footprint in their mining, REEs, in their end uses, often play an important role in the production of green energy. They are crucial in green technologies such as advanced wind turbines, solar panels and hybrid cars. The interest among states to develop green technologies as a means to meet $CO_2$ emissions reduction targets is perhaps nowhere more prominent than in China itself. Faced with a seemingly insatiable demand for electricity and increasing pollution from coal and non-renewable power generation, Beijing has placed unprecedented importance on boosting renewables in its energy mix. Electricity from wind turbines should increase dramatically from 2009 base rates of 12 gigawatts (GW) to 100 GW by 2020. Meanwhile, the installed capacity of solar energy is targeted to triple by 2017 to 70 GW.
5 Beijing's reorganisation of the rare earth mining industry, which is fragmented and made up of numerous small artisanal mines, is the reason for the contentious decrease in exports, according to conversations between the author and Chinese diplomats as well as public statements to the WTO. Beijing contests that the reorganisation was aimed at cleaning up the environmental impacts of the industry. Of course, a by-product of this reorganisation has been a consolidation of the industry that has resulted in greater centralised control where operations can be more closely monitored by Beijing. Beijing has also encouraged SOEs to diversify their businesses toward rare earth mining. Large SOEs such as Aluminium Corporation of China have begun investing away from their traditional areas of operation and into rare earth mining and processing.

## 162   E. Brennan

6 The ISA is an intergovernmental body established in 1994. The Authority, as explained in its mandate, 'is the organization through which States Parties to the Convention [United Nations Convention on the Law of the Sea] shall, in accordance with the regime for the seabed and ocean floor and subsoil thereof beyond the limits of national jurisdiction (the Area) established in Part XI and the Agreement, organise and control activities in the Area, particularly with a view to administering the resources of the Area.'

## References

Ali, S.H. (2014) 'Social and environmental impact of the rare earth industries', *Resources*, 3(1), pp. 123–134.

An, D.L. (2015) 'Critical rare earths, national security, and U.S.-China interactions— A portfolio approach to dysprosium policy design', *RAND Corporation*, available: http://www.rand.org/pubs/rgs_dissertations/RGSD337.html [accessed 20 October 2015].

Begley, S. (2010) 'Mining's final frontier', *Newsweek Magazine*, 20 September, available: http://www.thedailybeast.com/newsweek/2010/09/20/is-deep-sea-mining-bad-for-the-environment.html [accessed 20 Oct 2015].

Korean Central Broadcasting Station (2011) 'Kim Jong Il Visits Hyesan Youth Mine', Apr 21, as quoted in Bermudez J.S. Jr., 'North Korea's expansion of molybdenum production', *38North*, 23 January, available: http://38north.org/2015/01/jbermudez012315/ [accessed 11 October 2015].

Brennan, E. (2013) *Myanmar's Mineral Resources: Boon or Bane for the Peace Process?*. Stockholm: Institute for Security and Development Policy.

Brunk, C.G. (2012) 'Shaping a vision: the nature of peace studies', in C.P. Webel and J. Johansen (eds) *Peace and Conflict Studies: A Reader*. New York: Routledge, pp. 10–24.

Els, F. (2012) 'Rare earth mining in China: Low tech, dirty and devastating', *Mining.com*, 5 May, available: http://www.mining.com/rare-earth-mining-in-china-low-tech-dirty-and- devastating/ [accessed 20 September 2015].

Gardiner, N.J., Sykes, J.P., Trench, A. and Laurence, J.R, (2015) 'Tin mining in Myanmar: production and potential', *Resources Policy*, 46(2), pp. 219–233.

Haque, N., Hughes, A., Lim, S. and Vernon, C. (2014) 'Rare earth elements: overview of mining, mineralogy, uses, sustainability and environmental impact', *Resources*, 3(4), pp. 614–635.

Information Office of the Chinese State Council (2012) 'Situation and policies of China's rare earth industry', People's Republic of China White Paper, available: http://www.miit.gov.cn/n11293472/n11293832/n12771663/n14676956.files/n14675980.pdf [accessed 3 November 2015].

Keenan, R. (2011) 'Australia blocked rare earth deal on supply concerns', *Bloomberg*, Feb 15, available: http://www.bloomberg.com/news/articles/2011-02-14/australia-blocked-china-rare-earth-takeover-on-concern-of-threat-to-supply [accessed 3 November 2015].

McCauley D.J., Pinsky M.L., Palumbi, S.R., Estes J.A., Joyce F.H. and Warner R.R., (2015) 'Marine defaunation: animal loss in the global ocean', *Science*, 347(6219), pp. 247–254.

Mazza, M., Blumenthal, D. and Schmitt, G.J., 'Ensuring Japan's critical resource security: case studies in rare earth element and natural gas supplies', *American Enterprise Institute*,

*Rare earth diplomacy* 163

available:http://www.aei.org/files/2013/07/23/-ensuring-japans-critical-resource-security-case-studies-in-rare-earth-element-and-natural-gas-supplies_180131600240.pdf [accessed 2 November 2015].

Maurin, C. (2013) *Deep Seabed Minerals: A New Frontier in The Pacific Region*. Stockholm: Institute for Security and Development Policy, available: http://www.isdp.eu/images/stories/isdp-main-pdf/2013-maurin-deep-seabed-minerals.pdf [accessed 19 November 2015].

Mehta, L., (2010) 'Introduction', in L. Mehta (ed.) *The Limits to Scarcity: Contesting the Politics of Allocation*. Abingdon: Earthscan, pp. 1–8.

Morrison, W.M. and Tang R., (2012) *China's Rare Earth Industry and Export Regime: Economic and Trade Implications*. Washington, DC: Congressional Research Service, Apr 30, available: www.fas.org/sgp/crs/row/R42510.pdf [accessed 2 November 2015].

Mukherji, B. and Wright, T. (2012) 'India bets on rare earth minerals', *The Wall Street Journal*, 13 August, available: http://www.wsj.com/articles/SB10000872396390443437504577546772533972202 [accessed 2 November 2015].

Rayner, S. (2010) 'Foreword', in L. Mehta (ed.) *The Limits to Scarcity: Contesting the Politics of Allocation*. Abingdon: Earthscan, pp. xvii-xx.

SRE Minerals (2015) Pacific Century Rare Earth Minerals Limited [online], available: http://www.sreminerals.com/pcrem.php [accessed 15 November 2015].

Texas Rare Earth Resources Corp. (2015) 'U.S. Defense Logistics Agency Awards TRER Strategic Materials Research Contract', press release, 25 September, available: http://trer.com/news/press_releases/index.php?&content_id=155 [accessed 12 November 2015].

Tkacik, J.J. (2008) 'Magnequench: CFIUS and China's thirst for U.S. defense technology', The Heritage Foundation, 2 May, available: http://www.heritage.org/research/reports/2008/05/magnequench-cfius-and-chinas-thirst-for-us-defense-technology [accessed 3 Nov 2015].

US Geological Society (2015) 'Mineral Commodity Summaries: Rare Earths, January', available: http://minerals.usgs.gov/minerals/pubs/commodity/rare_earths/mcs-2015-raree.pdf / [accessed 3 November 2015].

Wedding,L.M.,Reiter,S.M.,Smith,C.R,Gjerde,K.M.,Kittinger,J.N.,Friedlander,A.M., Gaines, S.D., Clark, M.R., Thurnherr, A.M., Hardy, S.M. and Crowder, L.B., (2015) 'Managing mining of the deep seabed', *Science*, 349(6244), pp.144–145.

World Trade Organization (2014) *Chronological list of disputes cases*, 'DS431 China — Measures Related to the Exportation of Rare Earths, Tungsten and Molybdenum (Complainant: United States)'; 'DS432 China — Measures Related to the Exportation of Rare Earths, Tungsten and Molybdenum (Complainant: European Union)'; 'DS433 China—Measures Related to the Exportation of Rare Earths, Tungsten and Molybdenum (Complainant: Japan)', available: http://www.wto.org/english/tratop_e/dispu_e/dispu_status_e.htm [accessed 23 October 2015].

Wu, M. (2014) 'A free pass for China', *The New York Times*, 2 April, available: http://www.nytimes.com/2014/04/03/opinion/a-free-pass-for-china.html?_r=0 [accessed 11 November 2015].

Xenos, N. (2010) 'Everybody's got the fever: scarcity and US national, energy policy', in L. Mehta (ed.) *The Limits to Scarcity: Contesting the Politics of Allocation*. Abingdon: Earthscan, pp. 31–48.

# 10 Going with the flow

## Can river health be a focus for foreign policy?

*David Tickner*

## Introduction

In March 2010, Hillary Clinton, then US Secretary of State, gave a speech at the National Geographic Society in Washington, DC to mark the UN's World Water Day. In her remarks, Secretary Clinton said:

> the water that we use today has been circulating through the earth since time began. It must sustain humanity for as long as we live on this earth. In that sense, we didn't just inherit this resource from our parents; we are truly, as many indigenous cultures remind us, borrowing it from our children. It is my hope that by making water a front burner issue, a high priority in our national and international dialogues, we can give our children and our children's children the future they deserve.[1]
>
> (Hilary Clinton, 2010)

Secretary Clinton was not alone; in recent years, several other high-profile figures from the foreign policy sphere have emphasised the importance of water issues, including Baroness Catherine Ashton, then High Representative of the European Union for Foreign Affairs and Security Policy, who wrote that, 'we should listen to what history teaches us: there are superior causes that transcend any political interests. Water is such a cause' (Ashton, 2010: 12). A quick survey of publications such as *Science and Diplomacy*, *The Diplomat* and *Foreign Policy* and the websites of think tanks such as the Stimson Center, the Woodrow Wilson Center, the Oxford Research Group or Chatham House, suggests that in recent years water has attracted regular attention from international affairs commentators across Europe and North America. The potential for water resources to be a stimulus for, and a weapon in, conflicts is a recurring theme in the recent discourse, especially with regards to recent instability in the Middle East (Gleick, 2014). There has also been discussion in these arenas of the potential for water to be a focus for cooperation, peace and security.

The water on which people rely for irrigation, industrial uses, energy generation or domestic supply falls to earth as rainfall or snow. Much of it then gathers in rivers, lakes, wetlands and aquifers, which act as natural reservoirs

*Going with the flow*  165

from which society sources water. Rivers are the most visible, and often the most contested, components of this hydrological architecture. As linear, flowing features in the landscape, rivers connect economies, societies, cities and countries. In doing so, they act as foci for conflict or cooperation between different groups of people who need water or other goods and services that rivers provide. The ecological health of rivers—in terms of the physical flow of water, its quality and the condition of the plants and animals that live in or on it—can be thought of as a biophysical litmus test of whether societies manage water resources sustainably (Tickner and Acreman, 2013). But as the human population in many regions continues to grow, economies shift and climate change takes hold, global indicators of river health are in steep decline with knock-on impacts on strategically important ecosystem services (Dudgeon et al., 2006; Vorosmarty et al., 2010; Millennium Ecosystem Assessment, 2005). This chapter argues that, in some contexts, maintaining or restoring critical aspects of river ecosystem health can be a catalyst for cooperation between different groups of people and can mitigate socio-economic and geopolitical risks that arise when critical ecosystem services are compromised. As such, river restoration might present opportunities for the foreign policy community.

The chapter provides an overview of the important role rivers have played in the rise of civilisations, cultures and economies and the extent to which governance of rivers throughout history has been characterised by conflict or cooperation. It then briefly outlines the main causes and likely consequences of the ongoing collapse in the ecological condition of many rivers. Finally, it sets out possible solutions to the primary global challenges of river management and, based on 'six streams' of effort, suggests ways in which the foreign policy community in OECD countries and international organisations can make substantive contributions to designing and implementing these solutions.

## Civilisation and development, cooperation and conflict

Rivers host extraordinary concentrations of biodiversity (Dudgeon et al., 2006). They have inspired a wide range of art, music and literature (think of The Haywain by John Constable, Johann Strauss' *Blue Danube* waltz or the central role played by the Mississippi in Mark Twain's *Huckleberry Finn*). In many instances, they also hold great spiritual importance. For instance, the Whanganui iwi of New Zealand have a traditional saying that underscores the connection between rivers and ancestry: 'The great river flows from the mountains to the sea. I am the river and the river is me' (Young, 2005). The reverence in which hundreds of millions of Indians hold the 'mother Ganga' river is another example of this. In the context of foreign policy, perhaps the greatest significance of rivers lies in the role they have played in the rise of civilisations and economies and the way in which they have fostered cooperation and/or conflict between upstream and downstream groups.

166   *D. Tickner*

In his great book about the role of the Yangtze in Chinese history, *The River at the Centre of the World*, Simon Winchester wrote that the river was, 'the symbolic heart of the country, and at the very centre, literally and figuratively and spiritually, of the country through which it so ponderously and so hugely flows' (Winchester, 1996: 13). Archaeologists have dated fortified settlements along the Yangtze River to 6400–6100 BP and linked the rise of settlements and monarchs along the river to periods of fluctuating climate, shifting summer monsoons and the need for access to, and administration of, water for irrigation (Yasuda et al., 2004). Opponents of the construction of the Three Gorges Dam in the 1990s were concerned about the inundation of nearly 1300 known archaeological sites along the river's banks (Childs-Johnson and Sullivan, 1996) and scientists have suggested that the earliest human cultivation of rice took place in the Yangtze region (Normile, 1997). Similar evidence of the rise of civilisations and dynasties has been found along the banks of the Yellow River (Wu et al., 2016), the Ganges and Indus (Giosan et al., 2012), the Nile (Hassan, 1997), the Danube (Childe, 1927) and many other rivers. Arguably, the earliest civilisation of all rose along the banks of the Tigris and Euphrates in Mesopotamia (literally, 'the land between the rivers'). The presence there of naturally complex river channel networks and avulsion belts (areas subject to shifting river courses, especially as a result of flooding episodes) is thought to have provided conditions so good for irrigation that they allowed societies to settle and develop (Morozova, 2005). One such site, at the confluence of the two rivers at al Qurna, is thought to be the cradle of civilisation and birthplace of Abraham.

In modern history, river management has contributed significantly to economic development and has helped shape societies. In response to the Great Depression, the US Congress authorised the establishment of the Tennessee Valley Authority (TVA) with a remit to undertake huge hydropower and flood management infrastructure works in 1933 as a means of kick-starting the economy in the south-eastern US.[2] The TVA took to a new level the engineering-led, technical water resource management paradigm, which had emerged in Europe and North America during previous centuries. In doing so it provided a global blueprint for large water management infrastructure which has been, and continues to be, dominant in countries such as Ethiopia, Egypt, Mexico, Brazil and India (where Jawaharlal Nehru, the country's first prime minister after independence, described dams as the 'temples of modern India') (Pegram et al., 2013). Such 'hydraulic missions' (Allan, 2001; Swyngedouw, 1999) became part and parcel of nation and state-building efforts. Often, the construction and operation of dams, irrigation schemes and flood defences was closely associated with the building of political capital and the establishment of powerful administrative agencies. Nowhere is this truer than in China where multiple ministries, often called the 'nine dragons', share responsibilities for, and vie for influence over, water resources and river management (Yan et al., 2006) and where the building of the Three Gorges Dam fulfilled a nation-building vision held by Sun Yat-sen, Mao Zedong and Deng Xiaoping (Ponseti and López-Pujol, 2006).

Civilisations and cities have grown along rivers partly because of the proximity of water supplies for domestic use, irrigation and industry, but also because of the other important resources and services that rivers provide. Even today people in Cambodia obtain about 60–80 per cent of their total animal protein from the fishery in Tonle Sap (a large river–lake system). For Malawi, the equivalent figure is 70–75 per cent (Millennium Ecosystem Assessment, 2005). Rivers such as the Rhine, Danube, Mississippi and Yangtze have served as important long-distance transport routes, stimulating cooperation between upstream and downstream jurisdictions and populations (Sadoff and Grey, 2005). Even smaller rivers have historically facilitated economically important exchange of goods (Sherratt, 1996).

Sharing of water resources and riverine transport networks have been particularly important factors in the development of formalised frameworks for governance and cooperation approaches for river management. It is claimed that the world's oldest extant international organisation is the Central Commission for the Navigation of the Rhine (CCNR), established in 1868 to facilitate improved navigation for trade vessels along the river.[3] Management organisations, international legal frameworks or other cooperative mechanisms have been put in place for many of the world's 270 plus transboundary rivers[4] in the intervening 150 years. These include specific agreements between two neighbouring countries to share water, such as the 1944 Treaty between the USA and Mexico on the Utilization of Waters of the Colorado and Tijuana Rivers and of the Rio Grande;[5] basin-scale forums for information exchange such as the Mekong River Commission, the mission of which is to 'promote and coordinate sustainable management and development of water and related resources for the countries' mutual benefit and the people's well-being';[6] and supra-national bodies to which neighbouring riparian governments have ceded some degree of planning or decision-making authority such as the International Commission for the Protection of Danube River (ICPDR). At the global scale, customary law and practice on cooperation for the management of transboundary rivers was codified in the 1997 UN Watercourses Convention, which came into effect in 2014 when Vietnam became the 35th country to ratify it.

Although transboundary contexts pose particular governance challenges, rivers that flow within national boundaries can also be subject to competing interests. For this reason, most countries of the world have established institutional frameworks for river management. The nature of these frameworks varies in terms of scale of analysis and intervention, policy priorities and specific mechanisms. Public policy measures intended to promote cooperation have included, *inter alia*, mandating of local water resource users associations (e.g. in Kenya, South Africa or Tanzania), formulating river basin and sub-basin management plans (e.g. in much of Europe, as stipulated by the EU Water Framework Directive), convening multi-stakeholder information and planning forums (e.g. the Yangtze and Yellow River Forums in China) and instigating formal state level water plans within federal policy frameworks (e.g. in India and Brazil). Beyond the public policy realm, stakeholders will often collaborate informally to manage flood risk,[7] to spot trade water permits or abstractions (Brozovic et al., 2011) or to manage flows of water between neighbouring water users (Lankford and Hepworth, 2010). Such informal cooperation can be vital in avoiding or defusing potential riparian conflicts.

There have probably been more events related to cooperation for water and river management than there have been outright conflicts (Wolf et al., 2005). However, cooperation between nation states is not always what it seems and tensions and conflicts over river management have arisen in multiple guises. State engagement in transboundary river management may be more strategic than sincere, as shown by recent events on the Nile, which have led to Ethiopia's construction of the Grand Ethiopian Renaissance Dam despite objections from downstream states, especially Egypt (Cascão and Nicol, 2016). Recent or ongoing disagreements between Uruguay and Paraguay along the La Plata, between Laos, Vietnam and Cambodia on the Mekong, or between the USA and Mexico on the Colorado are just a few examples of non-violent conflicts. Genuine sharing of the benefits of rivers or large hydraulic projects remains an elusive goal (Phillips et al., 2006; Tawfik, 2015) and it has been argued that, despite appearances, all forms of cooperation carry with them an element of conflict (Mirumachi, 2015). Such events play out in terms of uneven treaty conditions, degradation of political relationships or decline in ecosystem health with the most powerful nation or state often able to effectively control river resources to the detriment of other riparian nations (Zeitoun and Warner, 2006; Wolf et al., 2005). Joint technical committees—whether between Palestine and Israel (Zeitoun, 2008), Syria and Jordan (Haddadin, 2001) or Turkey, Syria and Iraq (Çonker, 2014)—may even mask a deeper political conflict, thereby perpetuating it (Zeitoun and Mirumachi, 2008).

As well as being a stimulus for conflict, rivers and water can become weaponised during wars. In Iraq, Syria and Gaza, for example, reservoirs, dams and drinking water services have been targeted for military attack with devastating effects on vulnerable local populations (ICRC, 2015). Even in peace time, local conflicts can arise between different groups of river users, as has happened in Tanzania, for instance, where continued over-abstraction of the Great Ruaha River has led to conflict between upstream and downstream communities (Lankford et al., 2004; Walsh, 2012). The Water Conflict Chronology,[8] an online resource maintained by The Pacific Institute (a California-based non-governmental organization), lists a depressing array of violent water and river related conflicts including, in 2014 alone, 24 separate incidents in Europe, Asia, North America and South America. There remains much controversy about the prospect of genuine 'water wars' (e.g. Starr, 1991; Wolf, 1999; Swain, 2001; Zhang, 2016). Nevertheless, the onset of climate change and consequent unpredictability of rainfall and river flows, combined with steadily increasing pressures on river resources as a result of population growth and shifts to thirstier economic development models, seems likely to provoke further riparian disagreements, as well as stimulating new alignments between water users and between nations.

## Quantity, quality and timing

A number of factors affect the extent to which rivers can provide society with social, economic and strategic benefits such as riverine transport, water supplies, fisheries or replenishment of sediment to low-lying deltas. Built infrastructure is often required to harness and direct such benefits; functioning institutions are important if benefits are to be distributed among different groups of people in an equitable and efficient manner; and the health of the river ecosystem determines the quantity and quality of ecosystem services which underpin these benefits (Parker and Oates, 2016; Tickner et al., 2017). There is no accepted scientific definition of 'river health' but in general terms the interaction of a number of key elements influences the condition of freshwater ecosystems including catchment processes, flow regime, habitat structure, water quality and aquatic and riparian biodiversity (Speed et al., 2016). Figure 10.1 illustrates the interaction of these elements and the ecosystem services and social, economic or strategic benefits they typically provide. The relative role of each of these elements in determining river health and associated benefits will vary according to context. Nevertheless, freshwater ecosystem specialists have referred to the flow regime—defined in terms of the quantity, quality and timing of river flows—as the 'master variable' that governs the health of the river (Poff et al., 1997; Brisbane Declaration, 2007).

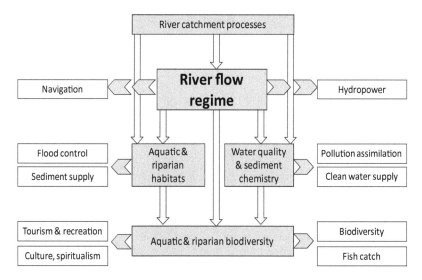

*Figure 10.1* Examples of freshwater ecosystem services and links to elements of river health

Adapted from Speed et al. (2016)

*Table 10.1* Selected examples of links between changes in the health of rivers and dimensions of conflict/cooperation

| River/wetland/ lake health element | Typical problems | Example river | Potential cooperation/conflict dimensions |
|---|---|---|---|
| Catchment processes | Degradation resulting from deforestation, urbanisation, agricultural expansion, climate change. | Mara | The Mara River provides the only year-round source of water to the iconic, and economically important, Maasai Mara and Serengeti conservation areas. Demographic change, climate change and conversion of forests to agriculture and grassland in the Mara Basin headwaters are likely to reduce dry season flows and increase peak flows, leading to greater water scarcity at critical times of the year, increased drought risks and potential competition for water resources between sectors and communities (Mango et al., 2011; Dessu et al., 2014). There are implications for transboundary land use and economic development policy within the East Africa Community (Albinus et al., 2008) and a transboundary water allocation plan is now being prepared under the aegis of the Lake Victoria Basin Commission. |
| Flow regime | Altered flows resulting from dam construction and operation and/ or water abstraction (especially for irrigation). | Nile | An emphasis on irrigation and hydropower as drivers of economic and social development, mean that Nile river flows are increasingly contested. Infrastructure development in upstream states has been pitted against established downstream agricultural livelihoods. Inter-state data sharing and technical exchanges have occurred but the political situation remains tense (Zeitoun et al., 2013). |
| Habitat structure | Wetland drainage and floodplain development for agriculture or urbanisation; riparian or in-channel sand/gravel extraction. | Danube | Conversion of the Danube River floodplains for farming and other development has degraded significant areas of floodplain, exacerbating flood peaks. Climate change is expected to further intensify flood risks. Ongoing floodplain restoration work commenced in 1993 and has encompassed various transboundary initiatives, including some in parts of Eastern Europe that had been affected by geopolitical transition and violent conflict. Along the lower Danube, restoration of floodplains by decommissioning under-performing flood protection infrastructure has resulted in improved capacity to retain and release floodwaters and remove pollutants, enhanced biodiversity and strengthened local economies through diversification of livelihoods. Drivers for restoration included the desire of some countries to join the EU and thus an imperative to fulfil EU legislative requirements on water management and nature protection (Ebert et al., 2009). |

| | | | |
|---|---|---|---|
| Water quality | Human health, water supply and amenity impacts from urban and industrial pollution and/or agricultural run-off. | Rhine | Decades of unregulated industrial and sewage pollution left the Rhine 'ecologically dead' by the 1970s. In response, the riparian states established the International Commission for the Protection of the Rhine in 1963 (the founding agreement, the Treaty of Bern, was superseded by the 1999 Convention on the Protection of the Rhine). Specific pollution events such as the 1986 Sandoz Accident (which resulted from a fire in a chemicals warehouse) focused the attention of the Commission and its member states and stimulated the establishment of the Rhine Action Programme for the restoration of the river. Although there remains debate about the influence of international cooperation on pollution levels, the water quality of the Rhine and of many of its tributaries has improved and the effects of heavy metals and other pollutants have diminished (Speed et al., 2016; Bernauer and Moser, 1996). |
| Aquatic and riparian biodiversity | Invasive species out-compete native wildlife; over-harvesting, e.g. inland fisheries. | Lake Victoria | Nile perch (*Lates nilotica*) were introduced to Lake Victoria in the mid-twentieth century in order to stimulate local fisheries, largely for export. Although the population dynamics are complex, it is claimed that the spread of Nile perch has contributed to the extinction of 200 endemic fish species, impoverishment of local populations and regional food insecurity. Recent expansion of fishing effort means that concern is growing that the species is in decline with potential associated economic and conflict issues (Lowe et al., 2000; Glaser et al., 2013; Geheb et al., 2008). Meanwhile, water hyacinth (*Eichhornia crassipes*) has infested large parts of Lake Victoria since the first report of its presence in 1988. Its spread directly reduces fish catch and increases pollution, thereby increasing pressure on local communities. Transboundary efforts to control the species have been supported by international agencies such as the World Bank (Lubovich, 2007). |

## 172   D. Tickner

Recent decades have witnessed a substantial upturn in water use, far outstripping increases in human population (UN Water, 2009), and a rapid and ongoing rise in the number of dams constructed around the world (World Commission on Dams, 2000; Zarfl et al., 2015). As a result, river flows have been significantly disrupted and habitats associated with 65 per cent of continental river flows have now been classified as moderately to highly threatened (Vorosmarty et al., 2010). Aquatic pollution, invasive plants and animals and direct impacts of climate change on rain and snowfall, and thereby on river flows, have added to these pressures. The consequences for river health include an average decline in populations of freshwater vertebrate species—akin to a global river health 'stock market index'—of 81 per cent from a 1970 baseline (WWF, 2016).

These trends have economic, social and geopolitical implications. Declining river, wetland and lake health has brought economic and social disruption to most regions of the planet in recent years and has stimulated or exacerbated conflicts and/or cooperation (Table 10.1). Many rivers that have been affected by pollution, over-abstraction or poorly planned infrastructure development flow through geopolitical hotspots, such as the Tigris and Euphrates, the Indus and the Mekong. A wide range of commentators—including the intelligence and security community (US Intelligence Community, 2012) and mainstream economists (World Economic Forum, 2016)—now consider that water risks merit policy attention beyond water and environment ministries. As well as being important to river health, the quantity, quality and timing of flows have also been described as the three issues to which all water disputes can be attributed (Wolf et al., 2005). Thus, while localised focus on pollution and other problems might be needed, the greatest alignment between the geopolitical arena and ecological dimensions of river health might be found in analysis of river hydrology.

## It's not the same river

It is not necessary for the flow regime to be entirely untouched by human activity in order for a river to be healthy. Rather, there should be sufficient volumes of water in rivers, and adequate variation of seasonal high and low river flows, to ensure that critical ecosystem processes—such as sediment transport to low-lying downstream deltas, dilution of pollutants or provision of stimuli to migratory fish such that they begin their reproductive journeys—can still take place. The science of defining 'environmental' flows, which can support these processes, and thereby guide river management efforts, has matured rapidly in recent decades (Acreman et al., 2014); but implementation of such flows remains more of a problem (Le Quesne et al., 2010). Implementation typically necessitates addressing tensions over three inter-linked technical water management issues: a) the siting, design and operation of dams and other water infrastructure that disrupt flow regimes; b) the allocation of water to different users along a river; and

*Going with the flow*   173

c) the remediation of water quality problems, including those relating to industrial, agricultural and sewage pollution.

Implementation solutions are emerging that can be useful if appropriately adapted to prevailing contexts. At the basin scale, frameworks that can help decision-makers and stakeholders put in place environmentally sustainable, socially equitable and economically efficient water allocation plans have been developed (Speed et al., 2013). These are now being tailored for use in river basins such as the Mara, spanning the Kenya-Tanzania border, and major rivers in China that cross provincial boundaries. Water efficiency tools and techniques that farmers can use to increase 'crop per drop' productivity are continually evolving, although there is lively debate about the impacts of these schemes on river and aquifer levels when they are implemented in isolation of robust water allocation plans (Batchelor et al., 2014; Lankford, 2006). River basin-scale models have been developed which can help decision-makers understand the trade-offs inherent in construction and operation of infrastructure that disrupts river flows (Opperman et al., 2015) and standards have been developed by industry groups and other stakeholders which can guide design and construction processes for dams (International Hydropower Association, 2011; World Commission on Dams, 2000).

Complex issues of governance and institutional capacity affect the development and implementation of effective and equitable solutions to these challenges. In many regions, government ministries and public water management authorities have struggled to resolve tensions and conflicts over rivers because of this. In some places, private sector actors who have become aware of strategic business risks from water scarcity are exploring and investing in mitigation actions that, with sufficient guidance and scrutiny from other stakeholders, could also bring broader benefits for communities and for river health (Hepworth, 2012; Newborne and Mason, 2012). However, it is debatable whether the private sector can or should take responsibility to oversee public goods such as river flows and water resources and there remains a substantial and significant river governance deficit at the global scale.

When the Ancient Greek philosopher Heraclitus remarked that, 'no man can enter the same river twice, for it is not the same river and he is not the same man' he might have been discussing twenty-first-century water challenges. Contests over river resources around the world present a bewildering range of political, cultural, economic, social and environmental contexts. It follows that measures to address river health and related water security problems must be context-specific and must take account of multiple stakeholder perspectives, future uncertainties and the complexities of local, national and transboundary political dynamics. 'Cookie cutter' approaches to river management challenges should be regarded with caution. An integrative, rather than reductive, approach is needed that draws on a wide range of expertise across social and environmental sciences and which is rooted in an understanding of local, national and regional political economies (Zeitoun et al., 2016; Tickner et al., 2017).

174  *D. Tickner*

## 'Six streams'

Foreign policy serves a number of different purposes, depending in large part on whose policy it is. The UK's foreign affairs (and so, water) objectives might be rather different from, say, Turkey's, which may in turn vary significantly from China's. The promotion of national interests is always a cornerstone, however, and such objectives can be pursued through improved cooperative arrangements with neighbours and partners and enhanced security of access to natural resources. For many states—typically including some that are members of groups such as the OECD and/or EU—the stated aims of foreign policy also include, at least in theory, promotion of international norms and practices with respect to good governance and/or facilitation of common responses to shared international challenges (Josephine Osikena, Foreign Policy Centre, personal communication).

Given the increasing scarcity of water resources in some geopolitically important regions, the transboundary nature of many rivers and the chronic (and sometimes acute) governance challenges presented by the management of contested watercourses, it is no surprise that Senator Clinton sharpened the USA's focus on the issue during her time as Secretary of State. In her 2010 speech, she referred to 'five streams', which could be 'channelled into a mighty river that runs across our entire diplomatic and development agenda.' These streams included:

1  *Building capacity* of water-stressed nations to manage scarce water resources.
2  *Elevating diplomatic efforts* to demonstrate a positive diplomatic precedent for fragile and water-stressed nations.
3  *Mobilising financial support*, including from the private sector, which might expect a return on investment.
4  Harnessing the power of *science and technology*, including new water treatment technologies and remote sensing technologies.
5  Broadening the scope of *global partnerships* with NGOs, the private sector and other governments.

To this list we might add another stream, which is, in most instances, essential for achieving positive water management outcomes and that might particularly draw on the position, skills and experience of foreign policy practitioners:

6  *Supporting international water law* as a pre-requisite for good governance and a key tool for achieving sustainable, equitable and efficient transboundary river management outcomes.

These six streams form the basis of a conceptual framing that might prove useful to resolve river health challenges and, in doing so, achieve foreign policy objectives (Figure 10.2). The framing shows schematically how the quantity, quality and timing of flows can be a useful lens through which the six streams can be focused in contexts where flow is the central issue for river health and a potential stimulus for conflict or cooperation. There are no panaceas or silver bullets; river health challenges can still be found in parts of the world, such as the EU, where the governance deficit is relatively small and where peace, security and stability is relatively well-established. Nevertheless, in many contexts, improving river health, especially by developing and implementing agreed river flows and water allocations, can aid, or be a focus for, cooperation; and, vice versa, improving security and stability can create conditions conducive to good river management and thus to improved river health.

Based on this conceptual framework and on recent and ongoing experience, Table 10.2 sets out practical measures that could be led or supported by the foreign policy community and that might contribute strategically to outcomes for flows, river health and peace, security and stability. Given the context-specific nature of water and river management challenges, and of cooperation and conflict situations, these examples should be taken as indicative suggestions of specific interventions that organisations concerned with foreign policy might be particularly well placed to make. It is not a definitive list. Further development of a typology of interventions could be a useful joint action for the foreign policy and river management communities of practice.

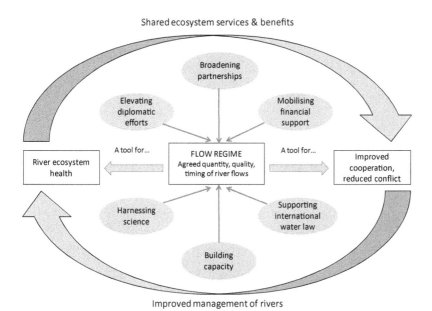

*Figure 10.2* Focusing 'six streams' of foreign policy interventions through the lens of flow regime to help attain outcomes for river health and for improved cooperation and reduced conflict

Source: inspired by Speed et al. (2016), Figure 2.2, p. 39

**Table 10.2** Indicative suggestions for foreign policy interventions to support improved cooperation for river health

| 'Six streams' of intervention | Types of measures that the foreign policy community might lead/support | Examples |
| --- | --- | --- |
| *Elevating diplomatic efforts* | Advise senior figures to take up appropriate opportunities to visit conflict/cooperation situations on specific rivers and to champion renewed dialogue between senior stakeholders interested and potentially impacted by river development. Balance this with encouragement of 'bottom-up' diplomacy, e.g. through sponsoring forums which provide a space for dialogue between upstream and downstream stakeholders along rivers. | In 2001, HRH the Duke of Edinburgh and the then President of Romania, Ion Iliescu, hosted a summit of 14 heads of state from Danube River Basin countries. The main output from the summit was a joint declaration about the need to encourage sustainable development in the basin at international, regional and local levels.[9] Funding from a number of European governments and EU institutions has helped support the establishment of local water user groups and associated discourse between upstream and downstream users in Eastern Africa, e.g. European Commission funding has helped create Water User Associations (WUAs) along the Great Ruaha River in Tanzania and a catchment committee through which such WUAs can convene; and funding from the Dutch Embassy has underpinned efforts to link stakeholders in the economically important Lake Naivasha Basin in Kenya. |
| *Broadening partnerships* | Develop partnerships with environment and development NGOs, researchers and international/national/local authorities to provide technical insights on specific river flow challenges. | The UK government, through the Department for International Development, supported WWF and The Nature Conservancy to lead an innovative research project—with input from the University of Manchester and in conjunction with multiple local stakeholders—into the potential for optimal basin-scale approaches to developing Myanmar's hydropower potential, balancing benefits (e.g. electricity generation) with non-financial costs (e.g. potential impacts on freshwater fisheries and indigenous people).[10] |
| *Mobilising financial support* | Convene financial institutions from private and public sectors to explore ways in which they can support water infrastructure investments that help to deliver on agreed river flows. | The OECD, working with the World Water Council (an NGO) and the Dutch government, has recently convened an initiative on water and finance, the aim of which is to water and finance communities (broadly interpreted) on how to overcome the global challenges of financing the investments needed for water security and sustainable economic growth. Although not specifically focused on river flows (it considers a broad range of water-related challenges), it has the potential to guide financial institutions towards investment practices and standards that could support agreements over quantity, quality and timing of flows.[11] |

| | | |
|---|---|---|
| *Supporting international water law* | Encourage widespread ratification and effective implementation of existing international water laws as well as development of new treaties and agreements for specific transboundary rivers where needed. | The 2014 entry into force of the 1997 UN Watercourses Convention and the spread of the 1992 UN Economic Commission for Europe (UNECE) Water Convention beyond Europe are recent developments that will require sustained diplomatic (more than financial) support. Some European governments are already providing such support, e.g. Switzerland hosts the UNECE Convention secretariat and France, Sweden and the Netherlands have acted as champions for the UN Watercourses Convention. Several other OECD governments have yet to ratify or accede to the 1997 Convention, including the USA, Australia and New Zealand. |
| *Building capacity* | Invest in capacity for negotiated solutions where river flow is contested, including governance, institutions, negotiation strategy and international law. Support the convening power of diplomats. | A number of European governments—including Denmark, the Netherlands, Norway, Sweden and the UK—have collaborated to provide funding to the Palestinian Negotiations Support Project (PNSP). The aim of the project was to strengthen Palestinian technical capacities needed to effectively pursue peace. The PNSP had a broad remit, part of which related to negotiations with Israel over environmental issues that affected long-term security of Palestinians, such as the shared water resources of the Jordan river. As such, one of the beneficiaries of the PNSP was the Palestinian Water Authority.[12] |
| *Harnessing science and technology* | A priority here is to encourage sharing of water data with other riparian stakeholders. As technology rapidly improves, support for the development and utilisation of remote sensing and earth observation tools to monitor river flows and water quality will be critical to overcome political and technical restrictions on accessibility of hydrological data. | There are many ongoing and planned scientific initiatives to harness the power of satellites, big data and remote sensing to aid river and water resource management. For instance, the Surface Water and Ocean Topography (SWOT) project—led by US, Canadian and French scientists—aims to make the first global survey of Earth's surface water, observe the fine details of the ocean's surface topography, and measure how water bodies change over time.[13] More generally, commentators have called for the USA, through its forthcoming Global Water Strategy (which it is required to produce according to the Paul Simon Water for the World Act 2014[14]) to leverage the capacity of agencies such as NASA, NOAA and the US Geological Survey to develop hydrological monitoring and early warning systems that, when combined with other diplomatic efforts, can help countries plan for the future.[15] |

## Conclusions

Interest in natural resource and climate risks seems to be on the rise in many sectors. As yet, however, few states have explicitly included cooperation or conflict over rivers as a headline priority in their foreign policy strategies. This is true even of many countries in the OECD and/or EU whose interests ostensibly include promotion of international norms and practices, good governance and regional or global responses to shared international challenges. Meanwhile, as pressures on water resources grow, the quantity, quality and timing of flows of water down many rivers continue to shift with implications both for peace, security and stability and for freshwater ecosystems. The future for the world's rivers, and those societies and economies that rely on them, is increasingly uncertain. Even where violent conflict over river flow is avoided, hegemony and inequality means that some nations, and some groups of people within nations, are likely to benefit far more than others from disrupted river flows.

History tells that, in most situations, officials in water or environment ministries and associated public sector authorities charged with managing rivers have insufficient influence to ensure that difficult decisions about water allocation and infrastructure are made on an equitable and sustainable basis, or to ensure that those decisions are reliably informed by good science. Despite Baroness Ashton's assertion, political considerations often take precedence. To ensure more equitable and sustainable (and, in the long term, more stable) sharing of river benefits, the active engagement of more senior policy sectors—including the foreign policy sector—will be needed.

There are good reasons for foreign policy practitioners to engage with river and water management issues, especially those relating to river flows, and there are straightforward conceptual links (based on the quantity, quality and timing of flows) between river health and stated foreign policy objectives. Moreover, there are already examples of valuable contributions foreign policy practitioners have made to river restoration efforts. Whether or not such engagement is a priority for the foreign policy community in the future will depend largely on specific hydrological, geopolitical and socio-economic situations. Regardless, given the global context of increasing water scarcity, however, it is likely that, at least in some regions, water resources and river flows will remain a front burner issue for those seeking to improve cooperation and reduce conflict.

## Acknowledgements

The author is grateful to Mark Zeitoun at the University of East Anglia who provided invaluable guidance on water resources, conflict and cooperation; and to Josephine Osikena at the Foreign Policy Centre, who provided helpful insights on the nature of foreign policy early in the drafting process.

## Notes

1 For the full transcript of Secretary Clinton's speech see http://iipdigital.usembassy.gov/st/english/texttrans/2010/03/20100322165432eaifas0.4756433.html#axzz4G5SbjRGy (accessed 1 August 2016).
2 See https://www.tva.com/About-TVA/Our-History for more on the history of the Tennessee Valley Authority (accessed 4 August 2016).
3 See http://www.ccr-zkr.org/11000000-en.html (accessed 5 August 2016).
4 At the time of writing, convention has it that there were 276 rivers in the world which crossed one or more national borders: see http://www.unwater.org/statistics/statistics-detail/en/c/211763/ (accessed 8 August 2016). However, the number changes frequently, largely due to geopolitical shifts including the break-up of large countries, such as the Soviet Union, into smaller ones.
5 See http://www.ibwc.state.gov/Treaties_Minutes/treaties.html (accessed 8 August 2016).
6 See http://www.mrcmekong.org/about-mrc/vision-and-mission/ (accessed 8 August 2016).
7 For instance, the townspeople of Pickering, a small town in Yorkshire, UK, 'decided to take matters into their own hands' following rejection by water management authorities of a conventional flood management plan on cost-benefit grounds. See http://www.independent.co.uk/news/uk/home-news/uk-flooding-how-a-yorkshire-flood-blackspot-worked-with-nature-to-stay-dry-a6794286.html (access 8 August 2016).
8 See http://www2.worldwater.org/conflict/list/ (accessed 8 August 2016).
9 See http://wwf.panda.org/wwf_news/?uNewsID=2246 (accessed 30 April 2017).
10 See https://thought-leadership-production.s3.amazonaws.com/2016/05/09/13/53/29/e26cf10b-9a56-463d-97fc-0309b1fde0d6/System-Scale%20Planning_Myanmar_Report.pdf (accessed 30 April 2017).
11 See http://www.oecd.org/environment/resources/roundtableonfinancingwater.htm (accessed 30 April 2017).
12 See https://www.google.co.uk/url?sa=t&rct=j&q=&esrc=s&source=web&cd=1&ved=0ahUKEwiCya7Q8czTAhWJHsAKHcZXCBAQFggnMAA&url=http%3A%2F%2Fiati.dfid.gov.uk%2Fiati_documents%2F3717226.odt&usg=AFQjCNEz3CWUjwqg0oyLN-sljgwOp0yk2Q&sig2=lG_TrPC7fxK6zbczheEMkQ&cad=rja (accessed 30 April 2017).
13 See https://swot.jpl.nasa.gov/ (accessed 30 April 2017).
14 See https://www.congress.gov/bill/113th-congress/house-bill/2901/text?overview=closed (accessed 30 April 2017).
15 See https://www.newsecuritybeat.org/2017/02/global-water-national-security-time/?utm_content=buffer7e875&utm_medium=social&utm_source=twitter.com&utm_campaign=buffer (accessed 30 April 2017).

## References

Acreman, M., Arthington, A.H., Colloff, M.J., Couch, C., Crossman, N.D., Dyer, F., Overton, I., Pollino, C.A., Stewardson, M.J. and Young, W. (2014) 'Environmental flows for natural, hybrid, and novel riverine ecosystems in a changing world', *Frontiers in Ecology and the Environment*, 12(8), pp. 466–473.

Albinus, M., Makalle, J. and Bamutaze, Y. (2008) 'Effects of land use practices on livelihoods in the transboundary sub-catchments of the Lake Victoria Basin', *African Journal of Environmental Science and Technology*, 2, pp. 309–317.

## 180 D. Tickner

Allan, J.A. (2001) *The Middle East Water Question: Hydropolitics and the Global Economy.* London, UK: I.B. Tauris.

Ashton, C. (2010) 'Foreword', in J. Osikena and D. Tickner (eds) *Tackling the World Water Crisis: Reshaping the Future of Foreign Policy.* London, UK: Foreign Policy Centre.

Batchelor, C., Reddy, V. R., Linstead, C., Dhar, M., Roy, S. and May, R. (2014) 'Do water-saving technologies improve environmental flows?', *Journal of Hydrology*, 518, pp. 140–149.

Bernauer, T. and Moser, P. (1996) 'Reducing pollution of the river Rhine: the influence of international cooperation', *The Journal of Environment & Development*, 5, pp. 389–415.

Brisbane Declaration. (2007) 'The Brisbane Declaration: environmental flows are essential for freshwater ecosystem health and human well-being', Tenth International River Symposium, Brisbane, Australia, pp. 3–6.

Brozovic, N., Carey, J. M. and Sunding, D.L. (2011) 'Trading activity in an informal agricultural water market: an example from California', *Journal of Contemporary Water Research and Education*, 121, pp. 3–16.

Cascão, A.E. and Nicol, A. (2016) 'GERD: new norms of cooperation in the Nile Basin?', *Water International*, 41, pp. 550–573.

Childe, V.G. (1927) 'The Danube thoroughfare and the beginnings of civilization in Europe', *Antiquity*, 1, pp. 79–91.

Childs-Johnson, E. and Sullivan, L.R. (1996) 'The Three Gorges Dam and the fate of China's southern heritage', *Orientations*, 27, pp. 55–61.

Çonker, A. (2014) *An Enhanced Notion of Power for Inter-state and Transnational Hydropolitics: An Analysis of Turkish-Syrian Water Relations and the Ilisu Dam.* Ph.D., University of East Anglia.

Dessu, S.B., Melesse, A.M., Bhat, M. G. and McClain, M.E. (2014) 'Assessment of water resources availability and demand in the Mara River Basin', *Catena*, 115, pp. 104–114.

Dudgeon, D., Arthington, A.H., Gessner, M.O., Kawabata, Z., Knowler, D.J., Leveque, C., Naiman, R.J., Prieur-Richard, A.H., Soto, D., Stiassny, M.L. and Sullivan, C.A. (2006) 'Freshwater biodiversity: importance, threats, status and conservation challenges', *Biological Reviews of the Cambridge Philosophical Society*, 81, pp. 163–82.

Ebert, S., Hulea, O. and Strobel, D. (2009) 'Floodplain restoration along the lower Danube: a climate change adaptation case study', *Climate and Development*, 1, pp. 212–219.

Geheb, K., Kalloch, S., Medard, M., Nyapendi, A.T., Lwenya, C. and Kyangwa, M. (2008) 'Nile perch and the hungry of Lake Victoria: Gender, status and food in an East African fishery', *Food Policy*, 33, pp. 85–98.

Giosan, L., Clift, P.D., Macklin, M.G., Fuller, D.Q., Constantinescu, S., Durcan, J.A., Stevens, T., Duller, G.A., Tabrez, A.R. and Gangal, K. (2012) 'Fluvial landscapes of the Harappan civilization', *Proceedings of the National Academy of Sciences*, 109, pp. E1688–E1694.

Glaser, S.M., Hendrix, C.S., Kaufman, L. and Mahoney, C. (2013) 'Conflict and fisheries in the Lake Victoria Basin: A coupled natural and human systems approach', APSA 2013 Annual Meeting Paper; American Political Science Association 2013 Annual Meeting.

Gleick, P.H. (2014) 'Water, drought, climate change, and conflict in Syria', *Weather, Climate, and Society*, 6, pp. 331–340.

Haddadin, M. (2001) *Diplomacy on the Jordan: International Conflict and Negotiated Resolution*. Dordrecht: International Development Research Centre and Kluwer Academic Publishers.

Hassan, F.A. (1997) 'The dynamics of a riverine civilization: a geoarchaeological perspective on the Nile Valley, Egypt', *World Archaeology*, 29, pp. 51–74.

Hepworth, N. (2012) 'Open for business or opening Pandora's Box? A constructive critique of corporate engagement in water policy: An introduction', *Water Alternatives*, 5, pp. 543–562.

ICRC (2015) *Urban Services During Protracted Armed Conflict: A Call for a Better Approach to Assisting Affected People*. Geneva: International Committee of the Red Cross.

International Hydropower Association (2011) *Hydropower Sustainability Assessment Protocol*. London: IHA.

Lankford, B. (2006) 'Localising irrigation efficiency', *Irrigation and Drainage*, 55, pp. 345–362.

Lankford, B. and Hepworrth, N. (2010) 'The cathedral and the bazaar: monocentric and polycentric river basin management', *Water Alternatives*, 3, pp. 82–101.

Lankford, B., van Koppen, B., Franks, T. and Mahoo, H. (2004) 'Entrenched views or insufficient science?: contested causes and solutions of water allocation; insights from the Great Ruaha River Basin, Tanzania', *Agricultural Water Management*, 69, pp. 135–153.

Lowe, S., Browne, M., Boudjelas, S. and de Poorter, M. (2000) *100 of the World's Worst Invasive Alien Species: A Selection from the Global Invasive Species Database*. Auckland, NZ: ISSG.

Lubovich, K. (2007) *Cooperation and Competition: Managing Transboundary Water Resources in the Lake Victoria Region*. Foundation for Environmental Security and Sustainability (FESS).

Mango, L.M., Melesse, A. M., McClain, M.E., Gann, D. and Setegn, S. (2011) 'Land use and climate change impacts on the hydrology of the upper Mara River Basin, Kenya: results of a modeling study to support better resource management', *Hydrology and Earth System Sciences*,15, pp. 2245–2258.

Millennium Ecosystem Assessment (2005) *Ecosystems and Human Well-being: Wetlands and Water*. Washington, DC: World Resources Institute.

Mirumachi, N. (2015) *Transboundary Water Politics in the Developing World*. London: Routledge.

Morozova, G.S. (2005) 'A review of Holocene avulsions of the Tigris and Euphrates rivers and possible effects on the evolution of civilizations in lower Mesopotamia', *Geoarchaeology*, 20, pp. 401–423.

Newborne, P. and Mason, N. (2012) 'The private sector's contribution to water management: re-examining corporate purposes and company roles', *Water Alternatives*, 5, pp. 603–618.

Normile, D. (1997) 'Yangtze seen as earliest rice site', *Science*, 275, 309–309.

Opperman, J., Grill, G. and Hartmann, J. (2015) *The Power of Rivers: Finding Balance between Energy and Conservation in Hydropower Development*. Washington, DC: The Nature Conservancy.

Parker, H. and Oates, N. (2016) *How do Healthy Rivers Benefit Society? A Review of the Evidence*. London: ODI and WWF.

Pegram, G., Yuanyuan, L., Le Quesne, T., Speed, R., Jianqiang, L. and Fuxin, S. (2013) *River Basin Planning Principles: Procedures and Approaches for Strategic Basin Planning*. Paris: Asian Development Bank.

182    *D. Tickner*

Phillips, D., Daoudy, M., Öjendal, J., Turton, A. and McCaffrey, S. (2006). *Transboundary Water Cooperation as a Tool for Conflict Prevention and Broader Benefit-sharing*. Stockholm: Ministry of Foreign Affairs.

Poff, N.L., Allan, J. D., Bain, M. B., Karr, J. R., Prestegaard, K. L., Richter, B. D., Sparks, R. E. and Stromberg, J.C. (1997) 'The natural flow regime', *BioScience*, 47, pp. 769–784.

Ponseti, M. and López-Pujol, J. (2006) 'The Three Gorges Dam project in China: history and consequences', *HMiC: Història Moderna i Contemporània*, pp. 151–188.

Sadoff, C.W. and Grey, D. (2005) 'Cooperation on international rivers: a continuum for securing and sharing benefits', *Water International*, 30, pp. 420–427.

Sherratt, A. (1996) 'Why Wessex? The Avon route and river transport in later British prehistory', *Oxford Journal of Archaeology*, 15, pp. 211–234.

Speed, R., Tickner, D., Naiman, R., Gang, L., Sayers, P., Yu, W., Yuanyuan, L., Houjian, H., Jianting, C. and Lilly, Y. (2016) *River Restoration: A Strategic Approach to Planning and Management*. New York: UNESCO Publishing.

Speed, R., Yuanyuan, L., Zhiwel, Z., Le Quesne, T. and Pegram, G. (2013) *Basin Water Allocation Planning: Principles, Procedures and Approaches for Basin Allocation Planning*. Paris: Asian Development Bank.

Starr, J.R. (1991) 'Water wars', *Foreign policy*, 82, pp. 17–36.

Swain, A. (2001) 'Water wars: fact or fiction?' *Futures*, 33, pp. 769–781.

Swyngedouw, E. (1999) 'Modernity and hybridity: Nature, regeneracionismo, and the production of the Spanish waterscape, 1890–1930', *Annals of the Association of American Geographers*, 89, pp. 443–465.

Tawfik, R. (2015) 'Revisiting hydro-hegemony from a benefit-sharing perspective: The case of the Grand Ethiopian Renaissance Dam', Discussion Paper No. 5/2015. Bonn: German Development Institute.

Tickner, D. and Acreman, M. (2013) 'Water security for ecosystems, ecosystems for water security', in B. Lankford, K. Bakker, M. Zeitoun and D. Conway, D., (eds) *Water Security: Principles, Perspectives and Practices*. Abingdon: Routledge, pp. 130–147.

Tickner, D., Parker, H., Oates, N.E., Moncrieff, C. R., Ludi, E. and Acreman, M. (2017) 'Managing rivers for multiple benefits—A coherent approach to research, policy and planning', *Frontiers in Environmental Science*, 5, 4, available http://journal.frontiersin.org/article/10.3389/fenvs.2017.00004/full [accessed 11 May 2017].

UN Water (2009) *The United Nations World Water Development Report 3–Water in a Changing World*. New York: UNESCO Publishing/Earthscan.

US Intelligence Community (2012) *Global Water Security*. Washington, DC: National Intelligence Council.

Vorosmarty, C. J., McIntyre, P. B., Gessner, M. O., Dudgeon, D., Prusevich, A., Green, P., Glidden, S., Bunn, S. E., Sullivan, C.A., Liermann, C.R. and Davies, P.M. (2010) 'Global threats to human water security and river biodiversity', *Nature*, 467, pp. 555–561.

Walsh, M. (2012) 'The not-so-Great Ruaha and hidden histories of an environmental panic in Tanzania', *Journal of Eastern African Studies*, 6, pp. 303–335.

Winchester, S. (1996) *The River at the Center of the World: A Journey up the Yangtze, and Back in Chinese Time*. London: Macmillan.

Wolf, A.T. (1999) '"Water wars" and water reality: conflict and cooperation along international waterways', in S.C. Lonergan (ed.) *Environmental Change, Adaptation, and Security*. New York: Springer, pp. 251–265.

Wolf, A.T., Kramer, A., Carius, A. and Dabelko, G.D. (2005) 'Managing water conflict and cooperation', in Worldwatch Institute, *State of the World 2005: Redefining Global Security*. Washington, DC: Worldwatch Institute, pp. 80–95.

World Commission on Dams (2000) *Dams and Development: A New Framework for Decision-making: The Report of the World Commission on Dams*. London: Earthscan.

World Economic Forum (2016) *The Global Risks Report 2016*. Geneva, Switzerland: World Economic Forum.

Wu, Q., Zhao, Z., Liu, L., Granger, D. E., Wang, H., Cohen, D. J., Wu, X., Ye, M., Bar-Yosef, O., Lu, B., Zhang, J., Zhang, P., Yuan, D., Qi, W., Cai, L. and Bai, S. (2016) 'Outburst flood at 1920 BCE supports historicity of China's Great Flood and the Xia dynasty'. *Science*, 353, pp. 579–582.

WWF. (2016) *Living Planet Report: Risk and Resilience in a New Era*. Gland, Switzerland: WWF International.

Yan, F., Daming, H. and Kinne, B. (2006) 'Water resources administration institution in China', *Water Policy*, 8, pp. 291–301.

Yasuda, Y., Fujiki, T., Nasu, H., Kato, M., Morita, Y., Mori, Y., Kaneharra, M., Toyama, S., Yano, A. and Okuno, M. (2004) 'Environmental archaeology at the Chengtoushan site, Hunan Province, China, and implications for environmental change and the rise and fall of the Yangtze River civilization', *Quaternary International*, 123, pp. 149–158.

Young, D. (2005) 'Whanganui tribes', Te Ara—The Encyclopedia of New Zealand, available: http://www.TeAra.govt.nz/en/whanganui-tribes/print (accessed 8 June 2017).

Zarfl, C., Lumsdon, A.E., Berlekamp, J., Tydecks, L. and Tockner, K. (2015) 'A global boom in hydropower dam construction', *Aquatic Sciences*, 77, pp. 161–170.

Zeitoun, M. (2008) *Power and Water: The Hidden Politics of the Palestinian-Israeli Conflict*. London: I.B. Tauris.

Zeitoun, M., Goulden, M. and Tickner, D. (2013) 'Current and future challenges facing transboundary river basin management', *Wiley Interdisciplinary Reviews: Climate Change*, 4, pp. 331–349.

Zeitoun, M., Lankford, B., Krueger, T., Forsyth, T., Carter, R., Hoekstra, A., Taylor, R., Varis, O., Cleaver, F. and Boelens, R. (2016) 'Reductionist and integrative research approaches to complex water security policy challenges', *Global Environmental Change*, 39, pp. 143–154.

Zeitoun, M. and Mirumachi, N. (2008) 'Transboundary water interaction I: reconsidering conflict and cooperation', *International Environmental Agreements*, 8, pp. 297–316.

Zeitoun, M. and Warner, J. (2006) 'Hydro-hegemony–a framework for analysis of trans-boundary water conflicts', *Water Policy*, 8, pp. 435–460.

Zhang, H. (2016) 'Sino-Indian water disputes: the coming water wars?', *Wiley Interdisciplinary Reviews: Water*, 3, pp. 155–166.

# 11 Don't forget the fish! Transnational collaboration in governing tuna fisheries in the Pacific

*Victoria Jollands and Karen Fisher*

## Introduction

The Western and Central Pacific Ocean (WCPO) is home to the world's largest, most valuable tuna fisheries (Hanich and Tsamenyi, 2010; Harley et al., 2014; Hunt, 2003; Langley et al., 2009; Parris, 2010; Parris and Grafton, 2006) and forms the backbone of the Pacific region's economy and culture (Chand, Grafton, and Petersen, 2003; Hanich and Tsamenyi, 2009). For distant water fishing nations (DWFN), the exploitation of tuna (*Thunnini, Scombroidei*) species for commercial purposes dates to the early 1900s. Liberalisation of trade policies, coupled with intensified utilisation of marine resources as a consequence of fisheries industrialisation, has increased socio-economic, political and environmental pressures in the Pacific and presents challenges to sustainable development (Pilling et al., 2015). Tuna fisheries in the WCPO exemplify the challenges to governing scarce fugitive resources where social, cultural and economic values are highly politicised, and tuna biology disrupts political and economic attempts to govern.

In this chapter, we understand fisheries scarcity to be socially constructed and a consequence of either demand or supply. The growing demand for fish driven by consumption fuels increased fisheries effort and can lead to over-fishing. On the supply side, the technology used to harvest tunas and tuna biology influence what is made available to the market. In addition, the 'race to fish' can lead to overfishing, since there are economic incentives to exploit the resource. The effects of both supply and demand subsequently lead to changes in targeted fish biology, populations and to ecosystem structure and function affecting resilience of socio-ecological systems (Walsh et al., 2006). Moreover, fisheries scarcity is increasingly acknowledged as being a conse-quence of governance failures requiring governance solutions (Hilborn et al., 2005). This is particularly so in the WCPO tuna fishery where scarcity is defined in socio-political terms.

In this chapter, we demonstrate how regional agreements emphasising cooperation and coordination enable multi-scale collaborative governance of tunas. In the WCPO, the tuna fishery faces two major challenges to achieving conservation and development goals: the need to collaborate because of the

*Don't forget the fish!* 185

fugitive nature of tunas and competing interests in relation to tunas; and the complex interrelated social and ecological issues that arise when managing a multi-species fishery. We elucidate the multi-scalar governance arrangements in WCPO tuna fisheries and consider the potential of these agreements to manage trade-offs (social, ecological and economic).

Our focus in this chapter is on extending previous research by exploring the concept of scarcity from a socio-political perspective to reveal how interconnections between socio-ecological systems interplay through myriad institutional arrangements influencing control of access to tuna stocks. We are particularly interested in tuna biology, tuna movement and the effects of the migratory and transboundary nature of tunas on national and international cooperation and governance, with the aim of understanding the trade-offs between social, economic and ecological aspects of tuna social-ecological systems.

## Tunas to consumers: characterising Pacific tuna fisheries

### *Implications of biology and ecology*

Tunas capture the attention of a wide scope of researchers. These fishes exhibit some of the most remarkable physiological and circulatory adaptations with sustained swimming, elevated cruising speeds and expansion of thermal niche (see Box 11.1). Adaptations include heat-conserving rete (increasing body temperature up to 20°C above ambient), high blood volume, more extensive aerobic red muscle, and streamlining modifications (Bond, 1996). The life history traits, foraging strategies, thermal and vertical niche, and ecosystem linkages are of critical interest to Pacific Island countries and territories (PICTs) wishing to develop their tuna fisheries, to DWFNs with considerable fishing interests in these areas, and to fisheries management organisations within the WCPO wishing to conserve them including, for example, the Western and Central Pacific Fisheries Commission (WCPFC), Parties to the Nauru Agreement (PNA) and Pacific Island Forum Fisheries Agency (FFA).

As active pelagic predators, tunas exhibit vast horizontal and vertical movement (see Box 11.1). Tunas are often incorrectly grouped as 'highly migratory'; however, only some are true 'migrators', while other tuna species show 'movement' and do not exhibit movement tied with specific life stages, or typical migration patterns. Two main categories of tunas can be used to describe movement of tunas (Itano et al., 2011). Temperate water tunas, including albacore (*T. alalunga*) and three bluefin species (Atlantic, Pacific, and South Pacific), are generally described as 'highly migratory' and exhibit ocean basin scale movements at specific life stages and between juvenile feeding areas and tropical spawning habitat. The second group of tunas, including skipjack (*Katsuwonus pelamis*) and yellowfin (*Thunnus albacares*), are described as tropical tunas that spawn, recruit and live within a single warm-water region. These tunas exhibit more restricted lifetime movements. Bigeye (*T. obesus*) tuna exhibit life history traits from both the temperate and tropical water tuna groups.

## Box 11.1    Factors influencing spatio-temporal horizontal and vertical movement of tunas and consequently that of tuna fisheries

### Accessibility of prey

Accessibility of tunas' prey is controlled by tunas' physiological limitations. For example, the unique endothermic traits of tunas have provided increased cold tolerances. The evolution of endothermic characteristics has been hypothesised as providing an expanded niche for tunas thereby increasing access to prey both geographically and horizontally in the water column (Madigan et al., 2015).

### Niche separation

Tunas exhibit niche separation in the water column where each species predominates different ranges of temperature and depth (Madigan et al., 2015). Yellowfin tuna occupy shallower, warmer waters (less than 25 m) with short infrequent dives below the thermocline. Albacore are found in intermediate depths associated with the thermocline (20–90 m). Bluefin tuna, such as Pacific bluefin tuna are the most extreme of the tuna species in their depth range and have been found to spend more time in the deeper, cooler water (190–450 m). The deeper-diving characteristic is thought to be an outcome of the tunas' hunting activity, causing forage species (e.g. sardine, jack mackerel, squid) to seek daytime refuge in deeper, sub-thermocline waters through diel vertical migration. This may also be the result of searching behaviour (Madigan et al., 2015).

### Foraging strategies

Strategies for foraging of prey depend on tunas' geographic location, stage of ontogeny, availability of prey and season. Albacore and yellowfin tuna diets exhibit more opportunistic feeding than other tuna species pursuing a wide range of species including small pelagic crustaceans, fishes and cephalopods (Hosseini and Kaymaram, 2016; Madigan et al., 2015). Conversely, even with a wider vertical and thermal niche, bluefin tunas show a preference for high energy, schooling prey when available. For example, Pacific bluefin tuna pursue sardine or anchovy, showing evidence for specialisation in the California Current Large Marine Ecosystem and Japan (Madigan et al., 2015). Larger Pacific bluefin tuna migrate further afield to subtropical spawning grounds and temperate foraging grounds.

## Oceanographic variability

Oceanography (water temperatures, currents, productivity) and climate dynamics impact on fishes' dynamics and fisheries (Lehodey, 2000; SPC, 2009). Such impacts have been shown to influence spatio-temporal horizontal and vertical movement of tunas in the WCPO. Generally, catches of tunas are mostly from the western equatorial Pacific warm pool—an area of low productivity and warm sea surface temperature. An example of a major oceanic process that affects the distribution of tunas in the WCPO is climatic changes of El Niño Southern Oscillation (ENSO). Tuna catches vary along the equator both seasonally and inter-annually due to the east–west movement of the warm pool-cold tongue pelagic ecosystem. Typically, during El Niño conditions, tuna catch is displaced eastwards.

Tunas' biology and ecology have implications for socio-economic organisation within and beyond PICTs. Sensitivity to scale is, therefore, important when dealing with the management of fugitive resources such as tunas that stretch beyond political and social boundaries. Here, scale is defined as 'the spatial, temporal, quantitative, or analytical dimensions used to measure and study any phenomenon', as defined in Cash et al. (2006, p. 2). Levels are the 'units of analysis that are located at different positions on a scale' (Cash et al., 2006). Interactions occur both within and across scale and in the WCPO tuna fishery this can become both complex and challenging. For example, the geographical location of tunas (place-based but also vertically in the water column) has implications for fisheries (e.g. fisheries gear required), but also the distribution of revenue gained (e.g. within or outside a nation's Exclusive Economic Zone (EEZ)) and ultimately determines what form of collaboration is required or developed to manage the fishery through national regulation, bilateral and multilateral treaties across local, national and international levels. Challenges are faced by society where such interactions are ignored, mismatched or generalised (Cash et al., 2006). Without taking scale and cross-scale dynamics into consideration, there is a risk of fisheries 'collapse' (Cash et al., 2006). The recovery of fisheries across the globe today is attributable, in part, to the shift towards a collaborative form of governance that engages stakeholders and interested parties.

### Diverse markets

Besides being unique species that have received considerable scientific interest, tunas are a highly valued and sought-after commodity in food markets around the world with demand concentrated in the EU, US and Japan. Tuna markets

188  *V. Jollands and K. Fisher*

are characterised by a range of product types that serve different market niches. The majority of catch landed is processed into canned tuna; but tunas are also processed into sashimi and other value-added products such as steaks, loins and smoked tuna products (Hamilton et al., 2011). Tuna fish markets are determined by a grading process based on fishing method (e.g. longline or purse seine) and the characteristics that make them exceptional such as fish body appearance, fat content, the 'redness' of fish muscle, freshness and external appearance (Blanc, 2002).

Bluefin tunas are the most prized commodity in the sushi market and also the most highly variable in price (Miyake et al., 2010). In 2010, bluefin tuna were reported to receive between 200 and 20,000 JPY per kg in the Japanese market (approximately between US$2 and US$210 based on the exchange rate on 31 March 2010 of US$1 = 93.3898 JPY) (Miyake et al., 2010). In 2013, a bluefin tuna became a million-dollar fish during the first auction of the year at Tokyo's Tsukiji fish market (US$1.76 million for a 222-kg bluefin tuna). Compared to bluefin, prices paid for fresh yellowfin, albacore and skipjack are lower but relatively more stable.

Tunas are also regarded as important to the food security, health and livelihoods of Pacific Island populations (Pilling et al., 2015). Globally, the potential for fish to contribute to food security has been the subject of debate. In some cases, fisheries have been (incorrectly, in some instances) identified as fully exploited or over exploited and, therefore, marine resources are not considered a sustainable source of food (Godfray et al., 2010). However, fish protein, in addition to agricultural production, has been identified as a panacea to feeding a projected nine billion people and redressing food insecurity particularly in regions such as the Pacific (Food and Agriculture Oranization of the United Nations, 2015; Godfray et al., 2010; Pilling et al., 2015; World Health Organization, 2015). While important to populations in the WCPO, local access to tuna fisheries for food security has been described as a local depletion and policy issue due to the industrialisation of tuna fishing such as purse seining of skipjack tuna (Pilling et al., 2015).

### Tuna harvest and monitoring abundance in the Pacific

The WCPO tuna fishery is considered the largest (by catch volume) and most valuable in the world. In 2014, the total value of the tuna catch in the Western and Central Pacific Convention Area (WCP-CA)[1] was approximately US$5.8 billion. The annual total catch has steadily increased since the 1960s, mostly due to growth in the purse seine catch. In 2014, purse seine catch of tunas was estimated to be 71 per cent of the record total catch at 2.9 million tonnes; this represented 60 per cent[2] of the global tuna catch (4.78 million tonnes) (FFA, 2015; Harley et al., 2014). In the same year, skipjack also reported a record catch at 2 million tonnes, which was 69 per cent of the total catch.

Four main species of tuna are targeted and managed within the WCP-CA: skipjack, yellowfin, bigeye and albacore. Catches are broadly distributed across the equatorial waters of the WCP-CA in EEZs of PICTs and in the high seas (Harley et al., 2014; Sibert and Hampton, 2003). Eighty per cent of tunas are caught within eight EEZs: Federated States of Micronesia (FSM), Kiribati, Marshall Islands, Nauru, Palau, Papua New Guinea (PNG), Solomon Islands and Tuvalu. In addition, there are a number of species caught in association with these targeted tuna species. Some are of commercial importance while others are discarded. The discarded species include fish of no commercial value, and endangered, threatened or protected species such as marine mammals, seabirds, sea turtles and sharks (a feature of fisheries exploitation discussed in Chapter 7).

The expansion of tuna fisheries in the WCPO has relied on scientific advances and improved understanding of biology and fisheries science. Knowledge of the tunas' life history traits and varying levels of movement across the Pacific and within the water column is fundamental to how tunas are managed. Science and technical organisations such as the Secretariat of the Pacific Community (SPC) examine tropical tunas' biology (movement patterns, reproduction) and exploitation rates in the WCPO. These research programmes provide data to inform fisheries and science managers and decision makers, including providing information on the status of tuna stocks.

A significant sustainability issue of the WCPO tuna fishery is overfishing of bigeye tuna. Besides fishing that targets bigeye tuna, a significant concern to their conservation is the exploitation of skipjack by purse seiners and the substantial quantities of bycatch of juvenile bigeye tuna. Recent stock assessments of bigeye tuna estimate spawning biomass levels to be below sustainable levels (16 per cent of the predicted biomass in the absence of fishing) (Harley et al., 2014). In order to rebuild bigeye tuna stocks, a reduction in both fishing mortality of bigeye and skipjack fishing effort is recommended (Harley et al., 2014).

## Governing the global industrialisation of tuna fisheries

The relationship between sustainable development and governance has occupied the attention of researchers interested in understanding how to create conditions to enable societies and environments to flourish (Bulkeley et al., 2013; Jordan, 2008). For researchers interested in governance across different scales or in relation to transboundary resources, this has led to a focus on interactive forms of governance (Ansell and Torfing, 2015; Bulkeley, 2005). Kooiman (1999; 2003) provides a theorisation of interactive governance that acknowledges the interdependence of actors in addressing societal problems and creating societal opportunities. Such an approach to governance focuses on interactions and relationships within particular contexts taking into account the diversity, complexity and dynamics of social, political and, we argue, ecological systems. This allows for multiple dimensions of scale (e.g. spatial and temporal), a diversity of actors (state and non-state) and advances in science and knowledge production to be considered in how institutional arrangements configure marine socio-ecological systems (Adger et al., 2005; Bulkeley, 2005;

Campbell et al., 2016). In characterising interactive governance, Sørensen et al. (2015) distinguish cooperation, coordination and collaboration. Cooperation is characterised as involving the 'exchange of ideas, knowledge and know-how', coordination requires 'mutual adjustments to reduce unintended consequences and create synergies', while collaboration refers to longer-term and institutionalised interactions in which 'actors are committed to negotiate diverging interests and develop shared governance goals, implement such goals in practice, and possibly share resources to meet these goals' (Sørensen et al., 2015: 333). Cooperation, coordination and collaboration are evident in the attempts to govern tunas and manage scarcity within the WCPO.

The 'highly migratory' nature of tuna species provided the impetus for cooperative, coordinated and collaborative approaches to regional governance (Hanich and Tsamenyi, 2010). The 1995 Agreement for the Implementation of the United Nations Convention of the Law of the Sea of 10 December 1982, relating to the Conservation and Management of Straddling Fish Stocks and Highly Migratory Fish Stocks (also known as the Fish Stocks Agreement or United Nations Fish Stocks Agreement (UNFSA)) and the United Nations Convention on the Law of the Sea (UNCLOS), provide the governance framework to manage the high seas fisheries and protect the common heritage of humankind. In accordance with these agreements, five tuna Regional Fisheries Management Organisations (RFMOs) were established to encourage and promote cooperation among coastal states and fishing nations to ensure the sustainable use of tunas.

There are two main RFMOs in the Pacific Ocean: the Inter-American-Tropical-Tuna-Commission (IATTC) and the WCPFC. The tuna fishery encompassed by the WCPO Convention Area of the WCPFC (WCP-CA) is one of the last largest healthy commercially-fished stocks in the world. The WCFPC was established in 2004 as an initiative of PICTs to address economic, social, political and environmental concerns and to match biological scales with management scales (Hanich and Tsamenyi, 2010; Parris, 2010). The aim of the WCPFC is to foster the conservation and sustainable use of (migratory) fish stocks in the WCPO (Miller et al., 2014). This regional body complements other efforts to manage tuna fish stocks and enable sustainable development, in particular, the PNA and FFA.

The WCPO is distinctive as a site of international cooperation because of the environmental and political challenges affecting tuna fisheries (Miller et al., 2014). The large areal extent of the WCPO, the fugitive characteristics of tunas, the cross-scale movement of tunas between EEZs and the high seas, and the competing claims to tunas from PICTs and DWFN provide the context for steering collective action and decision-making (Campbell et al., 2016; Cash et al., 2006; Adger et al., 2005). The regional tuna governance arrangements and mechanisms enacted through the WCPFC coordinate management of social-ecological systems and establish the framework within which decisions regarding tuna management in the WCPO are made (Schultz et al., 2015). The interactive nature of governance arrangements in the WCPO give rise to

Don't forget the fish! 191

a mode of collaborative governance that brings together multiple stakeholders, including the private sector and civil society, to enhance decision-making
(Ansell and Gash, 2008; Vierros et al., 2015).

### PICTs, historical relationships and tuna fisheries development in the Pacific

The economic and cultural importance of marine resources unites PICTs in
terms of governance, economics and management; nevertheless, coastal states
are highly diverse and range in economic, social, political and environmental
status. Geopolitically, the uniqueness of Pacific Island states can be characterised based on geographic size (land and EEZ) and location in the Pacific,
their colonial pasts, status of sovereignty and level of dependency on natural
resources (for tourism, tuna fisheries or mineral extraction). This heterogeneity
presents challenges for regional transboundary resource management.

Generally, many PICTs have a narrow resource base and limited access to
markets, limited land for agriculture, poor soil and are vulnerable to extreme
climatic events such as typhoons and droughts. Traditionally, subsistence life-
styles prevailed, and access to marine resources was, at least before the Second
World War, plentiful (Doulman, 1987). Natural resources vary from agricultural land that is relied upon by more than 50 per cent of the population for
subsistence living to marine resources including minerals in the seabed.

Tuna fishing became valued as a way for potential economic development
and self-reliance in the 1980s with the emergence of UNCLOS in1982, which
was seen as fundamental for supporting Pacific nations' acquired independence
(Doulman, 1987). The new regime extended countries' EEZs out 200 nautical
miles, resulting in PICTs controlling 38.5 million $km^2$ of ocean. While inshore
fisheries provided access for local communities to food, offshore fisheries gave
opportunities for economic growth and development of international presence
(both in markets and in political spaces), and continue to do so.

Fishing nations operate within the EEZs of coastal states under various bilateral and multilateral agreements. The US and Japan are two DWFNs that have
operated in the WCPO from the early 1900s, and have been leaders in the
industrialisation of tuna fishing in the region. In addition to modifications in gear
to suit the oceanographic environment, the US established tuna canneries in the
region and, later, home ports to shorten the supply chain and maximise efficiency. For its part, Japan was instrumental in demonstrating the viability of the
year-round fishery and efficiencies with using fish aggregating devices (FADs).

The presence of US home ports in the WCPO provided US vessels with
opportunistic access to some of the more productive waters in the region.
The agreement enabling this access arguably discounted the rights of the
coastal states over tuna resources by allowing US vessels to roam freely in the
WCPO (Gillet et al., 2002). The access afforded to the US was consolidated
through the Treaty of Fisheries between the Governments of Certain Pacific
Island States and the United States of America (the US Treaty), which entered

192  *V. Jollands and K. Fisher*

into force in June 1988. The US Treaty is a multilateral agreement providing 'broader cooperation' and access to US purse seiners to most areas in the WCPO (including the 16 PICTs party to the Treaty),[3] while creating development opportunities for Treaty partners. The US Treaty provides subsidised free-ranging access to the WCPO in which the US pays reduced access fees. The ability to range over the WCPO is an advantage due to the nature of the purse seine fishery, which requires vessels to search schooling tuna over vast distances (Gillett et al., 2002). The increased use of FADs, and the influence of climatic variation (e.g. the shift westward with the weak La Niña period (1995–1996) to PNG and FSM, and movement eastward in 1999 to the Gilbert Islands, Phoenix Islands and Tuvalu) have also changed the geographies of tuna fishing by moving fishing effort to match where the fish are.

The ever-increasing socio-economic demand for tuna products has led to the industrialisation of tuna fisheries whereby new technology, effort creep, increased capacity and development of relationships through multilateral agreements has enabled tuna fleets to venture into previously unfished areas of oceans and to increase fishing effort. Although tunas such as skipjack are fast growing, have high fecundity and are highly resilient relative to other tunas, fisheries expansion along with improvements in technology and the economic opportunities afforded by the fisheries have heightened concerns about marine resource scarcity. Moreover, concerns about the impacts of industrial fishing (and other anthropogenic impacts, such as climate change) on ocean ecosystems persist, as do concerns regarding the effects on coastal state communities that rely on these resources.

### Multilevel governance in the Western and Central Pacific tuna fishery[4]

The complicated web of governance arrangements in the WCPO reflects the complex array of actors implicated in the tuna fisheries. Actors include governments of DWFNs and PICTs, international trading partners of trade agreements, fishing vessel owners and operators, tuna processors, distributors and markets, scientists, policy makers, environmental non-governmental organisations (NGOs) and, ultimately, the consumer. The four main levels of governance are international, regional, sub-regional and national (as shown in Figure 11.1). Each of these levels of governance is supported by additional multi-scalar organisations, frameworks and movements including NGO initiatives such as Pacific Oceanscapes.[5]

Other regional governance arrangements in the WCPO include the FFA and PNA (Figure 11.2). The FFA comprises 17 member PICTs and was established in 1979 in response to the deliberation of the Third United Nations Conference on the Law of the Sea. The FFA provides a forum for member countries to manage, conserve and optimise the use of tuna resources in their EEZs and beyond. The body seeks economic determinism and sovereignty through UNCLOS and the establishment of 200-mile EEZs. Over the past four decades, FFA has displayed a strong level of collaboration among PICTs

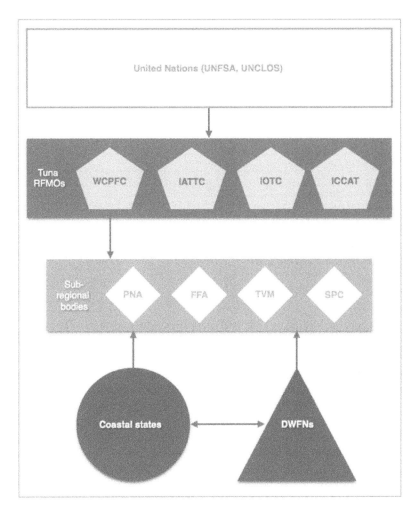

*Figure 11.1* WCPO tuna fishery governance arrangements
Source: authors

and has enhanced the capacity of the region to manage their fisheries and to negotiate with DWFNs. Regional collaboration through FFA has been effective for assisting PICTs in exercising their sovereign fisheries management rights and ecosystem based fisheries management. However, it has also highlighted the Pacific Island region's diversity and created some tension between PICTs who seek other goals. This led to the formation of additional sub-regional groups such as the PNA, which governs tuna collectively within its eight member countries' EEZs, and Te Vaka Moana South Pacific Fisheries Cooperation (TVM).

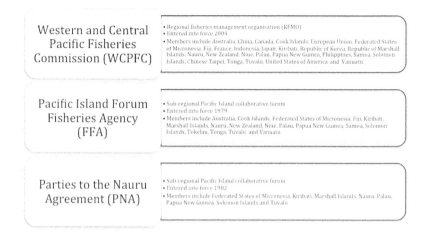

*Figure 11.2* WCPO tuna fishery actors
Source: authors

The PNA was established in 1982 and comprises eight members. The rationale for the establishment of the PNA was that more than 80 per cent of WCPO tuna fisheries resources were situated within eight of the 17 members of the FFA group. The PNA advocates the exercise of sovereign rights to realise the economic potential of tuna resources while ensuring sustainable use of tuna resources within members' EEZs. The PNA have become a powerful group within the Pacific with respect to controlling the largest proportion of tuna resources. Included in their success is the development of the FSM Arrangement, which entered into force in 1995. Among its objectives were: optimisation of economic benefits from tuna fisheries; development of domestic fishing fleets and a move away from dependency on access fees from DWFNs (Aqorau and Bergin, 1997) by giving preferential access to PICTs' vessels; the PNA Vessel Day Scheme, which sets overall limits on the number of days purse seine fishing vessels can be licensed to fish in PNA waters; the adoption of conservation and management measures (CMMs) prohibiting fishing in the high seas pocket closures and on FADs for three months of the year; and, the certified sustainability of the free school skipjack tuna fishery under the Marine Stewardship Council programme. FFA and PNA provide critical platforms for PICTs by promoting the coordination and negotiation of CMMs over multiple scales.

The main international frameworks influencing tuna governance in the WCPO are the UNCLOS and UNFSA. Article 64 of UNCLOS requires coastal states and fishing nations to '*cooperate directly or through appropriate international organisations with the view to ensuring conservation*'. The emphasis on cooperation and identification of international organisations to facilitate conservation is reiterated in the UNFSA. UNFSA was adopted in 1995 to address

*Don't forget the fish!* 195

growing concerns for global fisheries. Together, these agreements provide for the establishment of RFMOs[6] as the key mechanism by which nation states can fulfil their international obligations for cooperation and conserving and managing transboundary fish stocks.

UNFSA prompted coastal states and DWFNs within the WCPO to develop the Convention on the Conservation and Management of Highly Migratory Fish Stocks in the Western and Central Pacific Ocean (September 2000) for the conservation and management of tuna stocks within the WCPO. This led to the establishment of the WCPFC, which entered into force in July 2004. The Convention also established a Secretariat, the Scientific Committee, the Northern Committee and the Technical and Compliance Committee to provide recommendations to the Commission on matters including monitoring, control and surveillance, conservation and management of the fishery.

The objective of the WCPFC is to fulfil the broader conservation and resource requirements to ensure the sustainable use of tunas across the WCPO. The WCPFC is markedly different to other RFMOs since it covers both coastal states' EEZs and the high seas (Miller et al., 2014). As such, two distinctive institutional regimes exist. The first is a common-property regime based on shared transboundary tuna that flow between Pacific Islands' EEZs and controlled either individually or collectively through regional or sub-regional organisations. The second is an open access regime on the high seas that is accessible to any fishing nation. A mechanism deployed by the WCPFC and enabled under UNFSA is to pursue CMMs based upon the precautionary approach and the best available scientific information. UNFSA specifies that CMMs are to be compatible over high seas and nation states' EEZs and gives member states of regional fisheries bodies the mandate to board and inspect vessels on the high seas to ensure compliance, and to provide for peaceful settlement of disputes (Miller et al., 2014).

Each participant of the WCPFC represents multiple interests that broadly fit into security, trade, national (economic, social, political, environmental) and diplomacy interests. Key priorities of the WCPFC are to strengthen engagement through increased consistent dialogue, systematic and comprehensive strategic planning, and enhanced communication. A nation's tuna fishery (domestic and international) involves stakeholders from industry (catchers), markets, supply chain, sub-regional groups (Figure 11.1) and their citizens (social, cultural, and economic). The interests of these groups are also often fragmented. For example, catchers split into different gear type and target species catcher groups (i.e. purse seine, longline, pole and line, hand line) that have different needs and objectives that are often incompatible.

At the national level, there are a number of ways that nation states engage in the WCPFC's activities to further their interests. Each nation state represented in the WCPFC can be characterised by the following interests:

- Fishing nation (distant water, coastal or Pacific Island state).
- Target species and mode of fishing (principally purse seine or longline), and operational arrangements (e.g. joint ventures, foreign charter vessels).

196 *V. Jollands and K. Fisher*

- Political, economic (e.g. canneries) and market interests (exporter/importer).
- Fisheries management policies and mainstream discourses likely to influence policy development.
- Alliances (sub-regional groups, e.g. FFA, PNA).
- Historical relationships with tuna fisheries and main Pacific connections.

In some cases, the position of a specific delegation is heavily influenced or even dominated by a single stakeholder and a single economic or political interest (Hanich, 2011). In other cases, delegations may balance different, often competing or contradictory economic and political interests of different stakeholder groups. For example, PNG, Kiribati, Tuvalu, Nauru, FSM and the Solomon Islands are loosely referred to as 'purse seine/skipjack states'. FSM's largest fishery is the skipjack purse seine fishery; Japan has the highest volume of catch by flag for purse seines and 95 per cent of all tuna catch by FSM's domestic fleet was skipjack caught by purse seine. Significant quantities of tuna are also landed in FSM for transhipping to canneries in Asia.

The collaborative governance arrangements in the WCPO also provide opportunities for civil society engagement. Environmental NGOs (eNGOs) engage in the governance of tuna fisheries through advocating their agendas to multiple scales and levels of the fishery including the public, consumers, fishers and government (both nationally and internationally). Key messages have included the need to sustain the fishery and reduce bycatch of endangered species, the need for marine protected areas and, more recently, the imperative to ensure food security and development opportunities for small-island developing states (SIDS). A particular way in which eNGOs have engaged in the governance of WCPO tuna fishery is through advocating for sustainable procurement at the level of distribution (e.g. EU, US and Japanese markets). The US provides a good example of this and where eNGO advocacy has profoundly impacted the US tuna industry. By the 1960s, the shift towards the use of purse seine nets in the Eastern Tropical Pacific led to the incidental capture and mortality of an estimated 250,000–500,000 dolphins per year (Danaher and Mark, 2003). While efforts were made to reduce these numbers, such as the Marine Mammal Protection Act (1972), a considerable number of dolphins continued to be caught. In the late 1980s, a social movement, led by the eNGO Earth Island Institute, successfully changed this (Soule, 2009). In 1988, biologist Sam LaBudde captured graphic footage of the incidental mortality of dolphins on the tuna trawler *Maria Luisa*. This footage was later used by Earth Island Institute to leverage against the state to enforce the Marine Mammal Protection Act (MMPA) and to tighten regulation. Further, Earth Island Institute used the footage to raise public awareness using major television networks to air the controversial footage. This movement revolutionised the US market and in 1989 the Dolphin Protection Consumer Act was introduced, followed with an announcement by Tony O'Reilly, owner of StarKist Tuna, that they would supply 'dolphin safe' tuna. While this was an example

## Don't forget the fish! 197

of how eNGOs activities have made demonstrable change, to date there has been limited success in terms of influencing the implementation of sustainable policies to halt international tuna fisheries expansion, reduce bycatch across international waters and the high seas and otherwise improve sustainability in the transnational tuna fishery in the WCPFC. Moreover, NGOs face barriers that influence market and supply chains and drive WCPFC voting preferences. Barriers include duty free access, low costs of production (wages etc.) and intense competition (e.g. too many canneries operating worldwide).

The diversity of players in the WCPO tuna fishery impacts decision-making processes concerning the allocation of benefits and costs of the fishery. These decisions involve balancing the sustainability and development of the fishery such that it provides equitable allocation of catch to multiple players (historic players and new entrants including PICTs wishing to develop their own fishery).

## Mechanisms to improve tuna sustainability and why they don't work

In response to the critical status of bigeye tuna, CMMs, such as WCPFC's CMM 2008–01 (high seas and FAD closures), were introduced to reduce fishing pressure and allow more effective control over illegal fishing. The basis for developing CMM 2008–01 was to ensure political and economic alignment and it grew out of the PNA initiative to propose closures of the high seas. CMM 2008–01 went into effect on 1 January 2010 and closed two high seas pockets to purse seine fishing.[7] Those advocating for high seas closures, such as PNA members, argued that the benefits included accommodating the aspirations of SIDS, while addressing issues of overfishing and overcapacity as well as those of transhipment and illegal, unreported and unregulated (IUU) fishing. Those actors against high seas closures were countries such as New Zealand and the US, which have extensive purse seine vessel interests in the WCPO. While CMM 2008–01 sought to reduce effort in these areas, a number of factors undermined its success. First, exemptions were granted to SIDS and certain fishing nations based on diplomatic and other pressures, and historical 'friendships'. The exemptions for SIDS allowed for development of their domestic fisheries and can also be seen as an attempt to force DWFNs to fish in their EEZs and pay for the resource rents (Parris, 2010). Second, purse seine pressure increased elsewhere, under bilateral national agreements with PNA countries. For example, while the high seas pocket closure (2010–2012) resulted in a substantial decline in the domestic Philippines purse seine catch, the activities of Philippine flagged vessels fishing in PNG under bilateral agreements increased (Miller et al., 2014).

There has been considerable debate among the WCPFC, the Scientific Committee and independent researchers over the efficacy of high seas closures and whether they are effective at reducing effort and mitigating other issues such as IUU. Indeed, the WCPFC has been criticised for slow and uneven progress (Jollands, 2011). The ineffectiveness of CMM 2008–01 in reducing fishing effort (or to realise full economic potential for PICTs), and the inability to allocate the fishery is attributed to the difficulties of consensus decision-making and different interpretations regarding the role of the WCPFC. The FFA have sought to assert their sovereign rights through the WCPFC and added depth to the governance arrangements regulating access in member states' EEZs. At the same time, the WCPFC faces exceedingly complicated decisions regarding management measures to reduce fishing mortality while ensuring maximisation of the fishery profits and allowing development opportunities for PICTs. The unenforceability of resolutions, exemptions and the fact the Scientific Committee's information regarding the status of fish stocks is disregarded hamper the effectiveness of the WCPFC. The politicisation of the decision-making process in the context of multiple and competing interests means the WCPFC continually defers difficult decisions regarding allocation and conservation measures.

## Conclusion

Marine ecosystems are complex and require governance and institutional arrangements that work across multiple scales. Better management of fisheries across the globe today is attributable, in part, to the shift towards collaborative forms of governance that engages stakeholders and interested parties. As this chapter has shown, governance of the WCPO tuna requires multiscalar coordination over multiple domains (environmental, political, biological, organisational and social) and cooperation among actors across multiple levels (local to international) (Hanich et al., 2010; Miller et al., 2014; Sørensen et al., 2015). The complicated governance arrangements in the WCPO are made more complex, however, due to the varying membership of actors in the fishery to different agreements: some are party to the UNFSA, WCPFC, FFA and PNA, but others are not.

Regional and sub-regional governance of tuna in the Pacific has evolved for over 30 years. Sub-regional collaborative arrangements, FFA and PNA, have worked to strengthen the position of Pacific Island states. In particular, FFA and the PNA seek to manage migratory fishes with the objective of maximising economic benefits from tuna fisheries. For the FFA, the strong sense of solidarity among PICTs to protect their sovereign rights facilitates their collaboration in the WCPO and is an example of how PICTs have been able to negotiate competing interests and develop shared governance goals (Sørensen et al., 2015).

The WCPFC, as an RFMO, provides an important, though imperfect, part of the governance solution for tuna fisheries in the WCPO. The evolution of collaborative governance arrangements between DWFNs and PICTs, and the conflicts that manifest as DWFN effort increased, shaped how collaboration was understood, and have continued to influence the effectiveness of PICTs and DWFNs cooperation involving the conservation and optimal utilisation of tuna species in the region (Tarte, 2010).

The multiple and competing interests represented within the WCPFC make it difficult to obtain uniformity in positions since decisions can be undermined by PICTs who are members of FFA or PNA or who are acting as sovereign states.

Nevertheless, collaborative governance approaches in the WCPO have enabled fisheries managers to address scarcity of tunas in the Pacific, while also building social capacities and capabilities in the region. The WCPFC provides an overarching institutional structure that brings PICTs and DWFNs together in an attempt to balance conservation and sustainable use of tunas when stakes are high, time is limited and decisions are made based on incomplete information. In addition to these actors, regional collaborative forums have opened up a platform for eNGOs to advocate sustainable policy. Cooperation among members of the WCPFC has enabled better information about sustainability of tuna stocks to be collected and shared, which facilitates the optimal utilisation of tunas through trade and access. In developing shared governance goals and seeking to implement approaches to ensure the sustainable management of tunas, the WCPFC enabled the coordination among its members of compliance and observer programmes across the network of countries to support more rigorous surveillance and compliance.

In examining the shift towards regional governance in the WCPO through the WCPFC, this chapter has highlighted the challenges to managing fisheries where multiple claims of ownership to resources exist and must be reconciled with ambitions to utilise the fish and profit from such activities. Collaboration in this regard has magnified the complexities that exist at the sub-regional level and highlight those differing views held by DWFNs and PICTs.

## Notes

1 As defined in the WCPFC's Convention Text: *Convention on the Conservation and Management of High Migratory Fish Stocks in the Western and Central Pacific Ocean* (see https://www.wcpfc.int/convention-text).
2 The Indian Ocean represents 17 per cent of the global catch, the Atlantic and Eastern Pacific Oceans represent 10 per cent and 14 per cent, respectively.
3 Australia, Cook Island s, FSM, Fiji, Kiribati, Marshall Islands, Nauru, New Zealand, Niue, Palau, PNG, Samoa, Solomon Island s, Tonga, Tuvalu, US and Vanuatu.
4 This section (and following sections) is based on empirical research of Jollands, V. (2011) *It's not about the fish: Multi-scalar Governance in the Western and Central Pacific Ocean* (Unpublished master's thesis). University of Auckland, Auckland, New Zealand.
5 Oceanscapes is an initiative spearheaded by Pacific Islands Forum that involves a raft of participants including intergovernmental organisations, nation states and NGOs. The initiative seeks to protect, manage and sustain the cultural and natural integrity of the ocean for present and future generations and the broader global community.
6 At present there are five tuna RFMOs: Commission for the Conservation of Southern Bluefin Tuna (CCSBT), Inter-American Tropical Tuna Commission (IATTC), International Commission for the Conservation of Atlantic Tunas (ICCAT), Indian Ocean Tuna Commission (IOTC) and Western and Central Pacific Fisheries Commission (WCPFC).
7 WCPFC replaced the closures at its 2012 meeting with a measure that temporarily instituted input and output limits, observer coverage requirements, prohibited Philippines purse seine fishing in high seas pocket number 2 (Figure 11.2) and other measures (WCPFC, 2012). The 2012 measure was replaced at the WCPFC December 2015 meeting.

## References

Adger, W. N., Brown, K., and Tompkins, E. L. (2005) 'The political economy of cross-scale networks in resource co-management', *Ecology and Society*, 10(2), p. 9.

Ansell, C. and Gash, A. (2008) 'Collaborative governance in theory and practice', *Journal of Public Administration Research and Theory*, 18(4), pp. 543–571.

Ansell, C. and Torfing, J. (2015) 'How does collaborative governance scale?' *Policy and Politics*, 43(3), pp. 315–329.

Aqorau, T., and Bergin, A. (1997) 'The Federated States of Micronesia Arrangement for regional fisheries access', *The International Journal of Marine and Coastal Law*, 12(1), p. 44.

Blanc, M. (2002) 'Grading of tunas for the sashimi market', *SPC Fisheries Newsletter*, 29.

Bond, C. (1996) *Biology of Fishes* (2nd ed.). Fort Worth: Saunders College Pub.

Bulkeley, H. (2005) 'Reconfiguring environmental governance: towards a politics of scales and networks', *Political Geography*, 24, pp. 875–902.

Bulkeley, H., Jordan, A., and Perkins, R. (2013) 'Governing sustainability: Rio+20 and the road beyond', *Environment and Planning C*, 31, pp. 958–970.

Campbell, L. M., Gray, N. J., Fairbanks, L., Silver, J. J., Gruby, R. L., Dubik, B. A., and Basurto, X. (2016) 'Global oceans governance: New and emerging issues', *Annual Review of Environment and Resources*, 41, pp. 517–543.

Cash, D. W., Adger, W. N., Berkes, F., Garden, P., Lebel, L., Olsson, P., Pritchard, L., and Young, O. (2006) 'Scale and cross-scale dynamics: Governance and information in a multilevel world', *Ecology and Society*, 11(2), p. 8.

Chand, S., Grafton, R. Q., and Petersen, E. (2003) 'Multilateral governance of fisheries: management and cooperation in the western and central Pacific tuna fisheries', *Marine Resource Economics*, 18, pp. 329–344.

Danaher, K., & Mark, J. (2003) *Insurrection: The Citizen Challenge to Corporate Power*. New York: Routledge.

Doulman, D. J. (1987) *Tuna Issues and Perspectives in the Pacific Islands Region*. Honolulu: Pacific Islands Development Program.

FFA. (2015). *2015 Economic Indicators Report*. Honiara: FFA.

Food and Agriculture Oranization of the United Nations. (2015) *The State of Food Insecurity in the World: Meeting The 2015 International Hunger Targets—Taking Stock of Uneven Progress*. Rome: FAO.

Gillett, R., McCoy, M.A. and Itano, D.G. (2002) 'Status of the United States Western Pacific tuna purse seine fleet and factors affecting its future', available: http://www.soest.hawaii.edu/PFRP/soest_jimar_rpts/gpa_amer_samoa.pdf [accessed 22 July 2017].

Godfray, H. C. J., Beddington, J. R., Crute, I. R., Haddad, L., Lawrence, D., Muir, J. F., Pretty, J., Robinson, S., Thomas, S. M. and Toulmin, C. (2010) 'Food security: The challenge of feeding 9 billion people', *Science*, 327(5967), pp. 812–818.

Hamilton, A., Lewis, A., McCoy, M. A., Havice, E., and Campling, L. (2011) *Market and Industry Dynamics in the Global Tuna Supply Chain*. Honiara: FFA.

Hanich, Q. (2011) 'Interest and influence — A snapshot of the western and central Pacific tropical tuna fisheries', Australian National Centre for Ocean Resources and Security (ANCORS): University of Wollongong.

Hanich, Q., and Tsamenyi, M. (2009) 'Managing fisheries and corruption in the Pacific Islands region', *Marine Policy*, 33(2), pp. 386–392.

## Don't forget the fish! 201

Hanich, Q., and Tsamenyi, M. (2010) *Navigating Pacific fisheries: Legal and Policy Trends in the Implementation of International Fisheries Instruments in the Western and Central Pacific Region*. Wollongong: Ocean Publications.

Harley, S., Williams, P., Nicol, S., Hampton, J., and Brouwer, S. (2014) *The Western and Central Pacific Tuna Fishery: 2014 Overview and Status of Stocks*. Noumea: SPC.

Hosseini, S. A., and Kaymaram, F. (2016) 'Investigations on the reproductive biology and diet of yellowfin tuna, Thunnus albacares, (Bonnaterre, 1788) in the Oman Sea', *Journal of Applied Ichthyology*, 32(2), pp. 310–317.

Hunt, C. (2003) 'Economic globalisation impacts on Pacific marine resources', *Marine Policy*, 27(1), pp. 79–85.

Hilborn, R., Orensanz, J.M., and Parma, A. M. (2005) 'Institutions, incentives and the future of fisheries', *Philosophical Transactions of the Royal Society B: Biological Sciences*, 360, pp. 47–57.

Itano, D. G., Holland, K. N., Rooker, J. R., and Wells, R. J. D. (2011) 'Tuna management at sub-regional scales: scientific, ecological and socio-economic aspects of an old debate', Paper presented at the 62nd Tuna Conference: Data Challenges. Lake Arrowhead: California.

Jollands, V. (2011) It's not about the fish: Multi-scalar governance in the western and central Pacific Ocean. (Master of Science), The University of Auckland, Auckland.

Jordan, A. (2008) 'The governance of sustainable development: taking stock and looking forwards', *Environment and Planning C*, 26(1), pp. 17–33.

Kooiman, J. (1999) 'Social-political governance: overview, reflections and design', *Public Management: An International Journal of Research and Theory*, 1(1), pp. 67–92.

Kooiman, J. (2003). *Governing as Governance*. London: Sage.

Langley, A., Wright, A., Hurry, G., Hampton, J., Aqorua, T., and Rodwell, L. (2009) 'Slow steps towards management of the world's largest tuna fishery', *Marine Policy*, 33(2), pp. 271–279.

Lehodey, P. (2000) 'Impacts of the El Nino Southern Oscillation on tuna populations and fisheries in the tropical Pacific Ocean', Paper presented at the 13th Meeting of the Standing Committee on Tuna and Billfish. Noumea, New Caledonia.

Madigan, D.J., Carlisle, A.B., Gardner, L.D., Jayasundara, N., Micheli, F., Schaefer, K.M., Fuller, D.W., and Block, B. A. (2015) 'Assessing niche width of endothermic fish from genes to ecosystem', *Proceedings of the National Academy of Sciences of the United States of America*, 112(27), pp. 8350–8355.

Miller, A. M. M., Bush, S. R., and van Zwieten, P. A. M. (2014) 'Sub-regionalisation of fisheries governance: The case of the western and central Pacific Ocean tuna fisheries', *Maritime Studies*, 13(1), p. 17.

Miyake, M., Guillotreau, P., Sun, C. H., and Ishimura, G. (2010) 'Recent developments in the tuna industry: stocks, fisheries, management, processing, trade and markets', *FAO Fisheries and Aquaculture Technical Paper*, 543, p. 125.

Parris, H. (2010) 'Is the western and central Pacific fisheries commission meeting its conservation and management objectives?' *Ocean and Coastal Management*, 53(1), pp. 10–26.

Parris, H., and Grafton, R.Q. (2006) 'Can tuna promote sustainable development in the Pacific?' *The Journal of Environment and Development*, 15(3), pp. 269–296.

Pilling, G. M., Harley, S., Nicol, S., Williams, P., and Hampton, J. (2015) 'Can the tropical western and central Pacific tuna purse seine fishery contribute to Pacific Island population food security?' *Food Security*, 7, pp. 67–81.

Schultz, L., Folke, C., Österblom, H., and Olsson, P. (2015) 'Adaptive governance, ecosystem management, and natural capital', *PNAS*, 112(24): pp. 7369–7374.

Sibert, J., and Hampton, J. (2003) 'Mobility of tropical tunas and the implications for fisheries management', *Marine Policy*, 27, pp. 87–95.

Sørensen, E., Triantafillou, P., and Damgaard, B. (2015) 'Governing EU employment policy: does collaborative governance scale up?' *Policy and Politics*, 43(3), pp. 331–47.

Soule, S. A. (2009) *Contention and corporate social responsibility*. New York: Cambridge University Press.

SPC (2009) *Oceanographic variability*. Noumea: SPC.

Tarte, S. (2009) 'The convention for the conservation and management of highly migratory fish stocks in the Western and Central Pacific Ocean: Implementation challenges from a historical perspective', in Q. A. Hanich and B. M. Tsamenyi (eds) *Navigating Pacific Fisheries: Legal and Policy Trends in the Implementation of International Fisheries Instruments in the Western and Central Pacific Region*. Wollongong, Australia: Oceans Publications, pp. 204–220.

Vierros, M., Sumaila, U.R., and Payet, R.A. (2015) 'Main human uses of ocean areas and resources, impacts, and multiple scales of governance', in S. Aricò (ed.) *Ocean sustainability in the 21st Century*. New York: Cambridge University Press.

Walsh, M. R., Munch, S. B., Chiba, S., & Conover, D. O. (2006) 'Maladaptive changes in multiple traits caused by fishing: impediments to population recovery', *Ecology Letters,* 9(2), pp. 142–148.

World Health Organization (2015) *Food Security*. Geneva: WHO.

# 12 A world without scarcity?

*Marcelle C. Dawson, Christopher Rosin and Navé Wald*

What should be very apparent at this point is that the availability—or perhaps more accurately the accessibility—of resources is a topic that attracts the attention of a wide range of professionals, scholars and activists. In the resulting discourse, global resource scarcity is often regarded as a catalyst for conflict; yet, paradoxically, such scarcity also underlies some of the most important international collaborations. While some natural resources are irrefutably essential for life and human survival, others are more important for livelihoods and economic prosperity. Some resources derive their significance and value from how difficult they are to 'capture' and control, while 'market forces' determine the worth of others. The fact that natural resources underlie existing conceptions of economic security and achievement makes the capacity to control their access and exploitation highly desirable.

It is not hard to understand why this contested terrain of natural resources—when understood as a zero-sum game—pits key stakeholders against one another. Seen from the perspective of independent (and competitive) nation states, this situation points to an inevitable source of conflict especially in relation to those resources that are not contained within the undisputed jurisdiction of a single state. As discussed in this volume, the scarcity (perceived, created or real) of resources has the tendency to exacerbate the potential for conflict. Our intention in constructing this collection is not, however, to dwell on the inevitability of conflict; rather we suggest that the common desirability of and shared dependence on finite or limited resources can provide the impetus for cooperation in the governance of their exploitation, with the potential for more sustainable practices. This objective is reflected in the structure of the book, with chapters in Part II introducing some of the tensions associated with resources that experience demand that exceeds current or estimated future supply, while, in Part III, our contributors introduce examples of overtures towards international collaboration as a potential response to some of the sources of friction highlighted in Part II.

The chapters in this collection consider a range of social, political, environmental and economic factors that are at play in the exploitation of natural resources. Scarcity enters the conceptualisation of resource exploitation as a confounding factor. Implicit in the dominant treatment of scarcity is the expectation that increasing demand for resources (attributable to population growth, changing consumer preferences and insatiable human desires, for instance) will outpace supply and generate tensions around access to, and availability of, resources. The assumption that any gains by one group of resource users necessarily involve a loss among others creates the circumstances in which conflict becomes inevitable. Amidst ongoing talk of 'resource wars' (Le Billon, 2015; Morelli and Rohner, 2015) and fear-mongering around the urgent need to grab resources before it is too late (Klare, 2012)—views that work in the favour of greedy corporations looking to profit from the manufacture of scarcity—we are witnessing the emergence of alternative perspectives, some of which echo Marxist conceptualisations of scarcity in their questioning of how resources come to be regarded as scarce in the first place. These kinds of perspectives— underpinned as they are by a desire to challenge power and injustice—ask such questions as, 'Who has the power to capture a resource or determine its worth?' 'Whose interests are served by manufacturing the perception of scarcity?' 'Who stands to benefit from providing "solutions" to the "problem" of scarcity?' In attempting to provide answers to these questions, some of the contributors to this book argue that resource scarcity is not always a matter of an actual shortage in the supply of the resource. In some cases, a resource may be physically abundant, but access to it is limited for a range of reasons. In many instances, unequal distribution of resources is shown to be connected to state and corporate collusion. Some of the chapters in this book show how ordinary people and civil society groups work to challenge government policy and business interests. Still others highlight collaborative efforts within and between regions and nations of the world aimed at mitigating unequal distribution of, and access to, natural resources. The contributions to this part show that various forms of intervention, including policy recommendations, institutional change, improved resource management, and modifying human behaviour and values, have the potential to alleviate tensions and alter the way in which scarcity is understood. The achievements remain, however, emergent and tenuous, being subject to the tensions of competition among states.

The chapters in this volume contribute to our collective knowledge of issues pertinent to scarcity and natural resources. They depict diverse, contextualised and nuanced cases where the complexity of needs is being unpacked. In this sense, the book contributes to the convergence thesis, which stipulates the consolidation of different positions in the debate around scarcity of natural resources (Frerks, Dietz and van der Zang, 2014). But notwithstanding this convergence, Homer-Dixon's (1999) typology of the debate's main positions during the 1990s (neo-Malthusians, economic optimists, distributionists) can still be identified in the book's different accounts. For example, the Marxist-inspired distributionist approach is evident in the chapters by Mehta, Lahiri-Dutt and Hill, and it is usually associated with a more critical view of scarcity as a political social construct. The chapter by Lindström, Granit and Rosner, in contrast, has a stronger inclination towards economic optimism, where regional cooperation can mitigate the uneven physical distribution of a natural resource. In this sense, readers of the book can identify different elements of these various approaches, and appreciate how these are manifested within different contexts.

The interdisciplinary background of the book's contributors shifts the focus of the analysis beyond narrow theoretical treatments of international relations and resource diplomacy to broader examinations of the practicalities of cooperation in the context of competition and scarcity. Combining the insights of a range of social scientists, including sociologists, geographers, historians and political scientists, with those of engineers, ecologists, physicists and marine scientists—many of whom work as 'resource practitioners' outside the context of the university—has yielded refreshing insights. Tackling the question of global resource scarcity in this way has highlighted the tensions between 'thinking/theory' and 'doing/practice', which so often plague the process of social change. Indeed, the authors' contributions raise important questions about the ways in which a change in thinking can lead to changes in behaviour. Recognising that environmental loss or degradation is a loss for all and that there are sufficient resources to cater for everyone's needs, but not everyone's 'greeds' or excesses, lies at the heart of behavioural and policy change. In other words, conceived of in terms of a negative- or positive-sum game, resource politics have the potential to shift onto a terrain where allocation and access are determined by factors other than economic gain. While this may sound overly optimistic, possibly even naïve, evidence suggesting a linear relationship between scarcity and conflict is unconvincing. It denies the socially constructed nature of scarcity and undermines the ability of humans to develop alternatives that do not have economic prosperity as the ultimate objective. If controlling and monopolising a valued resource is seen as one possible response to ending the 'problem' of scarcity, can we think of alternatives that remove the impetus to compete? In other words, can we ultimately eliminate scarcity? Answering this question involves a thorough re-examination of human values and a deeper engagement with what the social, political and economic philosophies of 'degrowth' and *buen vivir* (roughly translated as 'the good life') could mean for sustained human existence on planet earth.

Rather than offering solid—and incontestable—conclusions, we believe the contributions to the book provide for a loosening of the definition of scarcity. In doing so, they open a space for discussions of resource exploitation that move beyond the strictures of competitive nation states to the conceivability of collaboration and cooperation. Thus redefined, it is possible to eliminate scarcity from the arena of allocation and access and more appropriately apply it to those situations in which an absolute and immediate scarcity can be met with the necessary resources to avoid humanitarian catastrophe. The suggestion that more cooperative conceptions of resource use are possible is, of course, not a novel one. In the Introduction, we already identified research focused on the potential for resources to facilitate peaceful relations where tensions exist in other interactions, with environmental peacebuilding being perhaps the most

# 206 *M. C. Dawson, C. Rosin and N. Wald*

ambitious. The interventions of our contributors suggest, however, that this collaboration can perform a broader and at the same time deeper role of realigning society's apparent infatuation with scarcity.

We remain fully convinced that collaboration is a potential (and highly desirable) response to resource scarcity. The contributions to this book demonstrate the already emergent collaborations around such essential, vital and potentially scarce resources as water, food, energy and marine resources. The tenuous nature of these achievements reminds us, however, of the continued need for dialogue among the diverse actors, disciplines, ontologies and epistemologies of resources and scarcity. Such dialogue should obviously involve reflections on peace building and incorporate the socioecological relations inherent to nexus frameworks. But they should not be limited to these framings, if such boundaries fail to account for the variety in representations of scarcity—some of which are so apparent in the chapters in this book. In the end, rather than solid, indisputable conclusions, we emphasise the need for continued engagement among those interested in and concerned with the relations of resource exploitation—and an engagement that acknowledges the insight to be gained from the distinctive representations of scarcity.

## References

Frerks, G., Dietz, T. and van der Zang, P. (2014) 'Conflict and cooperation on natural resources: Justifying the CoCooN programme', in M. Bavinck, L. Pellegrini and E. Mostert (eds.) *Conflicts over Natural Resources in the Global South—Conceptual Approaches*. Leiden, The Netherlands: CRC Press, pp. 13–34.

Homer-Dixon, T. F. (1999) *Environment, Scarcity, and Violence*. New Jersey: Princeton University Press.

Klare, M. T. (2012) *The Race for What's Left: The Global Scramble for the World's Last Resources*, New York: Metropolitan Books.

Le Billon, P. (2015) 'Resource wars and violence', in R.L. Bryant (ed.) *The International Handbook of Political Ecology*. Gloucestershire and Northampton: Edward Elgar Publishing, pp. 176–188.

Morelli, M. and Rohner, D. (2015) 'Resource concentration and civil wars', *Journal of Development Economics*, 117, pp. 32–47.

# Index

artisanal and small-scale mining (ASM) 74, 77, 79, 82

biodiversity 1, 7, 76, 92, 98, 108, 110–11, 117, 122, 134, 165, 169–71,
bycatch 110–11, 113–15, 189, 196–7

China 8, 22, 63, 98, 109, 149–61, 166–7, 173–4
climate change 8, 22, 32, 40, 43, 49, 51, 68, 108, 119–21, 134, 137, 142, 165, 169–72, 192
collaboration 2, 7, 12, 14–15, 40–3, 51–2, 76, 101, 121, 132, 184, 187, 190, 192–3, 198–9, 205–6; see also international collaboration
conflict 1–8, 11, 14–15, 22, 24–6, 30, 41–2, 44–5, 51, 73, 75, 81, 83, 89–90, 131, 138, 142, 146–7, 151, 153–5, 159–61, 164–5, 168, 170–3, 175–6, 178, 198, 203–5
conservation 5–7, 9, 110–11, 113–18, 122–3, 155, 170, 184, 189–90, 194–5, 198–9; of biodiversity 1,7; of dolphins 116; of sharks 114, 116
cooperation 1–4, 6–7, 11–16, 26, 39–45, 47–8, 50–1, 107, 113, 115, 123, 132, 136, 139, 164–5, 167–8, 170–2, 175–6, 178, 184–5, 190, 192, 194–5, 198–9, 203, 205
crisis 29, 66, 73–6, 98, 131–2, 154, 157; discourse 13; financial 22, 33; food 133, 137–8, 141; oil 156; water 29

dams 21, 31–3, 91–2, 94–7, 166, 168, 170, 172–3
developing countries 65, 78, 108, 111, 138–9
developing world 10, 29, 75, 108, 110

development 8–11, 15, 24, 26–7, 31, 40, 44–5, 49, 51, 65, 68, 78, 80–1, 91, 93–4, 99–101, 108, 111, 116, 133, 136, 139–40, 142, 146, 154, 156, 159, 165, 167, 172–7, 184, 192, 194, 196–8; economic 8–9, 12, 50, 60, 74, 85, 97, 136, 166, 168, 170–1, 191; of green technology 149; human 24, 29, 73, 85; hydropower 94; of peace parks 7; regional 39–42; 52; research and 64, 142, 154, 157; rural 50, 139; sustainable 9–11, 39, 176, 184, 189–90; underdevelopment 83, 97
diplomacy 100–1, 146–7, 159–60, 164, 176, 195, 205; international 15, 146

e-waste 156
economic growth 13, 21, 41, 44–5, 50–1, 73, 75, 97, 133, 176, 191
ecosystem 15, 27, 30, 39, 66, 92, 94, 107–8, 110–11, 114, 116, 118–20, 122, 134, 165, 167–9, 172, 175, 178, 184–7, 192–3, 198; services 6, 39, 89–90, 97–9, 101, 165, 169
electricity 12, 22, 39–41, 45–50, 52, 82, 94, 96, 101, 161, 176; market 45, 47, 49, 52
energy 12, 22, 27, 33, 39–41, 43–5, 47–52, 61, 65, 67–8, 82, 94, 97, 149, 154–5, 161, 164, 186, 206
environmental 2, 7, 39, 44–5, 52, 60, 65, 67, 76, 81–3, 92–4, 96, 99, 107, 117, 119, 134, 138, 149, 151–2, 155, 158, 161, 172–3, 190–2, 195–6, 198, 203; environment 7, 10, 24, 48, 59, 73, 75–6, 80, 82, 92, 95, 137–8, 141–2, 146, 172, 176–8, 189, 191; environmentalism 10; environmentalists 11; change 10, 24;

## 208  Index

conflict 22; damage 5; degradation 3–5, 9, 11, 13–14, 25, 81, 142, 205; flows ; management 5, 158; pressure 14, 184; security 24, 90, 98; scarcity 5–6; studies 6; wellbeing 15; *see also* sustainability and peacebuilding
exploitation 2, 7, 9, 13, 15–16, 63–4, 74, 116, 118, 132, 147, 151, 158, 161, 184, 189, 203, 205–6; overexploitation 107, 122
extractivism 13, 73–6, 85; new 75–6; old 75–6

farmers 14, 59, 61–3, 65–70, 77, 80, 94, 132–6, 138, 140–1, 173,
fertiliser 59–69, 94, 120, 135, 149,
fishery *also* fisheries 2, 7, 14–15, 92, 107–8, 110–17, 119–20, 133, 167, 169, 171, 176, 184–5, 187–93, 195–9; sustainability of 108, 111, 119; tuna 111, 116, 184–8, 190–2, 194–8
fishing 15, 107, 109–15, 117–19, 122–3, 153, 171, 184–5, 188–92, 194–5, 197–9; illegal 113, 197; overfishing 114, 184, 189, 197; sustainable 113
food security 13–14, 29, 59, 65, 79, 91, 108, 110–11, 116, 120, 133, 135–6, 138, 140–1, 188, 196
food sovereignty 14, 131–43
foreign policy 1, 15
fugitive resources 184, 187

geopolitical concentration 59
global demand 13, 60, 73, 108,
Global North *also* North 2, 21–2, 34, 132, 134, 139
Global South *also* South and Southern 2, 5, 8, 11, 13, 21–2, 34, 74–6, 78, 83–4, 132, 134, 138
governance 6, 8, 15, 40, 63, 65, 93, 111, 113, 139, 142, 146, 165, 167, 173–5, 177–8, 184–5, 189–91, 196, 198–9, 203; collaborative 7, 15, 184, 191, 196, 198–9; cooperative 7, 15, 187; centralised 151; democratic 132; frameworks 167, 190, 194; global 59, 63, 141; interactive 142, 189–90; international 13, 140; multilevel 192; multi-scalar142, 185, 199; of resources 7; of rivers 173; regional 40, 190, 192, 198–9; *see also* international *and* water governance

hunger 14, 25, 30, 131–2, 136, 138, 140–1
hydropower 45–6, 49, 94–6, 98, 166, 169–70, 173, 176

India 13, 21–2, 32–3, 63, 76–7, 82–3, 89–101, 109, 150, 157–8, 166–7
Indus 13, 89–95, 97–101, 166, 172
informal mining 73, 78–85
innovation 4, 8, 10, 22, 33, 70, 134, 147–8, 151, 154–5, 160–1
institutional arrangements 27, 31, 59, 70, 99, 185, 189, 198
integration 44–5, 50–1, 156; economic 41–5, 52; energy 43–4; market 44, 47, 49; regional 48–9
intensification; agricultural 89; labour 8; of farming 133; of production 142
international 2–3, 6–9, 13, 22, 26, 42, 63–5, 76, 89, 97, 112–13, 115–16, 119–20, 123, 132, 136–7, 140–1, 155, 158, 160–1, 164–5, 167, 174, 176–8, 187, 191–2, 194–8; boundaries 7; collaboration 1, 203; conflict 1, 147; cooperation 1, 7, 171, 185, 190; food policy 14; law 112, 167, 174, 177; peace parks 7; relations 1–2, 6, 15, 32, 40, 90, 205; *see also* diplomacy and governance
International Monetary Fund (IMF) 80
irrigation 33, 91, 93–4, 98, 164, 166–7, 170

La Via Campesina 14, 132–142
limits to growth 5, 9, 22, 34, 73

Malthus, Thomas 3–4; Malthusian 8–9, 32, 73; neo-Malthusian 4–5, 21, 25, 32, 94, 98, 204
marine protected areas (MPAs) 107–8, 117
metal 147, 149, 151–3, 156, 160–1; heavy 62, 171; precious 76; rare 156–7
mineral 2, 14–15, 73–85, 146–8, 151, 154, 158–61, 191

ocean; acidification 108, 119–22; warming 122

Pacific Island Countries and Territories (PICTs) 185, 187, 189–94, 197–9
peacebuilding 5–8, 14; environmental 205

*Index* 209

peak production 62
peasant 13, 73–4, 76–81, 84–5, 132, 134–5, 137–8, 141; extractive 73, 78, 84–5; livelihoods 81
perceived scarcity 1,26, 75, 148, 203
phosphate rock 13, 59–63, 65–6, 68–9
phosphorus 2, 13, 59–60, 61–70
Polanyi, Karl 24–5, 33
political ecology 8, 26, 32, 131, 138
population growth 3–5, 9, 22, 24–5, 31–2, 34, 59, 89, 142, 168, 204
power pools 41, 52

rare earth 146–7, 150–7, 159–61; minerals 2, 14–15; elements (REEs) 146–8
Regional Fisheries Management Organisation (RFMO) 7, 110–11, 113–15, 190
regionalisation 39, 42, 44, 51
renewable 47; electricity 45; energy 43–5, 47, 49, 51–2, 154; non-renewable 13, 60, 74, 161; resources 6, 12, 28; water 26, 28, 101
resource scarcity 1–16, 21–4, 32, 40, 50, 74–5, 89, 93, 97, 107, 142, 192, 203–6
resource substitution 5, 8, 15, 154, 157
river health 164–5, 169, 172–6, 178

scarcity discourse 1, 12–13, 21, 24–5, 32–3, 76, 131, 134, 142, 203;
scarcity postulate 4, 12, 21, 23–6, 34
seabed 158, 162, 191
security 3, 6, 13, 21, 22, 39, 41, 49, 59–60, 70, 82, 89–90, 98–100, 148, 154, 164, 172, 174–5, 177–8, 195, 203; energy 22, 39, 43, 45, 50–2; environmental 24, 90, 98; insecurity 6, 62–3; phosphorus 59–60, 64–6, 68, 70; studies 6; *see also* food security and water security
social construction of scarcity 21, 133
South Asia 13, 26, 81, 89–92, 94, 98–9, 101
substitution 5, 154, 157; *see also* resource substitution

supply chain 14, 82, 139–40, 146–9, 152–5, 157–61, 191, 195, 197
sustainability 10–11, 14, 27, 59, 75–6, 108, 110, 116, 132, 156, 189, 194, 197, 199; environmental 85; unsustainability 81
sustainable development *see* development; sustainable

technology 10, 22, 33, 74, 111–12, 146–8, 150–2, 154, 156–8, 160–1, 174, 177, 184, 192; biotechnology 32
trade 1, 24, 39–43, 45–7, 49–52, 63–4, 69, 74, 79, 81, 85, 114, 116, 132–3, 136–7, 139–42, 155–6, 167, 184, 192, 195, 199
transboundary 7,12, 14, 41, 50, 101, 170–1, 173, 185, 195; rivers 167–8, 174, 177; water 97–8, 170; water management 6–7, 14–15, 40; resources 189, 191

vulnerability 59, 63–5, 91, 147, 154, 161

water 21–34, 89–101, 164–78; deficit 22, 92; governance 26–33, 89–90, 90–4, 97–101, 164, 167–8, 173–8; grabs 22, 30, 138; management 7, 15, 27–32, 40, 68, 89–93, 98–100, 166–178; pollution 59–60, 67–8, 82, 121, 151, 165, 169–174, 178; quality 89, 91; resources 3, 22–31, 73, 81, 89–91, 93, 95, 99, 164–174; scarcity 6–7, 12, 21–2, 24, 26–33, 73, 89–100, 138, 173–4, 178; security 13, 22, 89–90, 92, 95, 98–100, 164, 173–4, 178; surplus 28, 92; wars 22, 24, 26, 98, 168
Western and Central Pacific Fisheries Commission (WCPFC) 110–11, 115, 185, 190, 195–9
Western and Central Pacific Ocean (WCPO)108, 115, 184–5, 187–99
World Bank 10, 27, 80, 82, 99, 133, 142, 171

# Taylor & Francis eBooks

## Helping you to choose the right eBooks for your Library

Add Routledge titles to your library's digital collection today. Taylor and Francis ebooks contains over 50,000 titles in the Humanities, Social Sciences, Behavioural Sciences, Built Environment and Law.

Choose from a range of subject packages or create your own!

**Benefits for you**
- Free MARC records
- COUNTER-compliant usage statistics
- Flexible purchase and pricing options
- All titles DRM-free.

**Benefits for your user**
- Off-site, anytime access via Athens or referring URL
- Print or copy pages or chapters
- Full content search
- Bookmark, highlight and annotate text
- Access to thousands of pages of quality research at the click of a button.

**REQUEST YOUR FREE INSTITUTIONAL TRIAL TODAY**

**Free Trials Available**
We offer free trials to qualifying academic, corporate and government customers.

## eCollections – Choose from over 30 subject eCollections, including:

| | |
|---|---|
| Archaeology | Language Learning |
| Architecture | Law |
| Asian Studies | Literature |
| Business & Management | Media & Communication |
| Classical Studies | Middle East Studies |
| Construction | Music |
| Creative & Media Arts | Philosophy |
| Criminology & Criminal Justice | Planning |
| Economics | Politics |
| Education | Psychology & Mental Health |
| Energy | Religion |
| Engineering | Security |
| English Language & Linguistics | Social Work |
| Environment & Sustainability | Sociology |
| Geography | Sport |
| Health Studies | Theatre & Performance |
| History | Tourism, Hospitality & Events |

For more information, pricing enquiries or to order a free trial, please contact your local sales team:
www.tandfebooks.com/page/sales

 | The home of Routledge books

**www.tandfebooks.com**

Milton Keynes UK
Ingram Content Group UK Ltd.
UKHW032340140224
437859UK00004B/16